THE
DEMONIC
TURN

The Power of Religion
to Inspire or Restrain
Violence

Lloyd Steffen

THE
PILGRIM
PRESS
Cleveland

The Pilgrim Press
700 Prospect Avenue
Cleveland, Ohio 44115-1100
pilgrimpress.com

08   07   06   05   04   03   5   4   3   2   1

Library of Congress Cataloging-in-Publication Data
Steffen, Lloyd H., 1951-
    The demonic turn : the power of religion to inspire or restrain
violence / Lloyd Steffen.
        p.   cm.
    Includes bibliographical references
    ISBN 0-8298-1563-5 (pbk. : alk. paper)
    1. Violence – Religious aspects. 2. Religion.   I. Title.
BL65.V55S74 2003
201'.7– dc22
                                        2003060141

To William Hamilton
in friendship

Contents

Contents

Contents

Preface

No other human interest has deluged the world in so much blood as religion; at the same time nothing has built so many hospitals and asylums for the poor... as religion. Nothing makes us so cruel as religion, nothing makes us so tender as religion.[1]

THIS STATEMENT, which could be made by any contemporary observer of religion, was actually offered over a century ago by a visitor to the United States, a Hindu reformer, Swami Vivekananda. The observation at the heart of this statement is the subject of this book. Vivekananda reminds us that religion is not one thing; there is no norm of religion. There are only forms of religion embedded in the contingencies of culture; and among the possible forms are those that advance the highest of human aspirations as well as those that bring what is good and noble in human life to ruin. Vivekananda observes that people can enact their religion in different ways, in ways that are life-affirming and ways that are destructive, and more than that, he goes on to suggest that religion presents us with options and that people have to choose how they will be religious. For that reason, in the New York City address from which the above quote is taken, Vivekananda would commend to his audience a "universal religion" that "would have no place for persecution or intolerance in its polity, and would recognize a divinity in every man or woman, and whose whole scope, whose whole force would be centered in aiding humanity to realize its Divine nature."[2]

Vivekananda understood that religion is powerful and dangerous; that it can serve different masters; that it ennobles as well as debases, creates as well as destroys. This book follows that insight and inquires into this difference. Why do people express themselves religiously the way they do? Why are some creative and peace-loving in their practice of religion, while others are destructive, even violent? Posing the issue this way suggests that people make decisions about how they will be religious and how they will enact their religion in the moral world of self-other relations. Religion inspires action, and the actions it inspires are open to moral critique, as is the religion itself.

What form of religious life people choose as their own depends upon a decision that is not in the first instance religious but moral. The question is whether they accept a form of religion that endorses and promotes a vision of goodness. How people choose to be religious and put their religion to work for various purposes related to the interests of their communities, even their own souls, to serve a broader moral vision is the critical issue of moral importance in the pages ahead; how people, both individually and in their religious communities, enact and embody their religious understanding reveals if that choice is ultimately life-affirming or destructive or, as religion itself identifies the destructive option, demonic. However religious people might agree or disagree over the content of Swami Vivekananda's faith perspective, the moral meaning of his words is clear — and not only clear, but luminous with respect to goodness, for he advanced a form of religious life and understanding grounded firmly in a life-affirming ethic. But religion, as we all know, need not go this way. The Aum Shinrikyo terrorist nerve-gas attacks in the Tokyo subways in March 1995; the thirty-nine Heaven's Gate suicides in San Diego in March 1997; the Branch Davidian disaster in Waco, Texas; the seventy Swiss and Canadians who perished in religious violence associated with the Order of the Solar Temple; and even the extremist Islamic movement that helped motivate the September 11, 2001, terrorist attacks all illustrate that religion can go another way. How can people who decide to express themselves religiously do so through violence and destruction? That is the question at issue in this book.

This book emerged as a response to two events: one an event of world historical importance, the other a lunch conversation.

In fall of 2001, I was scheduled to do some speaking engagements on the morality of the death penalty, and, as many things changed in the wake of the September 11 terrorist attacks, so did my presentations. I shifted attention from the death penalty per se to the issue of demonic religion and how religion provides resources both to incite violence and to restrain it. In these pages I have sought to respond to a question that a scholar of religion should be able to address, namely, "How can religion inspire violence and murder and even incite persons to suicide?" The fact is that violence has always been a dynamic of religion and religious expression, even as religion has attempted to keep violence at bay and outside the religious community. The explanation for how violence is provoked, however, goes to fundamental issues related to the power and the danger of religion. This book addresses those questions.

The events of September 11 provoked serious moral questions about religion, and in these pages I argue that people are religious the way they are because of choices they make about how to be religious. The moral dynamic of religion can be exposed by examining this decision and all that informs it, including such characteristics as intentionality, motivation, evaluation, judgment, affirmations of value, understandings of power, community, authority, and ultimacy, even the way visions of goodness can become involved with self-deception. Attention to the moral dynamics of religion allows us to see that a basic moral option presents itself to people in religious life and practice, given that people choose, both individually and in community, how to be religious. This book argues that people are religious in particular ways, and that how they construct and practice religion rests, finally, on a fundamental moral turn to be religious one way rather than another, either in a life-affirming or demonic way. The handle provided by this distinction goes a long way toward explaining the religious dimension of events surrounding September 11, not only the terrorist acts of murder and suicide, but also the evangelical Christian responses of Jerry Falwell and Pat Robertson, both of whom, in the immediate wake of the destruction of that day, declared that these events were God's righteous, albeit wrathful, judgment on an American society corrupted by feminism, homosexuality, and abortion rights.

This book also responds to the pressing question, "How can people find in religion justification for murder and suicide?" In the talks I gave in the fall of 2001, this basic moral insight about religion provided me with a key to helping others understand the religious dynamic relevant to those events. I provided examples not only of religious extremism as it appears in Islam, but also in Christianity and Judaism. Although the demonic dynamic is discernible in every form of religion, my emphasis in these pages is on the monotheistic traditions of the West. Not only are they my area of scholarly competence, but these religions also have set the conceptual and moral framework for so many of the problems we face in the modern world, including those that emerged on September 11 and which still plague the retaliation-riddled Middle East.

I wish to express my thanks to Professors Stuart Chandler and James Cahalan of Indiana University of Pennsylvania for their kind invitation to speak on their campus and for their generous hospitality. I also wish to thank the members of the Peace Forum and Rev. Dan Vander Ploegh in Duluth, Minnesota; Rev. Jeff Geary from the forum on peace and justice at the Setauket Presbyterian Church on Long Island; Rev. Bill Regan from Hope Church United Church of Christ in Allentown, Pennsylvania; and to friends at Lehigh University, especially Professor Gordon Bearn, who invited me to speak on "the demonic" at a Humanities Center event. I was also fortunate to have had the opportunity to test out some of these ideas at Cornell University, where I gave the 2002 Frederick C. Wood Lecture. I am most thankful to Rev. Kenneth Clark for extending the invitation to speak on these issues on the occasion of the fiftieth anniversary of the dedication of Annabelle Taylor Hall on the Cornell University campus.

I've addressed this book's context following the earth-shattering events of September 11, 2001, but I also said that this book is a response to a lunch conversation. A short story explains it.

One day at noon in the Yale Divinity School refectory, just as I was sitting down for lunch, a rather slight, elderly, white-haired gentleman asked if he could join me. Roland Bainton was his name, a legendary figure at Yale and a scholar whose work I knew well even before coming to Yale. I, of course, felt honored to be in his presence, and we exchanged pleasantries. Professor Bainton graciously inquired about my course work and I shared with him my enormous enthusiasm for Kierkegaard, whom I was studying rather seriously at that moment. I had just finished reading and discussing *Fear and Trembling,* a classic text that offers a remarkable distinction between the religious and ethical spheres of existence along with that philosophical kick about a "teleological suspension of the ethical." The book concerns Abraham's faith and the God who asks of Abraham something ethics could never understand, much less abide — the sacrifice of a faithful man's only son as a show of devotion to God. Bainton listened to me patiently, didn't interrupt me too much as I recall, and allowed me to go on about the philosophical profundity of this text. Then, as I finished speaking and lunch concluded, he rose from his seat, looked at me, and said something I have never forgotten: "What we need, son, is a good God."

The relevance of that comment should become apparent to anyone who reads through these pages. More than two decades after Roland Bainton said this to me, I am belatedly offering him my agreement. This book is a full-bodied endorsement of his insight. I do not leave Kierkegaard behind, for those who know his thought can find his influence everywhere here. But the heart of the message of this book lies in the moral message about religion Roland Bainton presented me and which has taken me many years to appreciate: "What we need, son, is a good God." Bainton, by the way, used to draw little sketches of people he enjoyed meeting and found interesting, sometimes even doing so on napkins. Many of my friends from Yale days received these little caricature portraits, these very personal signs of affection. I never did.

A few other acknowledgments are in order. I am grateful to my colleagues in the Religion Studies Department at Lehigh University, especially Professor Larry Silberstein — whose Religion Studies Faculty Seminar during the fall of 2001 focused on Foucault and power and started me thinking about the issue of power in different ways — and to Professors Ben Wright and Michael Raposa for discussing many of the issues in these pages with me. I am grateful to

Islamic scholar Simon Wood of Temple University, who reviewed the Islam material in the text and helped with critical comments.

Some of the Tillich material on the demonic and self-deception was developed in different form in an article, "Tillich, the Demonic, and Symbols of Self-Deception" in *Papers from the Annual Meeting of the North American Paul Tillich Society 1994,* ed. Robert Scharlemann (Charlottesville: University of Virginia, 1995): 55–62.

And I very much wish to thank Emmajane Finney, my spouse, for all of her support and encouragement as this project took form and came to conclusion. And I acknowledge what I take to be the implicit support of my sons, Nathan, Sam, and Will, all of whom think I worry too much about them. Maybe when they are older and look through these pages they will better understand their father's reasons.

I dedicate this book to William Hamilton, a dear friend who has been one of my mentors and intellectual companions. He will see more than resonances of his thought in these pages. I cannot repay him his many kindnesses to me over the years, but I can offer up a dedication, and I do so not only as a tribute and thank-you, but as atonement for my having been such a poor correspondent of late.

I accept responsibility for any mistakes of fact that may be here. Errors of judgment are, if not harder for the reader to identify, at least harder for the author to admit, but I know they must be there, and I have no doubt that they will be pointed out. I accept responsibility for them.

Part I

LIFE-AFFIRMING AND DEMONIC RELIGION: THE OPTION

Chapter One

The Power and Danger
of Religion

IN THE FOURTH CHAPTER of Genesis, the first brothers, Cain and Abel, sons of the first parents, tragically become the first murderer and the first murder victim. Living just outside of Eden, these brothers both offer sacrifices to God, Yahweh, who accepts Abel's sacrifice but rejects Cain's. The reasons for the rejection are unclear, but God appears to be either parsimonious or lacking in enough blessing to go around.[1] The text simply says, "For Cain and his offering, he had no regard" (Gen. 4:5). Cain, of course, feels the slight. Directing his indignation at his brother, Cain attacks Abel and kills him. Thus does the biblical account of origins include the story of the first sibling rivalry, which ends dramatically in fratricide.

This Genesis narrative concerning the first brothers exposes the costly, even lethal, consequences that can follow in the wake of a competition for divine favor. The story reveals something peculiar about the God whom these brothers worship. This God acts contrary to all one would expect of a God committed to realizing an idyllic vision of peace and harmony. Yahweh creates the conditions for a terrible conflict and does so seemingly oblivious to the emotional dynamics that would flow from a show of divine favoritism. The divine act of showing preference is followed by many more, and such acts emerge as a major biblical theme, finding their ultimate expression in covenant, a theological notion central in Hebrew thought. Preferential treatment, including covenant, provokes the problem of the insider and outsider; preferring some inevitably means rejecting others, establishing covenant with one group will necessarily exclude other groups. Preference seems always to come at someone else's expense, yielding serious and negative consequences for the "not chosen." The story of Cain and Abel shows that preferential treatment has a dark side, for being assigned to the ranks of the "not chosen" can, as the story of Cain demonstrates, lead to anger, resentment, and finally violence, even killing.

The Cain and Abel story does more than present a primal image of brothers in faith. More significantly, it presents a narrative in which violence enters into the dynamics of religious practice, even suggesting that the two notions are inextricably linked. In this story, religion becomes the occasion for brothers in faith to separate and oppose one another, even as they bring the best that is in them in religious offering to their common God. Whether inadvertent or intentional, the story reminds us that religion is a cause for violence, and this point is not a curious aside or a minor detail. The story emerges from the depths of mythic consciousness and in so important a context as a story about human origins — that of the first brothers.

What are we to make of this association of religion with violence? One response would be to deny any such association. Cain could be held totally responsible for all that transpires in the action of the story, and God's rejection of Cain could be interpreted as justified because God knew Cain was unworthy of blessing and then simply acted on this knowledge. God's role in this event could then be interpreted as a showing of divine impartiality: God offers a fair-minded judgment to which Cain then reacted irresponsibly. God is thus in no way responsible for the events that unfold. Only Cain is, and the cause of Cain's discontent is referred to the particularities of his personality and psyche, as if Cain's reaction is all internal matter.[2] The idea that God might have played a role in the outcome is thus dismissed.

But the text in Genesis 4 can support an alternative to this rather pietistic interpretation, for the text presents a God who acts not impartially but preferentially. The divine spurning of Cain in his moment of worship is not explained. Neither is Cain offered help. He is not given advice for improving his offering or for making amends for whatever offense he must have unwittingly committed. God, rather, after rejecting the sacrifice, offers only a cryptic comment to a crestfallen and angry Cain, saying that if he "does well," "will you not be accepted?" (v. 7). Cain must not have fathomed what "doing well" meant or, if feeling that he has been the target of an injustice, may not have actually believed that "being accepted" was in his future. Subsequent events present evidence that Yahweh's response fails to calm

Cain down, and a murder results. The story is transformed from an account of origins into a suggestion that a God who acts preferentially can arouse hostility and resentment, and that even acts of worship can provide the occasion for violence, up to and including murder. The Cain and Abel story connects religion and violence in an ancient text that refers to human origins, an indication that interest in this topic goes way back, even into the reaches of mythic time.

The Cain and Abel story is hardly sufficient for making the claim that religion and violence share some kind of deep, inextricable connection. Religion clearly need not express itself through violence. Innumerable acts of violence have nothing to do with religion, and violence is certainly not a defining characteristic of religion itself.[3]

But should it be? Is it possible that the Cain and Abel story provides a paradigmatic case for the intersection of religion and violence? Despite our refusal to acknowledge any necessary connection between the two, is there in fact something about religion that inevitably attracts, incites, or produces violence? Can we avoid encounter with story after story about religiously motivated destruction, oppression, exclusion, and death-dealing when we consider the history of religion? Does deity itself not appear in Western conceptions and even in sacred stories themselves as rather openly and dramatically destructive, even bloodthirsty at times? No apologist for Western religious traditions can avoid the fact that the God of the Hebrews curses and smites, that the God of Christian theology reconciles with humanity only at the cost of a terrible blood sacrifice, and that Allah vengefully punishes unbelievers and destroys corrupt societies. These ideas of God and tradition-bound notions of divine activity are all violence-related. Even if religion presents in its emphasis on love, joy and peace a powerful counterpoint to any claim that there might be an inherent religion-violence dynamic, is religion not in some ways connected to violence? Could we not even ponder the possibility that human religiosity inevitably expresses itself in violence?

Answering these questions does not require that we alter our definitions of religion so that violence is included along with other matters of definitional content, such as beliefs, symbols, rituals, ultimate concerns, and the like. What is required, rather, is that we attend to those features of religious life and practice susceptible to expression in, through, or as violence. Two such features of religion immediately suggest themselves, and when put in propositional form they express easily recognizable truths about religion, even if they do not fit into a formal definition of religion. One proposition is *Religion is powerful.* The other: *Religion is dangerous.*

Although religion means different things in different contexts, the wide variety of religious forms and modes of expression in human culture allows us to say with some confidence that religion is universal, complex, and diverse, and while integral in helping to construct community, religion is also, historically, a force of divisiveness. Religion provides human beings with the forms and structures that allow for interpreting those human experiences that are deemed transcendent, focused on ultimacy, or otherwise regarded as "religious" or "spiritual." As a cultural form, religion provides people with access to the symbols and structures of existence that allow them to meet psychological and spiritual needs for identity, power, community and belonging, and for meaning, ultimate meaning — that is, meaning tied to a relationship with ultimate values and transcendent realities. Religion offers pathways and resources to help people in their encounters and confrontations with mystery. These various statements describe religion as it plays an important role in human experience, both in terms of individual experience as well as in human culture.

To move beyond these broad statements and invite reflection on the idea that religion is powerful and dangerous allows us to say that in human culture religion is something people do. It is, in other words, an activity. Religious people act in the world and manifest their religious belief through religious practices and religiously motivated actions and behaviors. They claim that their behavior is itself religious and that to understand the meaning of their behavior requires appeal to religious categories and interpretive schemes that govern motivation and behavior. Violence, religious or not, is always a behavioral expression; violence, when publicly observed in certain contexts, can certainly reveal more about the religion-violence connection.

That religion is powerful and dangerous does not mean that religion must of necessity express itself through violence. The issue, rather, is that human beings can express themselves religiously in a variety of ways. Religion itself is so varied in culture and so complex in human experience that it can yield many different behaviors, including violence. But while religion can incite violence, it can also act as a restraint on violence. Given that religion can take many forms and provide a structure of meaning that incites people to act in certain ways, we can safely say that people who engage the world religiously, who act with religious intent or motivation, can express themselves as religious persons in ways that include both violent and nonviolent modes of behavior. Neither violence nor nonviolence is a necessary datum in defining religion. Violence, however, can reflect how people have chosen to enact their understanding of what it means to be a religious person as that understanding has been shaped by their traditions, community, practices, beliefs, and experiences. People can resort to violence to express themselves religiously, and while some do, many do not. Others, moreover, choose to express themselves religiously by opting for nonviolence.[4] Neither violence nor nonviolence expresses true religion; both can be authentic behavioral modes whereby people opt to express themselves religiously.

How and why violence might come to the foreground in religious behavior, or, conversely, be suppressed and even repudiated are important issues, but ones that religion is itself not adequate to answer. When religion is considered as human activity, as a motivator of action and as a system of interpretation that finds expression in the realm of human behavior, then religion presents itself for *moral* analysis.

Although human beings express themselves religiously in a multitude of specific ways, the moral point of view considers how these different ways of being religious are enacted. Moral attention focuses on the meaning of all that occurs in the specific sphere of the self's relations with others, the interpersonal realm of human interaction. From the moral platform created by this arena of relations, we can actually discern that people find all kinds of ways in the diversity of cultural systems to enact their religious beliefs and commitments. Furthermore, they actually choose how they are religious, how they enact their religion, and how they express themselves as religious in one manner rather than another. The argument I propose to defend in these pages is that understanding this moral platform is essential for understanding how people who have developed morally to be persons of a certain sort also choose to be religious in certain ways. Conversely, how people choose to be religious inevitably expresses moral anchors in the personality for which religion itself cannot account. Whenever violence, then, is chosen as a legitimate vehicle for the expression of religious belief or commitment, that violence, from a moral point of view, is consistent with an actual choice people make about how to be religious. Whether made explicitly or implicitly, that choice to be religious is grounded in the moral rather than the religious realm of meaning. To ask, therefore, why some people opt to express themselves by means of violence is to provoke a moral rather than a religious question. Even if a religious explanation denies the moral platform or offers a theology that explicitly denies such a moral backdrop for religious action, the moral point of view discerns this moral platform undergirding religious action and expression, and insists on its primacy when considering the meaning of religiously framed action. How people are religious is the result of moral decision making and determined by moral formation of the personality. To inquire into why people choose to be religious the way they do provokes consideration of the ways people engage one another fully as moral persons on the horizontal plane of human interaction and relationship, even when they understand their actions and engagements as an expression of their religiosity. What people do as religious people — how they pursue projects, interact with others, and make decisions — is eligible for moral analysis and critique, even when self-understanding is fully involved with religious explanations and interpretations.

My purpose in this chapter is to explore the way the moral and religious realms of understanding are both distinct and intersecting. The question about the relation of moral thought and religion can be better exposed by considering the moral options that present themselves as people decide how to be religious. I begin by considering the meaning of religion as it presents itself for moral evaluation. Religion, I argue, presents itself as a power, then as a dangerous power; to the extent that this power influences people's actions it is subject to moral critique. To understand why some people choose to express themselves religiously through violence depends upon making a distinction between religion and the moral point of view. The following discussion is offered to clarify the idea that people choose the manner in which they are religious.

Proposition One:
Religion Is Powerful

Any student of religion can study the history of religion and come to appreciate that religion is powerful, that it has played a dynamic role in history and culture, and that it has served to transmit knowledge and values. Religion has affected how people and societies have understood themselves, how they have gone about creating a meaningful order, or *nomos,* and how they have formed community around shared values and lived in the world with others. In contemporary America the power of religion is sometimes discounted based on a variety of cultural factors, including the dominance of secularization, a deep cultural preference for scientific explanation, and a pluralism that seems to fragment any authoritative religious center of political power. But even people who think of religion as a diminishing cultural force can never quite ignore it. Even as mainline religious organizations experience declining membership, and a majority of Americans believe religion is losing influence, 60 percent of Americans classify religion as "very important" to their lives, 95 percent hold that they believe in God, and 93 percent claim that they own a Bible.[5] Religion may have transmuted into more psychologized, nontraditional forms, such as self-help movements, spiritual exercises based on "I'm spiritual but not religious" claims, and even into such gathering activities as sports or, more recently, symbolic expressions of patriotism. Still, the power of religion as a cultural and even political power is not to be denied. The formation of voting blocs based in religion, exemplified on the American political scene by what is known as the "religious right," reminds us of the power of religious organization and religious leadership in shaping a national agenda. No serious politician ignores this power. Certain issues — abortion primarily, but also school prayer and flag burning — still have power to translate religious conviction into political force.

The power of religion to affect behavior is especially visible when it inspires violence. It takes a powerful motivator to incite a person to inflict intentional harm on others, even to kill, but it is an extraordinary power that is able to motivate suicide. Religious suicide is perhaps the best exemplar of religion's power, and examples are all too familiar, be it the suicides sponsored by Jim Jones in Guyana or Heaven's Gate in California, or the terrorist suicide bombings in the Middle East. The perpetrators of the September 11, 2001, attacks murdered and sacrificed their own lives in a cause that they apparently believed was religiously sanctioned. In this case, we see more than violence; we see the power of religion expressing itself through violence.

So why is religion powerful? Why is it even so powerful as to lead to murder and suicide?

Religion is powerful because it confronts *as a mystery* the mystery of existence. In the face of the most anxiety-generating questions of existence — questions about who we are, why we are here, and where we are going — religion proposes a structure of meaning whereby human beings can confront these questions and transform into mystery all that is uncertain and unknowable about life and death. Mystery is the unknown befriended. Engaging the unknown as mystery signals the displacement of anxiety by acceptance. Religion has the power to reframe thought and attitudes and even alter the natural logic of emotion; the grief that naturally attends death can, under the transformative power of religion, be turned into loving remembrance. Religion

[13]

thus has the power to affect how human beings understand the world and the mystery of human existence. Religion can create structures of meaning, shape attitudes, and transform understanding and emotion. If the universe is cold, religion has the power to warm it up and make it a home. This is an awesome power.

Religion also has power to affect human action and moral meaning. The moral realm, as already indicated, attends to all that is involved with human action and behavior, with the relations between self and others, and with all that is involved in the forming of dispositions and character. Moral meaning lies on a horizontal plane where human persons act and interact in freedom; where they form attitudes, intentions, and purposes, and make decisions; and where they develop character and build community centered on values. Asking the distinctively moral question, "Why do people do what they do?" allows us to see how religion connects to the moral realm, for religion affects in powerful ways what people do — and why they do it.

Given that motivation is a central feature of action and thus subject to moral scrutiny, we can say with certainty that religion is powerful because religion is a great motivator. Religion provides people with reasons for acting one way rather than another. Religion affects action by directing persons to the object of religious awareness, which is itself identified in terms of power. In the Western theistic traditions, that power is called "God." But "God" is itself a symbol for the object of religious attention, an object that is best described as *ultimacy*. Ultimacy is a "that which," a "that than which nothing greater can be conceived," as St. Anselm put it close to a thousand years ago.[6] Twentieth-century theologian Paul Tillich directed faith toward this object, which he identified as the object of "ultimate concern."

"Ultimacy" is a notion overflowing with power. For people to say that they do what they do because they are directed by God or by "that which" concerns them in an ultimate way is to say that they are guided in their decision-making and action preferences by a source of meaning that has no superior and cannot be transcended. When theists make this claim and say they are acting on what they take to be God's will they are saying that ultimacy, this center of meaning and value they identify with God, is directing their action and doing so with certainty. For God — "that than which nothing greater can be conceived" — is the end limit of conceiving and of power. And an all-knowing, perfect God directing human beings to act in conformity with the divine will offers certainty about the moral meaning of action. If God wills something be done, no errors or even perplexity need attend reflection on the meaning of action. That God wills something be done suffices as a moral justification. Religious persons who seek to conform their actions to God's will inevitably identify their actions and motivations as springing from divine purposes and intentions. The effect of this, in the sphere of human action, is to clothe human action with ultimacy — that is, with divine perfection. Making this move allows theists to claim that their actions are exempt from ordinary moral critique. Thus does that all too familiar sight appear: the religious person who grounds moral meaning in divine authority and thus achieves, through religion, *moral* certainty. The logic is simple, yet powerful: A reason for action grounded in ultimacy will trump any lesser reason, and in the face of ultimacy, all other reasons are by definition lesser reasons. Such is the power of religion.

Moral certainty inspired by religious belief is derived from the fact that action and motivation are tied to "ultimacy" — ultimate truth, ultimate reality, a center of meaning and value beyond which one cannot go. In the realm of the ultimate, nothing is more important, more true, more certain — or more powerful. This object of religious consciousness — this "ultimate" — is the final and authoritative arbiter of meaning and value. Those who commit themselves to it in faith will act in accordance with their religious understanding of what this ultimate reality wants them to do and how it wants them to live.

How people understand this ultimate reality and act in response to it differs not only from faith tradition to faith tradition, but even from individual to individual within traditions, so that all kinds of different actions can be traced back to the motivating power of the ultimate reality. But an action inspired by religious understanding is not any less religious for failing to conform to someone else's normative view of what religion requires. Religion is concerned at its heart with ultimacy, and anything can serve as the content of an ultimacy housed in the peculiar and indefinite language of "that which." For Western monotheists, the "that which" is God. But in another cultural context, it could be Atman-Brahman or any number of the 330 million gods of Hinduism; it could be the nontheistic Buddha of the Theravada tradition, or Elvis worship, or even atheism if atheism itself comes to hold ultimate value. But whatever its content, the "that which" of religion will present itself as powerful, for "that which" points to the heart of religion: ultimacy. The human desire to possess the kind of power religion makes available through ultimacy is part of religion's universal allure.

All kinds of possibilities present themselves when the person deciding to act is directed by a power that cannot be overridden. In relation to "that than which nothing greater can be conceived," everything else, even something so dearly cherished as life itself, can be relativized and subordinated. By any reasonable moral reckoning, life itself is a preeminent value in the hierarchy of the goods of life, but even the good of life is subject to subordination in the face of ultimacy.[7] It is an awesome and extraordinary power that can motivate a person to defy the basic moral injunctions of prudential reason and voluntarily surrender one's own life. Religion, however, makes a claim on exactly that power.

Religion's power derives from its focus on ultimacy. That power flows from the object of religious awareness, the "that than which nothing greater can be conceived." Whatever that object be — be it God or a god, or some more familiar construct of ultimate reality, such as one's career or love interest, connection to one's drug supplier, or money, or a sport, or rock and roll, or family or spirituality, or a piece of land or a nation or an idea for a nation — the relationship persons have to the object of ultimacy expresses itself in the moral realm of action as publicly observable behavior.

[17]

The object of ultimacy empowers persons to live a certain way, a way consistent with a vision of life that itself is sponsored by "that than which nothing greater can be conceived": ultimacy. And it will direct people into ways of meeting their spiritual needs for meaning, power, identity, and belonging. Ultimacy can unite persons into coherent personalities, fashioning out of the fragmented relations of the human self a unified self. This experience of "wholeness" can reflect a movement toward "creating greater unities," which is one way — Freud's way actually — to describe love. But the experience of wholeness can also be shaped around an ultimacy that is destructive rather than creative. Religion's power can be manifest destructively or creatively. Either way can express authentic religion.

Just as goodness identifies the center of all that pertains to the moral sphere of meaning, so does ultimacy play a similar role in religion. Religious people understand the meaning of their actions *as religious,* that is, as centered on a relationship to ultimacy. Their actions, attitudes, and behaviors, however, are expressed in the moral sphere of self-other relations, and as such are subject to moral scrutiny, moral interpretation, and moral evaluation. This is the case even in the face of an assertion of religious self-understanding and interpretation. The religious interpretation is not to be denied, but the moral point of view has integrity as a point of view, has validity and applicability independent of religious interpretation, and does not defer to the religious even as religion asserts itself in terms of ultimacy. An act is not good by virtue of being religious, but, rather, by virtue of being good. Moreover, goodness is the integrating core concept of all that pertains to the moral point of view. Goodness is what the moral point of view sees — or does not see. To the extent that religion is behaviorally manifest, that it motivates people to action, and that it provides bonds for the building of community and even the unity of personality, moral scrutiny can assess how well particular forms of religious behavior conform to goodness, so that a moral point of view can applaud or condemn certain religious behaviors, even particular religious values or forms of religious life themselves. Nothing human is off-limits or alien to the moral point of view.

•

A powerful dynamic in human life and culture, religion derives its power from the "that which" of ultimacy that lies at the heart of religion itself. Ultimacy is an idea intrinsically powerful, pointing to a "that than which nothing greater can be conceived," and it expresses itself as a power that can motivate and sanction, inspire and authorize human behavior. Religious people appeal to ultimacy to establish meaning, including the meaning of religiously inspired action. Although religious people are inclined to subordinate the moral point of view to the religious, the very fact that religion incorporates the moral point of view so that ultimacy is framed in terms of goodness (or the specific object of ultimate concern or attention is identified as good) bespeaks the deep interconnections between the moral and religious spheres. That religion can effect the incorporation of the moral point of view into itself and create visions of ultimacy in terms of goodness is but one more expression of religion's power. That ultimacy is assumed to be good — and even so good as never to be not good — is itself a move made possible through the power of ultimacy itself.[8]

Proposition Two: Religion Is Dangerous

Religion is dangerous the way fire is dangerous. If we strip away all value from the thought of fire, we discern in fire a phenomenon of nature created by fuel, oxygen, and an ignition source, the so-called "fire triangle." Disrupt the triangle and existing fires extinguish, potential fires are prevented. Fire, however, is never simply a matter for fire science. Fire is always interpreted through value constructs, so that we can say of fire many different things, positive and negative, depending on interpretive context. Fire can be life-preserving or life-threatening; it can enhance aesthetic pleasure or inflict searing pain. Fire holds a distinctive place in mythology as the Promethean force that helped bring about civilization itself. When controlled, it can serve as the creative catalyst for vital human activities; when uncontrolled it can destroy and kill. Fire is elemental in our experience of the world.

One meaning that human beings always attach to fire is that fire is dangerous. The destructive potential of fire is such that we expect all persons to understand fire, respect it, and be alert to its danger; learning control of fire constitutes a necessary life skill. We keep ignition sources away from children and immature persons, and do so for their protection and our own. Fire is also alluring, mysteriously — and that too contributes to its danger.

Fire is subject to interpretation and valuation, and societies construct sanctions of meaning around fire to prevent it from being used for harmful purposes. Reasonable people fear the prospect that fire might be accidentally or intentionally misused, and control of fire can never be assured with absolute certainty. Fire mindlessly follows fuel, and it continually threatens to breech whatever systems of control human beings place on it. That fire can wreak destruction and kill signals an awesome destructive power. Fire is always dangerous; it is never not dangerous.

Religion is like fire. As fire is an elemental phenomenon of nature, religion is an elemental phenomenon of human culture. It is, like fire, definable, and it can be interpreted through a "triangle" of sorts itself. Accepting for the moment that religion can be defined as "the varied symbolic expression and appropriate response to that which people deliberately affirm as being of [ultimate] value for them,"[9] an analogy to fire goes like this. Spiritual need and a longing for transcendence are akin to oxygen in a fire triangle in that they keep religion alive and moving. Religion has a sparking source — its ignition is the "that which" of ultimacy that lies at the heart of the religious enterprise. The spark ignites recognizable religion in the face of beliefs and practices, affirmations, symbolic expressions, and all the things religious people do to cultivate and sustain religious life, so that religious activity provides the fuel that makes it possible for religion to grow. To disrupt or eliminate any of these features is to extinguish religion.

As we understand fire in cultural contexts and through value interpretations, so too religion enters our discourse as a living, changing, and fluid concept, open to evaluation, assessment, and interpretation. So elemental is religion in our systems of thought and interpretation that religion becomes an interpretive tool that helps to identify forms of cultural life where ultimacy and its attendant symbols and symbol systems are at issue. Being religious is never a value-free experience, and religion itself can be identified as one of the goods of life that promotes human flourishing. It does so by providing a structure through which human beings can form intimate, even loving relationship with a "that which" source of ultimacy that is as basic a human good in the realm of the transcendent as friendship is in the realm of the interpersonal. Religion, then, identifies a vital, continuing project — important to peoples of every time and place. It is aimed at creating meaning in culture, in the world, in the vastness of all that is. By providing the cultural form whereby human beings meet basic spiritual needs for community, for meaning, for identity, for love, and for acceptance, religion contributes to cultural advance and to intellectual, moral, emotional, and aesthetic growth. In general religion functions culturally to make of an alienating world a home, and, from a moral point of view, can be counted as among the basic goods of human existence.[10] Religion, then, serves to advance a vision of goodness and recommends pathways for enacting and realizing that vision. It provides a way for human beings to contemplate ultimacy and express care.

But religion, like fire, is also dangerous. It is dangerous despite all the good that attaches to it. Religion is dangerous — and never not dangerous — because of the very thing that gives religion its distinctive power: its central and defining involvement with the "that which" of ultimacy, the "that than which nothing greater can be conceived" ultimacy that is the ignition source of religion. Ultimacy is an incendiary concept fraught with the potential for creating violence. But violence emerges from religion only when ultimacy is transformed and becomes equated with the idea of the Absolute. The distinction between ultimacy and absolutism deserves further attention.

Ultimacy as Absolutism

For many religious people, especially if not specifically monotheists, ultimacy — God — and absolutism are inseparably linked. One might ask, "How could ultimate reality, how could God, *not* be absolute or possess absolute power?" Although many who ponder religious ideas never seriously question the assumption that ultimacy is to be defined in terms of absolutism, absolutism and ultimacy are not synonyms or conceptual equivalents. Ultimacy can certainly be construed in terms that are not absolute.

Let me be clear about the distinction. In the old "that than which nothing greater can be conceived" language of St. Anselm, ultimacy refers to "that which" is most to be valued and cherished, and so valued and cherished that nothing beyond that can even be conceived. Although Anselm himself meant to be referring to God, this language can point to an ultimacy that is not theistically framed. Many things in the realm of human experience and human valuation can serve as the specific object of ultimate valuation. The concept of ultimacy identifies the heart of religion, and symbols — be they verbal, literary, visual, musical, or whatever — claim status as religious symbols to the extent that they invoke or evoke ultimacy. Without the "that which" of ultimacy, one does not encounter religion, but something best described in other, nonreligious terms. Where ultimacy is, there will religion be.

The content of the "that which" of ultimacy is open-ended and can include a wide variety of specific ideas and symbols, including all those that are specified in distinctive religious traditions. When religious people reflect on the content of ultimacy, they inevitably interpret ultimacy in ways that respect its tremendous power. But they sometimes make a move that is not necessary to make, which is to identify ultimacy with absolutism, even using at times "the Absolute" as a synonym for ultimacy. Absolutism is a totalizing or all-encompassing, all-enclosing philosophical idea that points toward a specific idea of ultimacy as unconditioned and unrestricted, all-powerful, all-knowing, and unlimited. The idea of "the Absolute" inevitably entails the religious understanding of ultimacy, even when absolutism is advanced in secular philosophical terms. Absolutism includes within its boundaries of meaning the idea of "that than which nothing greater can be conceived." Invoking the idea of the absolute identifies the absolute as a particular way of thinking about ultimacy itself; that is, absolutism identifies a particular way of conceiving "that

than which nothing greater can be conceived." Absolutism
entails ultimacy, which is why it is so easy to assume a necessary connection between the two concepts, even that the
two ideas are synonymous.

Associating ultimacy with absolutism and thus with absolute power leads to disastrous results. In politics, absolutism
ultimately expresses itself in totalitarian despotism. In religion, absolutism leads to the crushing of spiritual freedom.
Philosophically, ultimacy defined in absolutist terms is only
one particular way of conceiving ultimacy, and this particular meaning transforms ultimacy into a concept that suffers
no restrictions, admits no limitations, and allows no exceptions. The idea of "the Absolute" points to an ultimate
reality that is self-contained and independent of relationship
outside itself; it encompasses and gathers into itself all that
is, and it is fraught with problems.

Because it is self-contained and exceptionless, absolutism
is a totalizing notion that encompasses everything. Incorporated into the absolutist conception is all that defines the
Absolute positively, but it includes more than that. As a
totalizing perspective, absolutism necessarily encompasses
all that is, including all that opposes the Absolute, all that
defines the Absolute negatively. Because absolutism encompasses all things, both positive and negative, the Absolute
contains self-opposition. The peculiar philosophical problem that results is that the Absolute necessarily contains
within itself its own contradiction, which is the case not
only logically but empirically. Absolutists are logically committed to contradicting themselves. To accept ultimacy as
"that than which nothing greater can be conceived" and

absolutism as necessarily contradictory is to draw an important — and fascinating — conclusion. If ultimacy is really "that than which nothing greater can be conceived," then a noncontradictory idea of ultimacy is "greater than" one that is contradictory. If absolutism entails contradiction, and does so necessarily, then a notion of ultimacy that avoids any such entailment of contradiction would be "greater" than one that does. An ultimacy that avoids absolutism, then, is "greater" than an absolutist ultimacy that makes claims to being "all powerful," "all-knowing," and the like.

I raise the point about the relationship of absolutism to ultimacy because doing so is relevant to the subject of religion as dangerous. My case is that ultimacy leads to harm-producing destruction and violence when it becomes associated with absolutism. Absolutism is the source of destructive, life-defying religion. Absolutism is the central reason and the main cause for religion becoming dangerous.

Absolute ultimacy inevitably endangers reason itself and thus poses threats to moral and religious well-being. The association of ultimacy with absolutism raises the classical problem of evil and God's role in the origins and the persistence of evil. We need not detain ourselves long on this point, but consider that the classical formulation of the theodicy problem arises because of an absolutist conception of ultimacy. The question to be asked is both simple and reasonable: why would an all-powerful ultimate reality, imagined as an omnipotent and omniscient God, allow evil or not act to prevent evil if, in fact, it is within the grasp of ultimate power to prevent it? If God is construed as absolutely powerful — that is, lacking any imperfection or deficiency with respect to power — then why does God not exercise that power to defeat and eliminate evil? If God is absolutely powerful, why does evil exist and persist?

This problem — the so-called "theodicy" problem — arises solely from the absolutizing of religious theism, where ultimacy is identified with God and God is then configured as absolute. Eliminate the absolutism, construct a God not absolutely powerful and thus not sufficiently powerful to prevent evil, and the theodicy issue drops out. Evil may still exist and persist, but God is not then positioned as the cause of that evil. If, on the other hand, God is conceived as absolutely powerful yet does not act to oppose evil, then God becomes responsible for evil and its perpetuation. A good God conceived of in absolutist terms shipwrecks on the logical conclusion that the absolutely powerful God is not absolutely powerful — a contradictory notion; or it may invite reflection on the prospect that the good God is not really good, the assumption being that a good God able to act to prevent evil would do so. Evil might exist and persist before an absolute God if God is either mad or evil, which in a different way raises a contradiction about God.

Theists do not typically attribute evil directly to God, but if they absolutize God, such a move is finally unavoidable. Of course attempts have been made to resolve the contradiction, as Luther did when he said, "Let God be God." Luther's solution was quite ingenious. His thought was that God is so far beyond the human ability to conceive that the effort to understand God in relation to evil is a sinful attempt to encapsulate God in the small and inadequate categories of human reason. So Luther placed faith and reason in opposition to one another, going so far as to call reason a "whore," as is well-known.

Luther's move to elevate faith above and outside the reach of reason is a familiar theological response to the theodicy problem. The problem with placing faith in opposition to reason, however, is that locating God beyond the grasp of reason also locates God beyond goodness, since reason is able to grasp goodness. The result is to raise the theodicy question in another way. A God of absolute power who acts beyond the goodness that reason is able to discern acts in such a way that reason is unable to discern goodness in God's act — and what is that except to discern in God's own act evil itself? The contradiction arises again, with God now the logical source of evil and the party solely responsible for its continued existence. The "let God be God" ideology moves God beyond reason and thus beyond goodness itself, yielding a God who is either evil or mad.

The source of this classic problem lies not in ultimacy per se, but in absolutism. Absolutism entails a notion of ultimacy and invokes a particular conception of ultimacy, but ultimacy is itself distinct from absolutism and not bound to it by any tie of logical necessity.

Conceiving of ultimacy — God — in absolutist categories or as "the Absolute" inevitably creates contradictions and problems, insurmountable obstacles even, for rational thought. But the most serious problems provoked by appeal to absolutist categories of thought are not rational and intellectual, but moral. When people try to act in accordance with the demands of the Absolute, they provoke behavioral contradictions that pose threats to human well-being. One way to gain access to the nature of these problems is to consider the role that goodness plays in both ultimacy and that particular form of ultimacy that we are terming "absolute."

From a rational and moral point of view, the human relationship with ultimacy points to a basic good of life. Ultimacy, as it is made available through religion, can — and ought to — contribute to human flourishing. This is a moral evaluation of religion, and religion, from the moral point of view, can be deemed a commendable human activity, one that promotes the goods of life, and even goodness itself. When the human relation to ultimacy is transmuted into absolutism, however, the goodness that attends ultimacy is counterbalanced by all that opposes goodness, for the Absolute will take up into itself not only goodness, but all that contradicts goodness. Absolutism, recall, encompasses everything, and for every positive good encompassed by absolutism, its negative opposing force is also encompassed. In religious life, negative behaviors show themselves contradicting goodness because of their inclusion under the category of the Absolute. These negative behaviors are invested with religious meaning, and they oppose goodness. Such behaviors appear when absolutism authorizes, in the name of ultimacy, violence, hatred, destruction, repression of freedom, and at the furthest extreme, killing. Nothing in the concept of ultimacy itself leads to such outcomes; absolutism necessarily makes room within the Absolute itself for the association of these behaviors, attitudes, and actions with ultimacy.

Absolutism, not ultimacy, demands for itself full and total freedom, which thereby denies freedom to human beings.

Absolutism, not ultimacy, invites people into self-deceptive interpretations about moral meaning, insisting that acts it commands be deemed good even when they are destructive of goodness.

Absolutism opposes itself and will, out of itself, contradict the goodness to be found in the human relationship to ultimacy. The contradiction will appear in destructive, disintegrating, and harmful acts, even as those who undertake such acts do so in an effort to express the goodness of the ultimate reality authorizing them. Those who commit destructive, violent, and harmful acts against others do so believing that ultimacy has authorized such actions. Because relationship with ultimacy is itself a good of life, a relationship that promotes goodness and human flourishing, people who commit such acts necessarily believe that what they are doing is good. Acting consistent with what they believe to be the divine will, they reasonably assume that the divine will is good, and they see goodness in what they do. The contradiction arises from moral critique. Reason and moral discernment judge harmful actions from the moral point of view, assessing the meaning against goodness rather than against the standard of ultimacy. Reason and moral discernment also refuse to attach goodness to deeds, attitudes, and behaviors that contradict goodness. The moral point of view even goes so far as to evaluate the moral standing of the God who authorizes acts harmful to human well-being and destructive of goodness: such a God is not a good God. Acting in defiance of goodness, the Absolute God who identifies enemies only to destroy them, whether through battle, flood, or plague, exhibits a destructive nature that cannot be conformed to goodness. Destruction follows absolutism, and the great irony of absolutism is that persons who follow the Absolute God in obedience to the will of the Absolute time after time find themselves acting contrary to whatever they conceived the central identity of this ultimate reality to be.

The idea that an absolute ultimacy entails evil is hardly hidden even if it is sometimes not noticed. Absolutism necessarily requires that the presence and persistence of evil are located in the absolute itself, for the absolute encompasses everything. Familiar mythologies of evil show how the inexorable logic of absolutism plays out, as our poets have discerned. In *Paradise Lost,* for instance, John Milton's prideful Lucifer is clearly shown to be a rebel in heaven. Lucifer was a creation and friend of the Most High God — the Absolute God. In this epic poetic portrayal, the origins of evil and its embodiment in Lucifer, although claimed to be located in Lucifer's pride and vice, are ultimately attributable to the one who made him, the omniscient God who knew what would become of this favorite son of heaven, and who, additionally, possessed power sufficient to defeat Lucifer, at least to the point of stamping out the rebellion in heaven and expelling the rebels. Lucifer originates in God, as does the Satan tempter who, under God's condoning eye, plagues Job in the Wisdom book of that name. The forces that tempt persons away from goodness are always in some way attributable to ultimacy when ultimacy and absoluteness become equated. When, in the New Testament story, Jesus asks God to "lead us not into temptation," he reveals his understanding of the source of such temptation by locating ultimate responsibility with the addressee of the prayer: "Our father." That Jesus should express himself this way reveals that at the time he offered this prayer he was committed to an absolutist conception of God.

Contradictions in one sense simply identify oppositions in language or thought. They pose no danger to life or limb. In logic, at least since the time of Aristotle, the law of contradiction holds that because a statement and its opposite cannot both be true in the same respect at the same time, asserting that they are renders discourse meaningless. Contradictions, then, pose problems for meaningful speech.

Moral and religious contradictions, however, lead to much more serious consequences. In the moral realm, a behavioral contradiction can arise when people act believing that their actions are good, yet their actions oppose goodness, and even defy it; contradictions in the religious realm reveal ultimacy itself as contradictory. Religiously motivated action conformed to the will of an ultimacy believed to be good can yield action, attitudes, and behaviors that from a moral point of view are anything but good. Actions conforming to the divine will are, when the divine itself is conceived as an absolute, destructive of the goods of life, even destructive of goodness itself. Claims made about an absolute God inevitably expose contradictions in God. So God, when conceived of as Absolute, can never be unified but must always reveal self-opposition — a strange thing to say about an absolute, omniscient, omnipotent, monotheistic God. But who can fail to see God's self-opposition: the God of peace in one place, a God of war in another; the God of exclusive relation with a covenanted people in one place, yet a God who transcends exclusivity and expresses nonexclusive universalism. The God of love can be a God of hatred and jealous wrath; the God of forgiveness can be a God of extended retributive punishment, even toward future generations not involved in the offense; the God of creation and preservation can be a God of aggression and destructiveness; the God of liberation can endorse subjecting alien peoples even to slavery.[11]

In the Western monotheistic traditions, when God is conceived as an absolute power, the picture of God that emerges is contradictory. This inevitable consequence of absolutist thinking is only really a problem on the moral front — at the point where human beings seek to conform their action and behavior to the will of this absolute ultimacy. Contradiction, ironically, is a consistent feature of absolutism, and one of the troubles with interpreting a book as rich and as complicated as the Bible is that one can find in it support for contradictory views of God, so that attempts to associate God with only one idea — one Absolute idea — are doomed to failure. The deeper irony is that people who are able to see the contradictions opt to suppress the contradictions by attacking reason itself as an enemy of faith, as when Luther calls reason a whore and resolves the contradictions by saying they are not resolvable through reason but only beyond reason and in omnipotence itself: "Let God be God." Ultimacy is a concept that, even by definition, trumps all others, which is why ultimacy always holds power and always possesses a potential for danger.

Absolutism poses a danger not so much in the arena of logic but in the arena of action, for the simple reason that absolutism yields to contradiction and the contradictions it enables are then enacted behaviorally. The contradiction appears in the difference between an act and its meaning, specifically, between the best, most reasonable interpretation of an act and the interpretation offered by the person gripped by absolutism. Bizarre as this may sound, absolutism claims power sufficient to provide sanction, legitimation, and justification for any action deemed authorized by the absolute power. Those actions can easily conform to a vision of goodness, because relationship with ultimacy is itself a good of life and promotes goodness. But the Absolute entails its own opposition, and in that opposition to goodness, human well-being is put at risk and human beings themselves are under threat of divinely sanctioned destruction.

Absolute ultimacy does not recognize or answer to anything higher than itself, so the legitimate authorization for action need only conform to the will of the absolute. Whether the act conforms to a vision of goodness is not itself a relevant concern in the religious realm. That is, of course, not the case in the moral realm. The moral point of view can critique action and establish the moral meaning of deeds considered harmful and destructive, even evil. But absolutism is so powerful that it can transform moral meaning. Absolutism is so powerful that it can authorize evil acts, suppress moral critique, and then motivate people lured to act by goodness to conceive their evil act as good. Absolutism not only inspires action but then commands how acts must be interpreted. Absolutism, when expressed in the moral realm as action, insists upon subjecting action to interpretation through the totalizing hermeneutic of moral goodness.[12] If God is good — and as a symbol of ultimacy, reasonable people should expect God to be good — then what God commands should be good. When God is not only ultimate but absolute, whatever God commands will be perceived as good, even when the Absolute contradicts goodness, as it must, and authorizes actions destructive of life and goodness. This situation is dangerous. The danger arises from the inability to discern moral meaning. The danger appears as acts discernible to reason as harmful, destructive, and evil are interpreted not as evil but as good, and good because they conform to the will of the divine. Such acts express ultimacy itself, and ultimacy, being absolute, is not to be questioned and certainly not subjected to a moral critique that simply cannot understand the transcendent good that rests in God's own self-understanding, to which human beings have no direct access.

An absolute God lies beyond the categories of good and evil, so absolutists caution that judging God through reason or with the resources of moral thought is to presume a power of discernment human beings cannot claim. Moral and religious explanations and interpretations come into conflict. So a religiously motivated person, holding to a belief in the Absolute, kills another person for some purpose deemed consistent with the divine will. The action may easily fail the test of goodness and be deemed by reason and morality to be an evil deed. But if authorized and sanctioned by the Absolute, the meaning of the deed is referred to a higher realm of legitimation — a realm above the moral, beyond good and evil, where one can only "let God be God."

Absolutism always has power to trump goodness. Thus does Abraham leave with his son for the land of Moriah to offer him up in burnt sacrifice. That he does not succeed is because of ultimacy eschewing absolutism and intervening as a good God. Goodness itself seems to let out a sigh of relief.

•

My claim has been that religion is dangerous, and the central danger I have identified is that created by equating ultimacy with absoluteness. The legitimating and sanctioning power of the absolute can be, and often is, used to justify harmful and destructive deeds as if such deeds were good — good because they are authorized by the ultimate "that which" at the center of religion. Religion becomes dangerous when it affirms an ultimate "that which" in absolutist form; when it accepts this absolute as good but turns a deaf ear to the contradiction that absolutism necessarily entails; when, in the name of goodness and on behalf of the absolute, it authorizes and legitimates actions that defy goodness. Religion thus has power to motivate people to undertake destructively harmful acts of violence, as if they were good.

As we proceed to explore the issues that help to reveal how religion and violence are related, we should note that violence performs the work of establishing, clarifying, asserting, and overthrowing power relationships, and doing so by means of force. We locate power relationships in the realm of politics, but now we are able to say that religion is also concerned with questions of power, particularly with the question of ultimate power. Religion is likewise concerned with the politics of human relationship. What distinguishes the religious from the political has to do with the kind of power religion claims as distinctively its own, and that is the power of ultimacy — ultimate meaning, ultimate value, and ultimate power.

Violence is always political, even when undertaken for religions reasons or with religious sanction. Politics is always susceptible to being affected by the religious dynamic, for religion is concerned with power relationships — the subject matter of politics. Politics is concerned with violence in that violence is one way that people attempt to define, and construct or rearrange, power relationships. Religion comes to the fore when people refer violence to the realm of ultimacy for legitimation. In nonreligious uses of violence, no such appeal to ultimate authority is made.

Religion can motivate and sanction violence, having the power sufficient to legitimate harmful acts in a realm of ultimate meaning and through ultimate authority. In that it possesses power to do these things, religion is dangerous. We must disabuse ourselves of the idea that peaceful religion is true religion or that violence-producing religion is false religion. Both express ways of being religious. Both are authentic expressions of religion's power, and any act can be deemed "religious" to the extent that ultimacy motivates it and sanctions it, be it the crucified Jesus forgiving his executioners, a Zen Buddhist meditating on a koan, Gandhi denouncing English colonialism or the Indian caste system, or King David slaughtering eighteen thousand Edomites in the Valley of Salt (2 Sam. 8:12–13) with the explanation of record being, "And the Lord gave victory to David wherever he went" (2 Sam. 8:14).

So prone are religious people to equating ultimacy and absoluteness — and it happens in every religious tradition, in every form of religious expression — that destruction and violence are always possible expressions of religious belief and practice. Symbols of ultimacy can be absolutized. As a symbol is a tool to mediate understanding relative to the culture in which it is embedded, a symbol ought always to be open-ended and appreciated as participant in the reality to which it points, yet not identical to that reality. When symbols of ultimacy are absolutized, an absolute identity between symbol and reality is forged. The symbol itself, in all of its contingency and relativity, becomes the bearer of meaning in such a way that to deny the symbol is to defy relationship with ultimacy itself. This relationship occurs in religious fundamentalism, in which certain symbols are denied status as symbols and the symbol becomes ultimacy itself. Literal interpretations of sacred Scriptures, associated with some forms of fundamentalism, are products of such an absolutizing process, and people who hold to a literal interpretation of Scripture wind up denying that they are in fact offering a particular interpretation but, rather, have in some sense a hold on the reality of ultimacy itself.

An absolutized symbol is a symbol that is denied status as a symbol. Thus we see again the contradiction in the absolute — the symbol that is not symbol — but always the moral consequences are the more serious ones. To construct a symbol so that it bears the full weight of ultimacy makes the symbol the test of truth itself, which has moral consequences and affects the relationships of human beings to one another. The move to absolutize symbols assists in identity formation, not only individually, but communally; and the community that develops is knit together in its common insistence that its symbols are unique and distinct — and absolutely true — signifiers of ultimacy itself. Forming community around absolutes necessitates the construction of a boundary of exclusion against any and all who deny a symbol this absolute status, and the creation of exclusionary boundaries eventuates in resentment, anger, hostility, and violence. The Cain and Abel narrative masterfully demonstrated this outcome.

Conclusion

Ultimacy, this core of religious reality, opens up a realm of power like no other. Religion, then, is powerful because it deals with the elemental dynamics of life and life's big questions, and does so within a framework of ultimacy. I have argued that despite the tendency of human beings to elide ultimacy into absolutist conceptions, ultimacy is not absolutist in its "default" position. Human beings accept across cultures and even within religious (and political) communities diverse visions of ultimacy, and some — many — of those conceptions are absolutist. Ultimacy, however, is always mediated through symbol systems. People who practice religion accept certain symbols and even whole systems of symbols as meaningful in a normative sense, and that move can easily come to mean that they do not then continue to acknowledge those symbols as contingent and relative vessels to convey meaning about ultimate things. Religious people shed conscious attachment to relativity in symbols for the practical purpose of working the symbols in their individual as well as communal life as religious persons. This process is, in fact, normal, because it is not typical for a Christian or Muslim reciting a creed, or a Buddhist or Jew reading a text, or a Hindu at prayer to pause to reflect on the contingent and relative nature of the symbols they accept and then use in their religious practice. Absolutism threatens when religious people lack appreciation for the contingent nature of their symbols of ultimacy.

Absolutizing the symbols of a religious tradition inevitably opens religion itself to contradiction. Absolutizing religion finally expresses itself in a totalized conception of ultimacy so encompassing that it necessarily entails everything, even its own contradiction. Moreover, absolutizing religion will express itself though absolutized, literalized symbols, which then deny symbols their character as contingent and relative. The move toward absolutizing ultimacy itself leads to the formation of community built around excluding any and all who reject the absolutist picture of ultimacy. As has been argued, the logic of such exclusionary boundary building eventuates in resentment, anger, hostility, and violence.

Religion that absolutizes symbols — conforms them to an absolute ultimacy — asserts its own identity in opposition to those deemed outsiders or "others." As in the primal story of Cain, or as in the biblical stories of the conquest of Canaan or the Davidic subjection and enslavement of noncovenanted peoples, religious identity formation inevitably foments a politics of anger and resentment and beyond

[40]

that — violence. Barrier building generates a politics of insiders and outsiders, saved and lost, winners and losers; barrier building is inherently violent.[13]

Religion is, as a basic phenomenon in the matrix of human culture, both complex and multiform. What can be included under the conceptual umbrella of the concept of "religion" are all those things that appeal for meaning to ultimacy, which is a very wide spectrum of beliefs and practices indeed. Religion is subject to analysis from various points of view, and my interest is to examine religion from the moral point of view. Evaluating the concept of religion from the moral point of view allows us to say with some confidence that religion promotes goodness, particularly the good of human relationship to ultimacy. Religion can thus be counted as one of the goods of life and can serve to promote greater human flourishing. Religion provides a means of access to human beings who aspire for a relationship with the mysterious "that which" of ultimacy. That relationship holds at its core a vision of goodness that people, both individually and in community, seek to embody in action, attitude, and the formation of greater unities.

But religion is a cultural form created and used by human beings for a variety of purposes. From a moral point of view, it would be folly to say religion is itself good — or bad. Religion is, morally speaking, what people do with it, which is subject to moral interpretation and evaluation. Religion, as I have argued, always holds potential for turning destructive and going down the road to absolutism. Religion can create identity and sustain community at the expense of "others" who are barred and excluded and, finally, demonized. It can express itself as a destructive fanaticism that calls for domination out of its certain claim to absolute truth, creating resentment and leading to violence and destruction.

Religion is a powerful dynamic in human culture, perhaps the most powerful and volatile variable in human experience. Although religion is an enormous power that can undoubtedly be a creative force, it is used as human beings use any power, which is to say that they use religion for morally worthy and positive purposes as well as for ends that are destructive and self-serving. A moral critique of religion affirms both possibilities. We can say religion is a good of life, but if we do, we ought to qualify that statement and say that it is a good like fire; like fire, religion is always dangerous. To understand religion is to understand that it is never not dangerous.

Chapter Two

Being Religious:
The Life-Affirming Option

DESPITE ALL THE WAYS that religion can take form in
human culture, the focus of religion on the "that
which" of ultimacy renders religion powerful. Ultimacy is,
as argued in the last chapter, a power concept, and human
beings exercise the power of religion as they go about daily
living. Religion motivates people to make choices, adopt attitudes, and engage in various activities and practices that
affect other people. Religion affects such basic matters as
what people value, both individually and in community, and
how people decide to live and act in a world of cultural,
spiritual, and political meaning where ultimacy is at issue.
In that religion expresses ultimacy in and through action, it
is subject to moral critique, as is all action, as are all those
things that are enclosed by the moral sphere of self-other
relations. Religion motivates people to act in ways that conform to ideas about ultimacy, and in this religion possesses
great power.

[43]

But that power, as noted in the last chapter, can be dangerous. Ultimacy is mediated though language, culture, and symbols, which is to say that ultimacy is itself subject to the relativities and contingencies of human culture. Human beings undertake to interpret, even to create, symbols of ultimacy; in that interpretive activity lurks danger. Religion can come to express visions of ultimacy that are creative and connected to life and goodness, or they can turn destructive and become involved in death-dealing. The human activity of interpreting ultimacy allows for different responses, even within recognized religious traditions, and even this interpretive activity, because it is activity and relevant to the moral realm of self-other relations, is subject to moral analysis. Religion, therefore, is never simply to be equated with goodness or a normative vision of the Good, but must always be approached critically, which always includes the moral point of view. The moral point of view seeks to understand, assess, and evaluate the meaning of human actions, attitudes, and behaviors, even when they are put forward as expressions of religious belief or understanding. Moral meaning need not conform to religious meaning, and a moral evaluation of what people do as religious people may offer insights and conclusions quite at odds with a religious interpretation. For example, human beings can form community around an idea of ultimacy and create that community at the expense of outsiders. They can invoke ultimacy to justify destructive and harmful acts; religion can authorize violence. It need not do so, but this authorization is certainly within the reach of religion's power. The result is that the power of religion must be regarded as dangerous — from the moral point of view.

Because religion is a variable enterprise subject to interpretation and diverse forms of expression, the question arises, "Why do people wind up being religious the way they do?" That is, why do some express their religion in ways that are inclusive of others, while others are exclusive; why are some prone to judgmentalism and others not, or some given to justifying out of religious resources violence, while others, even within the same tradition, commit themselves to principles of nonviolence? In short, the question provoked from a moral point of view is this: "Do people choose to be religious one way rather than another?" If so, how — and why — do people choose to be religious the way they do?

How and why people are religious the way they are does not usually look mysterious to us. We are religious in the first instance because of the transmission of religious culture through basic structures of social organization, particularly the family. Most of us owe whatever religion we know to our parents and the instruction they provided or saw to it that we received. People are not religious in the first instance because of having direct mystical encounters with divine reality. Religion is a mediated activity transmitted through culture and social institutions.

Although many people who are religious may never seem conscious of having made a choice to be religious, at some point, we do choose to be religious, and we choose how to be religious. Each person who receives a religious identity through the structures of society, and for whom the transmission of religious value has actually worked, at some point decides to be religious in some way, sometimes explicitly, sometimes implicitly. This decision to be religious, and to be religious one way rather than another, is made in freedom as people come to particular understandings of ultimacy, join particular communities, and commit themselves to particular ways of acting that conform to what they believe ultimacy requires.

When we look at the issue of religious violence, we discern that religious people approach this issue in different ways. Some religious people support a principle of noninjury; others find religion a source of sanction for the worst kinds of injury imaginable, including inquisitional torture or religiously inspired warfare and killing, including at times even suicide. But always at issue is the moral insight that religious expression gives rise to different actions, attitudes, and behaviors, and all are fraught with moral meaning, all subject to moral analysis and critique.

From a moral point of view, the question of importance concerns not only the moral meaning of the behaviors, but the deeper problem concerning the decision people make to be religious one way rather than another. That decision may confirm the tradition as it was handed down through the family. It may be a decision to reject that inheritance of religious identity and to take on something else. Some find a form of religious life that seems to fit their values and personality; others opt for an identity not affiliated with a specific tradition, that now-familiar "spiritual but

[46]

not religious" identity. Many, especially in American society, direct their religious attention to a nontraditional ultimacy, some object of value "than which nothing greater can be conceived"; such a substitution may not look religious at all. Whether that object is a focus on one's career, relationships, or some other driving and defining passion, the personality attaches to some object invested with ultimate meaning and value. That object is chosen in freedom; relationship with that object unifies the personality and inspires action that is itself expressive of the ultimacy that lies at the core of religious thought and action.

To say that human beings choose religion and how to be religious is to propose that freedom and choice, basic categories of moral thought, intersect with religious life and practice. To ask why people choose to be religious the way they do provokes reflection on symbols of ultimacy and the efficacy of particular symbol systems. Asking why people, both individually and as communities, choose to be religious and express themselves religiously in the particular ways they do can undoubtedly help to illumine religion as religion, as a cultural formation and societal structure that focuses on ultimacy, meets spiritual need, and helps create a world of meaning. This question, though, is even more significantly a moral question. To ask why we are religious the way we are evokes moral questions about human action and motivation, freedom and decision making, and human interaction and self-other relations.

My view is that a fundamental religious option presents itself in any and every form of religious life and practice.

That choice is between two ways of being religious. One of those ways is "life affirming," the other being what religious thought has typically described as "demonic." Religion presents this option in such a way that religious people can be on one side of this option at one time, on the other at another time. The option is fixed, but the people who exercise this option are fluid; being religious itself is fluid. Every person who confronts the possibility of entering into some kind of relationship with ultimacy faces a choice about how to be religious. The distinction between life-affirming versus demonic is advanced not as a sociological observation, but as a divide recognized in religious life itself. By attending to this distinction, we can expose how religion understands itself in relation to a question that is at its heart a moral question concerning the human relationship to ultimacy and how that relationship gives rise to behavioral expression in the moral world of self-other relations.

Characterizing religion as "powerful" and "dangerous" helps to provide a full account of what religion is and how it functions in human culture. The distinction to which I now turn arises out of the resources of religion itself. The distinction is a generalization, yes, but in an age when religion still has power to surprise us with its dangerous power, the life-affirming/demonic distinction is worthy of our consideration, because it provides us with access to the phenomenon of religiously inspired violence.

Life-Affirming Religion

When people are shocked upon learning that religion has played a role in an act of violence, the shock itself is revealing. Such shock reveals that a deeply held assumption has been affronted. That assumption is that religion ought not to be contributing to death and destruction, but on the contrary should be opposing destruction and violence and affirming the value of life.

Religion does indeed value life. How deeply and intensely religion values life can be discerned by considering the way religion understands death to be meaningful. Death is meaningful not because it is the end to life, but because it is continuous with the mystery of life and thus an expression of concern with ultimacy.

Religion, of course, concerns itself with death. There are some thinkers, like the twentieth-century Christian theologian Karl Barth, who have argued that religion is fundamentally about death. That religious resources structure meaning in the face of death through various rituals and practices, as well as beliefs, provides ample evidence to support this claim. But religion, in that it concerns itself with ultimacy and with the mystery of ultimacy, holds that life, not death, is the great mystery. Death can, of course, participate in this mystery, but when it does so it presents itself as continuous with the mystery of life.

Philosopher Gabriel Marcel once said that mystery is self-involving and is to be "thought of as a sphere where the distinction between what is in me and what is before me loses its meaning and its initial validity."[1] He distinguished mystery from problem, holding that problems are subject to techniques and manipulations, but that mystery transcends technique. In light of this distinction, death can be approached either way — as problem or mystery. When death is approached as a problem, it is because death generates anxiety in human life. In the face of this anxiety, human beings can objectify and problematize death in order to manipulate more easily the variables involved with the mystery of death — the dread of spiritual and psychological anxiety, the physical breakdown, the loss of control, the actual fear, the experience of loss. To subject the mystery of death to manipulation and technique confirms an understanding of death as a problem in Marcel's sense, and to manipulate this problem, to control the anxiety or stave off the fear, resources are summoned that have the effect of keeping death at bay and "out there." Deep anxiety has created a market for widespread cultural response, and resources have been made available in the arts and entertainment; in economic activity, including advertising; and in medicine, psychology, and religions of certainty. The attempt to keep death "before me" but not "in me," in Marcel's words, involves human beings in activities that objectify death, making it a manipulable problem, something to be solved, even eliminated, as it presents human beings with the unknown, with the threat of nonbeing, and thus with deep anxiety.

But death need not be addressed as an unknown, as an objectified "out there" problem that can be solved the way a problem in mathematics is solved or a physical symptom of illness is relieved. When we integrate death into ourselves as a part of who and what we are, we acknowledge death as a mystery at the heart of existence. Its meaning is affirmed not apart from life, but in the midst of life. Spiritual masters, as is well known, have "deproblematized" death. St. Francis, for example, actually made friends with death. The Buddha saw death as an achievement. The Prophet Muhammad said, "People are asleep, and when they die, they wake up."[2] Coming to understand death within the context of the mystery of life is a spiritual feat not easy but certainly possible to accomplish. The meaning of death can be shifted so that people confront death not as a problem to be solved but as a mystery, the meaning of which can be affirmed within the context of human subjectivity. That is to say, death can be so "deproblematized" that its meaning does not rest so much in anxiety as in the understanding that grasps death as integral to human experience and central to awareness of the mystery of being human.

When the "out there" of death is finally integrated into the self-understanding "in here," death, from its status as problem, is lifted into continuity with the mystery of life itself. Religion provides a diverse array of beliefs and conceptual frameworks for sanctioning discussion and speculation about what this is or might be; in this move, religion seeks to assist in the process of deproblematizing death and reframing its meaning by subsuming the meaning under the essential category of mystery, which religion so intensely values.

Life-affirming religion points to a way of being religious that transforms the meaning of death. Life-affirming religion expresses itself in a multitude of behaviors, attitudes, and actions, but it will, in the first instance, so value life that death itself comes to be understood as continuous with the mystery of life rather than as life's negation or final end. Death, in other words, always means something more than life with a negative sign in front of it. This transformation in the meaning of death is, I believe, the most dramatic evidence for understanding just how central the value of life can be in religion. From this argument it follows that life, not death, is the great mystery; furthermore, religion then demonstrates in its stories and beliefs, in its rituals and practices, how life is itself grounded in mystery — in a mystery of origins and destiny, of creation and dissolution, of meaning and interpretation and understanding. Thus do religious people confront the mystery of death as if its meaning is to be extracted from the concept of life itself, as in beliefs about an afterlife as well as in the religiously ordained move whereby emotions like grief are turned over to loving remembrance, where those who have died continue to live on in memory and meaningful presence. In such movements of mind and emotion and spirit, death is not problematized, but confronted and accepted and transformed by the overpowering mystery of life.

That religion is able to affirm life with such dramatic power is of course a familiar feature of religion. When we pause to reflect on the content of religious life and practice, it is simply astounding to see the extent to which religion concerns itself with promoting life and the value of life. A religion turned in a life-affirming direction provides the means for interpreting life as meaningful within the context of ultimacy itself. In practical terms, life-affirming religion provides the forms and structures that assert the prime value of life within human society and confirms that valuation within a *nomos* of meaning itself grounded in ultimacy.

How do we see religion affirming the value of life? We see the value of life affirmed in the central myths of religious traditions. It appears in creation myths where order is brought to chaos so that meaningful life can issue forth into the world. In the Hebrew Bible, which so influenced Christianity and Islam, we see this affirmation of life in the creation itself, with God bringing forth life and then subjecting it to evaluation as "good." We see it in the creation of the natural world that teems with abundant life in the sea, on the land, and in the air. We see it in the first commandment of the Hebrew Bible in the first chapter of Genesis (v. 22): "Be fruitful and multiply." This command comes as a blessing but also obliges human beings to participate in the God-giving fecundity, accepting the gift of life and passing it on. This Genesis text identifies a foundational affirmation of the value of life (and sexuality) in Western religion, but this religious story associates, even integrates, ultimacy with the moral point of view. Divine activity, itself the result of divine intentions and purposes, aims at creating life. This occurs, but the activity of calling into being and creating life is then subjected to a moral evaluation, and what the text records is the result of that assessment — that it was good. The divine acts of creation become subject to moral assessment, interpretation, and evaluation, as do any and all acts undertaken in freedom. Thus do the writers of Scripture in their first presentation of divine activity subject even God's actions to the moral point of view and integrate that point of view into God's self-understanding.

The affirmation of life appears in all that God does to preserve and protect the lives of the people of Israel as they journey from bondage to freedom in a new home. It appears in numerous ways, even in the seder remembrance of the enemies who lost their lives seeking to destroy the people of Israel.[3] The Scriptures acknowledge that life derives from God's creative activity, and the essential goodness of life is affirmed in many different ways. One classic scriptural expression of life's goodness is contained in the divine recognition that human beings are, as free and spiritual creatures, able to make choices for life, and against it. But when deciding how this good of life is to be valued, Yahweh does not hesitate to offer the divine recommendation: "I have set before you life and death. . . . Choose life" (Deut. 30:19).

Christianity reasserts this valuation of life's goodness, not only in the central image of Christian faith as "life in Christ" but in central doctrines such as resurrection and the development of a whole theology of an afterlife. Life is a gift of God and as such is good, Christianity asserts, and in its eschatological mode it affirms that even the dead will ultimately be restored to God and to the way of life that is God's loving hope for humanity. One description of the Christian message is that love and life are integrally connected, that life is itself a gift of God's creative love, and that in resurrection, love is stronger than death. Love is so powerful an exemplification of God's identity in the Christian understanding that it identifies and sustains life that endures beyond time. Islam, too, acknowledges this creator God who not only shows the faithful how to live in faithfulness to God's command but presents them as free to decide for submission to God. Those who follow the faith enjoy life and will receive the reward of an afterlife, for Allah preserves the lives of the faithful. In other religious traditions, too, life is centrally valued. One can see it in the precepts of right living in Buddhism; in the Hindu belief in karma and *samsara,* where life cycles and recycles; and in every form of religion where practices and rituals and beliefs enshrine the religious significance of life.

Ritual, so central to religion, confirms the central valuation religion can place on life. Ritual practices function to promote life and to secure it from harm. Cultural anthropologist A. M. Hocart writes, "the object of ritual is to secure full life and to escape from evil";[4] this thought is echoed by Ernest Becker, who observes that "Ritual is a technique for giving life."[5] When ritual functions to create cultural order by excluding from the community threats to life posed by violence, ritual serves to preserve life. René Girard's theory of violence and the sacred explores this meaning of ritual. Girard interprets ritual as action that allows a community to flourish. Sacrificial ritual, he argues, imitates and reenacts violence so that actual violence is sublimated into symbol and thus kept "outside the community."[6] This interpretation of ritual emphasizes the life-preserving and life-enhancing character of ritual practice.

In Christianity the ritual acts of the sacraments provide structures of meaning that preserve and promote the value of life. The significant events of life, from birth to death, are invested with sacred meaning through sacramental acts. Roman Catholic and Orthodox Christians enter the Church, which is understood theologically as the *living* body of Christ, to find new life in community; the sacraments provide a pathway to preserve this new life and keep it connected to God. For all that sacraments may mean in particular, the sacramentalizing process intensifies the value of life and connects an individual's life to ultimate sources of meaning. Sacraments allow individuals to enter the community of faith (baptism, confirmation), find therein a home, then enter a form of life where they are continually connecting directly to God through forgiveness (confession). Maintaining faith through repeated participation in the sacrifice of Christ (Eucharist), they become people able to take a sacramentalized vocation, either to "be fruitful and multiply" (marriage) or to serve directly in the Church under holy orders (ordination). The sacraments provide ritualistic action as people pass from life into death under the continued hope of life yet to come (extreme unction or last rites). The Roman Catholic position on abortion can be understood as a particular way of extending a sacramentalizing valuation to fetal life. This moral teaching on abortion rests on a sacramentalized view of the fetus, which is then explained as a deep concern to protect developing life when it is deemed "innocent" (i.e., sinless) yet susceptible to moral and, even more significantly, religious devaluation by those considering abortion.[7]

In Protestantism, the sacraments function to remind the community of the presence of God so that life in community might be strengthened and preserved. The Christian sacraments, then, honor and sustain, preserve and promote the value of life. Sacraments are life-affirming rituals. Islam has no formal sacraments, but the *umma*, or community of faithful, preserves and sustains the value of life in a kinship of faith that obliterates all distinctions of race and class before God. Karen Armstrong has observed that the *umma* holds "sacramental importance" in Islam, and the *hajj,* or pilgrimage, becomes a ritualistic performance wherein faithful Muslims experience a sacramental-like integration into the community where the central bond of unity is God and life with God.[8] Monotheistic religions affirm not only that God is the author and creator of life, but that life is to be treated with the utmost respect as itself a gift of God honored and valued by God.

Nowhere is the life-preserving emphasis of religion seen more clearly than in a faith tradition's moral directives. Religious codes of behavior reference the central value of life by demarcating what is allowable from what is not. Ethical instructions drive religious practice and seek to affect dispositions so that behavior will embody beliefs. Those actions that affirm life, that promote and protect it, receive divine sanction. "Thou shalt not kill," the Torah commands, and this is repeated though qualified in the Qur'an. "You shall not kill any man whom Allah has forbidden you to kill, except for just cause" (Qur'an 17:33). "Turn the other cheek" and "do good to them who hate you," says Jesus, thus eschewing violence as a response to hatred and provocation. Moral guidelines and teachings are the concrete expression of those requirements, suggestions, and prohibitions that enact God's desire for human beings to live in community and in conformity with a divine vision emphasizing abundant life. That these guidelines are directed, in the main, toward promoting the value of life and preserving the life of the community that is in faithful relation to God can be discerned by review of the Torah's 613 commandments, Jesus' and Paul's ethical prescriptions, and Qur'anic teaching. The emphasis on enhancing, promoting, and protecting the value of life runs through all religious ethical reflection, and any book today that one would pick up to learn more about the ethical teachings of the world's religions would manifest this central theme. Promoting and preserving life is to a large extent the focus and purpose of religiously framed ethical injunctions. These injunctions are, of course, not all consistent with one another, but all are put forward as a way of enacting a religious vision in which life itself is centrally valued.

Religion, we can conclude, provides a primary cultural support for advancing and promoting the value of life. Moreover, the act of affirming religion as life-promoting is one of the central ways people come to hold life itself as a primary good of life. By coming to this moral stance through religion, people come to hold that life is not only a central value but a value expressive of ultimacy itself. The high moral valuation placed on life itself can be framed religiously and attached to ultimacy directly, which is what occurs when religious people sometimes claim that life is "sacred."

A life-affirming religious stance obtains only because people conform their religious thought and practice to an ethic of respect for life. Nothing in religion itself requires them to make this interpretive move, and we know examples of religious people who seem not to do this, especially those who, like Heaven's Gate members or even the September 11 hijackers, commit suicide. Although in the next chapter I offer another option for being religious — the demonic option — at present what I wish to defend is the life-affirming option as a moral perspective that defines a particular option for being religious in a certain way, in a life-affirming way. This is to identify an ethic underlying the religious perspective, and religious people, in whatever religious symbol system they happen to be, can endorse this ethic and interpret their religion in order to conform religion to it. Religious people need not conform their religious activity to life-affirming values, nor ground their conceptions of ultimacy in such a value perspective. Religion can be life-affirming, but it need not be, and empirical evidence to this effect abounds in the history of religion.

Examining religion from a moral point of view allows us to discern a life-affirming option for how people may choose to be religious. How people enact their religious beliefs and understanding in the realm of action, attitude, and behavior is, properly speaking, an issue of moral significance, and while a religious ethic is certainly not irrelevant to religion, my argument is that an ethic always undergirds religious expression and practice. Analyzing religion from the moral point of view exposes in the backdrop of religious expression the moral options that people confront in their practice of religion. The moral point of view allows us to discern that people actually make choices about how to be religious, and this in turn illumines the moral meaning of religious violence — and religious response to violence.

The Lure of Goodness:
Where Religion and Ethics Meet

If religion identifies the cultural forms through which human beings connect to the ultimate mystery and meaning of existence, does it not follow that human beings would, in accord with their religious commitments, treat others with kindness, regard life with profound respect, uphold the value of peacefulness, and shun violence at every turn? The simple answer to this question is "no." Religion is not, in itself, constrained by a normative moral vision that happens to uphold these particular life-affirming identifiers. A life-affirming religious stance is life-affirming not because religion necessarily supports and structures such a stance. A religious stance becomes life-affirming only when human beings commit themselves to a moral vision that accords with life-affirming values. Religious persons accept those life-affirming values as expressions of ultimacy itself, and in so doing, they associate those life-affirming values with the moral center of ultimacy. That moral center comes to the fore whenever questions are asked about who God is and what God wills, and even in so basic a question as what it means, in an ultimate sense, to be human.

So what makes religion life-affirming?

My answer to this question is located in the heart of a moral rather than a religious vision. My answer is that religion that is deemed life-affirming expresses a vision not of God, nor of ultimate reality — but of goodness.

Goodness is the central or core value of moral reflection, holding the same position in the moral sphere that ultimacy holds in the religious. Affirming the value of life "as good" arises from moral understanding. When the Genesis story tells of a God who moved over the face of the waters and then began creating, what God created had no meaning until God interpreted what had been done and evaluated it as good. God, then, is shown in the Hebrew Bible not only creating through the exercise of religious power, but undertaking the work of moral valuation and interpretation. In this moral dimension of the creation story, human beings attribute to God a moral self-understanding and conform their conception of God to a moral, not simply a religious, vision. The *meaning* of creation cannot, therefore, be confined to the religious sphere simply because God is the actor. Moral meaning infuses the interpretation and evaluation of the creative act, and God, subjecting the divine act to evaluation, determines that it is good.

So God creates life and life is good. Is life good because God created it? Or is life good and God recognizes it as such? If God defines what is good simply out of God's own nature, as if the creation were an extension of God's power, then calling an act of God's "good" is simply to acknowledge that God's power is such that it defines goodness out of God's own self. Goodness, in other words, is whatever God wills. The other way to consider the issue is that God understands goodness and seeks to conform divine acts to it, so that the goodness of God is God recognizing, acknowledging and assenting to goodness. This is not the same as determining goodness. God thus is endowed with the capacity to know and understand and evaluate goodness. God is thus able to evaluate all things in light of goodness, critically, apparently even God's own act. In the Genesis creation story, God is not just a religious mystery, an ultimate power, but an agent who intends to act in a certain way and accomplishes certain ends by acting in the ways chosen. The creation activities are then subject to assessment in the recognition that, as Scripture says, "God saw that they were good."

Even in so deeply a religious story as the Genesis narrative concerning creation, knowledge and recognition of goodness are shown to spring from capacities that are moral rather than religious. "Moral" refers to the sphere of self-other relations and the qualitative evaluation of human action in light of goodness. "Moral" is a notion that encompasses all that attends human action in a context of freedom. It discerns and evaluates the values that inform action and are expressed in and through action. It attends to motives, intentions, and purposes. It attends to action-guides that establish what is good, right, and fitting in the realm of action, attitude, and behavior. It attends to principles governing action, to concerns for justice and the expression of care, and to the consequences of action and the formation of virtuous character. It attends to the issue of choice and questions of responsibility, both personal and communal, as well as to all that is involved in the effort to embody a vision of goodness in action and being. As religious vision is connected integrally to the concept of ultimacy, moral vision is essentially related to goodness, and evaluations of action employ goodness as a normative concept against which the achievements and the deficiencies of goodness are to be measured.

When human beings engage one another in the world and do so on the basis of their religious beliefs and commitments, their engagements are subject to moral critique. Their actions are subject to moral evaluation, as is the religion that governs the action. Life-affirming religion points to a particular way people enact religion and even to a particular way they choose to be religious. It is religion not so much qualified by a moral perspective as grounded in a moral commitment to being religious one way rather than some other, and it is a choice to be religious in the direction of promoting, protecting, and advancing life and the goods of life. Life-affirming religion characterizes a way of being religious that is itself grounded in a vision of goodness, so that ultimacy itself — "that than which nothing greater can be conceived" — is expressive of goodness. Goodness identifies the key normative concept in that realm of meaning we identify as "moral."

Most people who are religious think of the kind of religion they hold dear as being good and life-affirming, which accounts for the fact that when they see religion turning destructive and expressing death-dealing activities in the name of ultimacy, they sometimes conclude that such religion is perverse or somehow false religion. But that is not the case. Religion can motivate people to violence and destruction; it can even inspire murder and suicide, or endorse torture or slavery. The condemning of such actions as unworthy of the best that human beings can do arises not from religious assessment — religion may have actually instructed such actions — but from moral assessment, moral evaluation, moral critique. Murder, suicide, torture, and enslavement are repugnant, condemnable acts, but not from a religious point of view. They are deplorable from a moral point of view, and they are acts to be condemned because they fail to embody a vision of goodness. An action is not good simply because it is religious. All kinds of morally questionable, even reprehensible, actions, attitudes, and behaviors can be sponsored as legitimately religious under the rubric of ultimacy.

In the moral realm, goodness — not ultimacy — is the normative concept against which everything else is to be assessed and evaluated. An act of killing that is authorized and sanctioned by the object of ultimacy would be a religious-inspired killing, the meaning of which would be referred to ultimacy. The question at issue is whether the killing was performed as religious authority required or instructed. The moral meaning of that act, however, whether it be a good act or not, would appropriately be referred to the moral point of view for evaluation and assessment. The question to be asked from a moral point of view would be this: Did that religious act manifest goodness? Was goodness luminous?[9]

At the heart of the moral life is attention to the normative value of goodness, which is the touchstone of moral meaning. Goodness cannot be confined to a particular time or place or relativized to the point that its meaning extends no further than to a group or to an assertion of power — that good is whatever the most powerful says it is.[10]

But what is goodness? As one who has been teaching ethics and philosophy for over twenty years, I wish I had more to say about this than I do. I think goodness may be very much akin conceptually to happiness, at least as Aristotle conceived happiness. Happiness, Aristotle wrote, is always an end people choose for itself and never for any other reason — it is, therefore, intrinsically valuable, and it is acquired not by direct pursuit, but by functioning well and so living that happiness accrues from living a good, virtuous life.[11] Goodness is similarly "contentless." Goodness is to be associated with certain things that exemplify or embody goodness or in some way contribute to its promotion, but the idea of goodness itself is one of those intrinsically valuable notions to which other things are referred for meaning. Goodness informs about the quality of other things referred to the idea of goodness, but goodness itself is not simply definable as this particular quality or that. After all, goodness is appropriately applied in judgment to the sensual delight of taste and smell of a good cherry pie as well as to the excellence of a good surgery that helped a patient recover to full health, or a good constitution that regulated the affairs of a state fairly; these things are hardly commensurable. Goodness directs meaning one way rather than another, and to move in that direction is to involve an evaluation and assessment of qualities that are desirable, fitting, suitable, beneficial, or excellent with respect to whatever is qualified as good.

The moral point of view seeks out goodness in human action, attitude, and behavior: goodness provides the normative concept against which moral meaning is discerned and actions evaluated. The archetypical religious text related to goodness provides access into the meaning of goodness: that Genesis account of creation where God creates and, as the text says, "God *saw* that it was good."

One of the things we can say about goodness is that certain metaphors illuminate how we gain access to its meaning, such as the visual metaphors of vision or seeing. Appeal to visual metaphors allows access to the idea that a vision of goodness is not and cannot be hidden from view, but that goodness shows itself and can be seen. This particular metaphor, one that the writers of the Genesis creation account employed, assumes the capacity for sight. This particular visual metaphor, even if it is of limited usefulness in that it works for sighted persons but not for others, suggests that goodness is, in a metaphorical sense, luminous — shining forth and showing itself — which assumes that human beings in general are equipped with the appropriate capacities to discern goodness.

Along with luminosity, the archetypal story of creation in Western religious thought suggests other points relevant to understanding the moral meaning of goodness. We see that goodness is not defined but offered as a characterization, as if goodness is something intrinsically valuable that attaches to activities and even things produced through activity. We can infer that the activity of creation was aimed at goodness and that the divine comment was a statement not of surprise — as if what was created turned out to be good when God had given such a result no consideration — but of an intention fulfilled and a desire realized. The moral point of view would infer that God had intended to create something good, then succeeded in doing so. Goodness was intended and a purpose in the creative activity. Furthermore, the Genesis account associates goodness with a judgment on creation. Goodness attaches, then, to the product of creation; to the world and all that is in the world, including human beings; and to the activity of creation itself. Goodness, then, in its archetypal usage, attaches to activities that express creativity, acts that express imagination and aim at bringing into being, realizing fitting ends, building up, and promoting the value of things like life, diverse forms of life, freedom, beauty, truthful words, and all that is affirmed "as good" in the creation.

The Genesis creation story, a religiously framed narrative infused with moral meaning, associates goodness with capacities and qualities that are good and thus intrinsically valuable. Moral thought has affirmed this idea of a human capacity that allows people to recognize and discern goodness. Especially in the Western natural law tradition, moral thought has so construed reason as to attribute to it a power of discernment able to recognize and understand — "see" — goodness. Goodness is not only seen but associated with certain things that seem to be intrinsically good given that they are essential if goodness is to be realized in human existence. Reason would bid human beings to pursue these particular "goods" and promote them to the end of bringing about their realization in human life.

The specific goods of life, all of which exemplify goodness and express intrinsic good, are limited, but reason's discerning eye is able to recognize the goodness in them. These goods of life are the following:

- Life itself

- Physical integrity, self-consciousness, and the capacity for interacting meaningfully in one's environment

- The capacity to experience pleasure and aesthetic enjoyment

- The freedom and ability to work, play, and pursue speculative knowledge

- The capacity for forming loving relationships with other persons (friendships) and with a transcendent other (religion)

- The development of a personal identity that reflects character and a cohesiveness of personal integrity

- Practical reasonableness, which is a good of life that connects being and action and grounds all moral reflection[12]

These goods of life ground a moral ontology of human being, identifying intrinsically valuable goods discernible to reason as goods to be enjoyed, pursued, desired, shared, and promoted. These specific goods are the concrete expressions of a vision of goodness; they make goodness specific. Each particular points to some desirable aspect of life essential to human flourishing. Goodness shows itself through these particular goods, and the goodness is not hidden but visible to reason and to moral insight. Even if our attempts to give content to goodness fail, we see goodness manifest in human life, and human beings are possessed of the capacity to recognize goodness when they see it.[13]

The goods of life can come into conflict with one another, giving rise to moral problems and dilemmas. None of these intrinsically valuable goods is ever absolute in the sense that one good is possessed of such power that it can always trump any other good. The goods of life are always in relation to one another, and sometimes the messiness of life conspires with human imperfection to create a need for decision making about how to act and which goods to emphasize or diminish. The good of life is preeminent for the simple reason that without life no other good can be realized, but even life can come into conflict with other goods. Life is not an absolute good, which explains why lethal force can at times be used with justification, although justifying the taking of life is perhaps the most difficult moral chore. Some opponents of abortion rest their opposition to abortion on the claim that life is an absolute good, but closer examination of the absolutist "pro-life" position reveals that usually such proponents do not absolutize the good of life but only fetal life, and that for particularized religious reasons. The goods of life, from a moral point of view, are not absolute, but relational and subject to evaluation in the messiness of the moral life where decisions about what to do are always present in a context of freedom.

The goods of life listed previously identify two primary goods involved in life-affirming religion. Life is itself a good of life to be valued as intrinsically good, as is the religious relationship to ultimacy, to a transcendent other, to a "that than which nothing greater can be conceived." Religion that is appropriately life-affirming is directed toward promoting the good of life. Furthermore, religion constructs a relation

[69]

to ultimacy in such a way that the exercise of religion itself becomes expressive of goodness. Life-affirming religion is turned toward goodness. It is turned in the direction of realizing the goods of life and manifesting goodness in religious activity and expression. Life-affirming religion emphasizes creativity, as already noted, but also seeks to preserve life and promote the value of life. It emphasizes freedom and supports the furthering of knowledge and understanding through religion, not only of the world but of the self. It employs practical reasonableness to establish expectations for behavior — for what goodness in the religious realm requires of persons in their interpersonal relations, which gives rise to religiously framed moral instruction, such as the Ten Commandments, the Sermon on the Mount, or the Dhammapada. Life-affirming religion turns toward enhancing life and doing so by means of expressing goodness. It generates not only religious thought but behavioral action guides and expectations that are themselves grounded in a moral understanding of goodness. In short, it conforms religion and religious expression to goodness, for it insists that religious life come to fruition in such a way that goodness itself is realized.

Life-affirming religion turns toward creativity, building up persons and communities so that goodness itself might be further realized. Life-affirming religion always turns toward freedom so that human beings can use their capacities for evaluating and deciding in such a way that, in a context of freedom, they seek to conform action and being in the context of a relation with ultimacy. Human beings thus come to accept responsibility for who they are and what they do as religious persons. When life-affirming religion is in play, the goodness that undergirds it is not and cannot be hidden; such goodness is luminous and shows forth. Of such religion, the moral point of view will examine it, evaluate what is thought and done in the name of religion, and establish that what is thought and done conforms not only to a theological belief or understanding, but to goodness itself. To the extent that goodness illumines the religious thought and practice, the religion itself will be deemed, from the moral point of view, good.

Conclusion

The claim has been made that the hijackers who attacked the United States on September 11, 2001, were doing so at least in part from religious motivations. If that is true, those persons would have understood their actions in religious terms as being consistent with what they took to be the divine will. In other words, they would have assumed that because God was endorsing their actions, their actions would necessarily embody goodness even if the enemies of goodness could not see it. By what right can someone outside that particular community of understanding say that it was not good?

My case is that whenever religion inspires human beings to action, the critical evaluative issue from a moral point of view is to determine how or whether those acts express a vision of goodness. The terrorist attacks of September 11, 2001, failed to embody any vision of goodness. Those particular acts were not luminous with respect to goodness;

they did not show forth the illuminating effects of goodness. Although at least in part inspired by religion, those acts fall within the critical scrutiny of the moral point of view, which commands the simple insight that the willful destruction of human life is not a good to be promoted. Killing, whenever undertaken and even when undertaken for religious reasons, does not express goodness, even as goodness is manifest in that particular good of life we associate with religion: the relationship to ultimacy. Moral discernment focuses on goodness, and goodness is luminous, shining forth and making itself visible. The perpetrators of the September 11, 2001, attacks created a metaphor for their deeds. A thick, light-obscuring debris storm rolled through New York streets following the collapse of the World Trade Center towers, making darkness at midday their metaphor. The only thing luminous about those attacks was the momentary flash of exploding jet fuel.

Assessing the meaning of violent acts like those of September 11, 2001, or the Heaven's Gate suicides, or the killing and suicides in Jim Jones's Guyana, whether religiously inspired or not, is a moral task, not a religious one. About particular events involving religion and destruction many different kinds of questions can and should be asked; the September 11 attacks, in particular, press on Americans questions that many people are reluctant to consider, such as the reasons for the deep hatred and contempt with which so many in the world hold America.[14]

But if what guides moral assessment is a vision of goodness, then nothing that occurred in the destruction of that

particular day, the killing of innocent persons and the suicides of the perpetrators, allows the luminosity of goodness
to show forth. No good is to be seen in what occurred. That
good has and might yet come from these events has nothing
to do with assessing the moral meaning of the acts themselves, which were not in any way luminous with respect
to goodness. That those acts may have violated laws, even
sacred laws such as prescribed religious commandments —
the Qur'an, for instance, without qualification forbids suicide — is not critical to their moral interpretation. Those
acts must be adjudged and evaluated against the standard
of a vision of goodness. That is what it means to be moral
and to be in moral community beyond the contingencies and
relativities of culture.

September 11 provided a unique moment for Americans
to experience and even affirm the reality of the moral community of which they are a part, even if for many it shall
not prove an enduring experience. But the events of that
day provoked for many an encounter with the luminosity
of goodness — a direct experience of knowledge by acquaintance at the heart of the moral enterprise. That experience
exposed the reality of the moral community to which all
rational persons of goodwill belong. Unfortunately, the experience and awareness of moral community so pronounced
in the wake of the events of September 11, 2001, were then
obscured, even degraded, in the days that followed by a
nationalistic turn and its call for retaliation and vengeance.

Life-affirming religion is religion that has submitted to the
moral vision in which the luminosity of goodness provides
the norm for what is and what is not life-affirming. Life,

from a moral perspective, is itself a good of life, even a preeminent good. So the idea that life-affirming religion is what religion is or should be must itself be tested against this standard or norm: does it or does it not embody a vision of goodness? To say that life is good is to evaluate life as itself participant in the luminosity of goodness — its meaning as good is there to see.

Religion is a good of life, but it may come into conflict with other goods. It can even be so manipulated as to turn away from goodness. Religion may or may not be life-affirming. From the moral point of view, how people choose to be religious is an open question, and their actual decisions are open for testing against a vision of goodness. To say that religion *should* be life-affirming is to prescribe a certain way of being religious, one that must itself become transparent so that goodness can show forth in religious behavior and practice. Persons who accept a religion must determine how they enact their religion in a world of self-other relations. They must choose the ethical stance that they want their religiosity to express and embody in the world, and choose they must, for ultimacy must be interpreted and given symbolic shape and form. Morally speaking, ultimacy ought to be interpreted and constructed on a moral foundation so that it conforms to goodness. When people affirm ultimate reality, they of course assert beliefs and avow the efficacy of certain symbols as adequate to the chore of expressing those beliefs. But more than that, they also make manifest in their lives as religious persons their commitment to a moral vision wherein ultimacy becomes the vehicle to "divinize" a vision of goodness.

Life-affirming religion provides one option for how people choose to be religious, but it is a way of being religious that is, at its conceptual core, *moral,* because it embodies a vision of goodness in the practice of religion itself. Life-affirming religion is not a religious norm, but a way of being religious that checks and constrains religion in light of a moral vision of goodness. Religion is life-affirming to the extent that it seeks to embody goodness while finding sanction for that vision of goodness in ultimacy itself. Life-affirming religion is a way of being religious that subordinates religion and its defining concern for ultimacy to a moral vision in which ultimacy is itself constrained by and inextricably bound to a vision of goodness.

Although many inherit their religion, people at some point also choose the manner in which they are religious, even if implicitly. We may accept religion in the form it is handed on, modify or reject it, or opt for a form of religious thought and practice more compatible with larger issues of identity and existential self-understanding. But being religious is a choice, and we choose to be religious in the multitude of ways that we have devised for expressing ultimate concern in beliefs and religious practices. Whatever form that choice may take, the choice to be religious expresses the willingness to confront the givenness of existence as if it were a mystery, a transcendent mystery, even a gift; that decision affirms that life itself is participant in this mystery. In that life itself is a central value in religious thought and practice, the decision to be religious can be itself a way of affirming this high valuation of life. Life-affirming religion is a way of being religious that connects the meaning of life to the mystery of ultimate reality. In practice, life-affirming religion holds that life is to be treated with respect, is not to be destroyed, and is to be regarded as deriving its meaning and value from ultimacy itself.

The life-affirming option in religion is always open, but religion, being complex, powerful, and dangerous, ought not to be thought of as life-affirming by definition. The simple fact is that people can choose to express themselves religiously in ways that are not life-affirming, and doing so does not make them somehow "not religious."

Chapter Three

Being Religious:
The Demonic Option

MOST PEOPLE live their religion in domesticated form. They integrate religion into their lives and experience it as familiar, comfortable, and comforting. They find that developing a relationship with ultimacy through religion is itself a cherished good of life worthy of being preserved, protected, and promoted. They understand their religion to conform to moral ideas of behavior and action that emphasize moderation and concern for the well-being of others. They embrace religion as a primary cultural transmitter of moral meaning and values. They actually experience religion as an "ultimate" expression of goodness. For most people, the symbols of religious expression embody goodness and in no way oppose goodness or subvert moral ideals.

People can express themselves religiously in ways that a moral point of view would clearly evaluate as life-affirming, but religion itself is never reducible to the "life-affirming" norm. Religion is a complex phenomenon in human culture; as people construct, interpret, experience, enact, and manipulate religion and its symbols to serve spiritual need or to realize the good of relationship with the "transcendent other" of ultimacy, religion can take form in ways that subvert the life-affirming mode. The life-affirming way is, of course, the preferable, even optimal mode of religious expression from the moral point of view. Given that religion is complex and variable, however, people can, both individually and collectively, so engage themselves with ultimacy that their religion takes form in a way that distorts or even defies the vision of goodness on which life-affirming religion is based. People who are religious can, as religious people, turn away from life-affirming values. They do not cease being religious when they do so.

No student of human culture, history, or religion can fail to grasp that people sometimes express themselves religiously in life-denying and destructive ways. Religious people do not deny this possibility, although for most people the idea that religion can be tied to extremism and violence, fanaticism, and destruction is abstract, because that is not how most people "do" their religion. How people do their religion — how they enact it and practice it in the world of self-other relations — opens religion to moral critique. Such a critique can be offered by observing religion from the outside, describing religious practices and sponsored activities, and then evaluating their moral meaning. But the resources of religious thought can themselves provide access to this moral critique. Religious thinkers have long reflected on responses to ultimacy that turn destructive, even those responses within their own traditions of religious life and understanding. They have discerned that religion itself provides conceptual tools to evaluate and critique religion caught up in opposition to life-affirming modes of behavioral expression.

"Demonic" is the term often employed from within religious resources to describe religion turned destructive. The term "demonic" always points toward ultimacy and qualifies ultimacy. The term "demonic" also qualifies action. The demonic points to a movement away from life-affirming values while at the same time moving toward a life-denying destructiveness and disintegration. "Demonic" identifies one way of being religious, and the power and danger of religion cannot be fully appreciated without taking account of religion in its demonic mode of destructiveness. Understanding religion requires appreciation of the demonic possibility, for religion can convey human beings to ultimacy through demonic as well as through life-affirming means.

The turn toward demonic destructiveness is well-known and often discussed in other arenas of human experience. The term "demonic" has often been explicitly invoked as a metaphor to describe a certain kind of politics (fascism, for example) or art (Dadaist suicides as well as "snuff films" come to mind); even certain psychosomatic conditions, such as epilepsy, delirium, and schizophrenia, have been named "demonic." Although the term "demonic" can evoke meaning outside the religious realm, its distinction lies with its irrevocable attachment to the realm of religious discourse and meaning. "Demonic" invokes ultimate values, ultimate concerns, and ultimate meaning — the religious realm.

The idea of demonic religion allows us to explore the moral meaning of religious activity more completely. Religion is, of course, many things besides activity, but it is beyond dispute that religion sponsors and motivates certain kinds of actions, that it structures moral meaning and leads to expression in publicly observable behaviors. A moral critique of these behaviors is necessary to understand how people choose to be religious in certain ways and why they make the particular choices they do.

The claim that people choose how they are religious only makes sense if religion itself presents an option. Thus far I have suggested that religion in the life-affirming mode presents one option. People can also express themselves religiously in ways that do not affirm life or promote action grounded in a vision of goodness. This demonic option presents an alternative way of being in relation with ultimacy. My assertion is that people actually choose this option, and their reasons for doing so are similar to those that lead others to direct their religious life and practice in a life-affirming direction.

This demonic alternative, so prevalent in human religious experience and so often chosen by religious people as the preferred mode of religious expression, requires further elucidation.

The Demonic as Fanaticism

The demonic option expresses a turning away from life-affirming values because of a relation to ultimacy that suppresses, distorts, and even defies the vision of goodness on which life-affirming religion is based.

The demonic takes form in different ways in human experience, and moral philosophers and psychologists often invoke the demonic by referring to "fanaticism." Although fanaticism associates closely with political extremism, fanaticism also invokes the idea of ultimacy, and its presence in religious life is undeniable. If it is true that where ultimacy is, there will religion be, then fanatics are persons who attach to some object an ultimate valuation and then attend to that overvalued object with what is recognizable as a kind of religious devotion. Fanatics engage in single-minded pursuits around values or objects that are, for all practical purposes, objects of ultimate value. They "overvalue" these attachments, placing on a particular idea "too much psychic energy and intensity."[1]

Such overvaluation rests on a very human need for living what analytic psychologist Josef Rudin calls "a value-filled existence." Affirming and cultivating values in life expands our being, enhancing and enriching our very existence. Values dispose us to action; as Eduard Spranger has written, values signify "a perfection and thus induce striving."[2] No life can be thought meaningful without values being affirmed and incorporated into life as action guides. Those action guides reflect attitudes and orientations that finally settle in dispositions to action, and thus they become integral to character and identity. The values that become subject to fanatical overvaluation are avowed unambiguously and take on the character of absolute values beyond contingency and condition. Absolute values necessarily convey ultimate meaning, and, given that ultimacy is the core relational possibility in the religious realm of meaning, absolutized and overvalued objects come to participate in religious reality. Fanaticism, then, takes on a religious character to the extent that fanatical overvaluation expresses an extremism of thought and action, and does so in relation to some object deemed to be of ultimate, even absolute, value.

The object of fanatical and absolutized overvaluation could be practically anything, from atheism to certain symbols in a particular religious faith tradition — a cross or a Torah; from low carbohydrate diets to vegetarianism; from trickle-down capitalist economics to Marxism; fanatical overvaluation could also spin out from almost any political ideology, from libertarianism to despotism.

Fanaticism results from the absolutizing of passion. Passions themselves identify a concentration of value, an intensity of valuation around which all aspects of the personality congeal. They help integrate and unify the personality. Passions, as intensifiers of thought and feeling, focus attention on certain values in life, and they open up the possibility for an overvaluing process that becomes a necessary, though not a sufficient, condition for the development of fanaticism. Passions can be directed toward the realization of positive value, and passion even in religion need not generate the overvaluation that we associate with fanatical absolutism. Kierkegaard, for instance, although sometimes identified as a person with extreme religious views, played an almost moderate Aristotelian card when he endorsed religious faith as a "happy passion."

Passions concentrate value, and such concentration gives depth of meaning to life. A religion that did not inspire persons to passionate commitment, a moral philosophy that failed to call forth a passion for justice, or an aesthetic that denigrated a passion for beauty would hardly be worth the effort of attending to in any serious way. In a passion itself, however, even in the movement toward overvaluation, nothing is unusual or pathological. But passion left unchecked by the restraints of reason and other-regardingness opens up the dangerous prospect of fanatical overvaluation. Fanatical overvaluation can be discerned from various perspectives: psychology, ethics, politics, and, yes, religion.

Psychology recognizes this fanatical overvaluation in its analysis of obsessional disorders. Certain objects become the targets of a totalizing obsessional attachment, which so interferes with self-acceptance and social interactions that it creates illness and dysfunction and may be deemed pathological. Psychological descriptions of overvaluation gone pathological never fail to invoke the move into absolutism. Morality itself can become the object of such obsessional attachment. The following quote presents a psychological description and ethical interpretation of a moral absolutist, a fanatic of the ethical form:

> Let us clearly emphasize that what the fanatic of ethical form experiences is external conformity of action with the ethical form, with the "law." The more exact and complete this conformity manifests itself the more perfect is the experience of ethical form. Unyielding, integral behavior according to the strictest standards of

the moral code becomes the supreme value, the *fanum*. Ethical forms are absolutized and are in the center of thinking, feeling and action. Therefore to fulfill the last letter of the moral code under any circumstances and without exception is for these types a constant and entirely consuming task. Even authentic inner development and love for a supreme being and fellow man retreat before the force of this obligation. [These types thus experience] a strong sense of security . . . ; conceptual rigidity and externality generally drive them into behavior alien to life and reality.[3]

What I would focus on in this picture of moral obsession is how the fanatic is governed by absolutized conceptions that are entirely consuming, self-enclosing, and disregarding of exceptions. What is gained from such absolutizing is a psychological benefit — a deep and unchallengeable sense of certainty and thus security. This security is purchased at the price of "conceptual rigidity" and issues in behavior "alien" to life and reality. The fanatic, here a moral extremist but as likely to be formed out of political or religious interests, subordinates everything to the object of devotion and absolutized valuation. Even the value of life itself can be subordinated and thus rendered instrumental to an object of fanatical devotion. Life can also serve as the object of fanatical attachment, but even then, the dynamics of absolutism lead to contradiction, with life itself being destroyed in the effort to honor its value as absolute. Absolutism eventuates in relativizing, then denigrating the value of life as a preeminent good, subordinating it to a sacrificing impulse so that the object of overvaluation can be preserved, advanced, and promoted at all costs — even when the object of overvaluation is life itself.

If psychology examines the overvaluing personality and follows it into the pathology of obsessional disorder and absolutist thinking, ethics looks at fanatics and concludes that they are, as philosopher R. M. Hare writes, "those who aim at perfection in disregard of the interests of other people," for they "disregard others' interests in pursuit, not of human perfection, but of some supposed 'absolute' duty."[4]

This reference to duty signifies the important role of duty in moral reflection and the functioning of reason. In deontological ethics, one does one's duty as a free moral agent because reason itself bids that it be done. But what happens if duty itself becomes the object of fanatical overvaluation? Reason can necessarily turn against itself and in the grip of fanaticism overrule reason's own resistance to fanatical and absolutist overvaluation. Reason itself does not "cure" the pathological obsession, and it is not able to withstand an absolutism that undermines its effort to value other interests and goods of life. Absolutist modes of thought actually engage reason in order to blunt reason's own critical capacities, devaluing and disempowering reason's critical functions.

How absolutism overrules critical reason can be demonstrated by examining one consequence of absolutism: the fanatic's devaluing of life, which necessarily involves fanatics in devaluing their own lives. This consequence arises from an appeal to duty and acceptance of the rational imperative whereby reason itself bids one to do one's duty.

The logic of self-devaluation emerges from a premise itself rational to hold, which is that rational persons ought to acknowledge a prudential concern so to regard the good of life — including, especially, one's own — that they can afford their life necessary protection. Fanatic absolutism undermines this premise. A fanatic is not simply a person with a passion, say, akin to the passionate hatred a Nazi might have for a Jew. What makes the Nazi a fanatic is something more than hatred, even passionate hatred. The fanaticism arises as the hatred issues in action that overwhelms and defies so basic a rational concern as self-preservation and self-protection. So from hatred of Jews to the desire to see all Jews dead, the fanatical Nazi expresses fanaticism by holding that the duty to eliminate Jews is an absolute duty. Nazi absolutists would universalize hatred for Jews and say that Jews are so unworthy of life and such fitting objects of extermination that were they Jews themselves, they would consent to their own elimination. Fanaticism leads to destruction because it eventuates in the willing sacrifice of anything and anyone to the object of fanatical devotion. Moreover, fanatics themselves may even sacrifice themselves so that the destruction left in the wake of absolutist overvaluation — fanaticism — eventuates in a totalizing destruction.

Fanatics are committed to such a form of self-destructive reasoning. They employ reason to serve the absolutized object of overvaluation, thus denying reason a role in criticizing the fanatical effort to act against the most basic kind of rational self-interest: self-preservation. Fanatics do so this in order to advance their fanatical aims and desires. We can assume that those men who piloted airplanes into the September 11, 2001, targets were "fanatics" in this sense, persons so committed to an overvalued, absolutized object that to serve that object they not only willingly participated in murder but also consented to their own destruction.

Values affect action, and overvaluation leads to action that can be characterized as fanatical because it is absolutist; and we can discern this movement into absolutism in an ethical context quite apart from psychological descriptions. Religion, too, is familiar with the behavior we have been describing, and religion offers out of its own resource a means of analyzing the phenomenon of fanaticism when the object of overvaluation is a religious object and thus an object centered in ultimacy. Religion itself understands that objects grounded in ultimacy can be overvalued to the point that they become absolutized. While moral thought would continue to describe such a development as "fanatical," religion itself invokes another term. Religion calls this overvaluing absolutism "demonic."

What Is the Demonic?

Paul Tillich, a prominent twentieth-century Christian theologian, attended to the demonic form of religious expression: "In the sphere of the Holy itself there arises the polarity of the divine and the demonic. The demonic is the Holy (or sacred) with a minus sign before it, the sacred antidivine."[5] Tillich in this statement calls attention to the character of the demonic not as something alien to religion, but as something integral to it — a term of dialectical relationship within the sphere of religion itself. "The Holy," Tillich calls it, the realm of ultimacy.

Tillich is careful to say that the demonic does not stand outside of religion or over against it as the negation of religion. Rather, the demonic arises within the religious realm as a term of internal opposition, a negative valence within religion that has the effect, in Tillich's terms, of "distorting" the holy. Tillich held that the demonic effected such a distortion by enclosing the human — thus finite — religious aspiration to divinity, that mad desire to become the holy itself. Tillich, of course, would have assumed out of his own Christian theological tradition that such an aspiration is inevitably doomed to failure. Because only what is finite can aspire to be infinite, only something that is not the holy can aspire to be the holy; even the aspiration to holiness within the religious realm of meaning itself is a movement of demonic opposition to the holy. Tillich grasped that the term "demonic" could be used meaningfully to characterize authentic forms of religious expression. Its applicability as a term of opposition within the religious realm of meaning and discourse is, Tillich argued, discernible from even a causal look at the history of religious mythology: "Demons in mythological vision are divine-anti-divine beings. They are not simply negations of the divine but participate in a distorted way in the power and the holiness of the divine. The term must be understood against this mythological background."[6]

Tillich extends "demonic" into the world of human affairs and applies the term interpretively in discussions of religion, art, politics, and even psychology, but before doing so he reminds us that the demonic is grounded in religion as a term signifying relation to ultimacy, so that its power to evoke meaning is always tied in a basic way to the realm of religious meaning.

The particulars of Tillich's analysis of the demonic have been subjected to some scholarly analysis, and although more is needed, my purpose here is not to reiterate such work[7] but to explore the demonic itself.

The first thing I want to say about the demonic is that it is an authentic expression of human religiosity. The content of demonic religion is certainly translatable into other categories and systems of thought — say, the psychological, the ethical, and the political — and there are similarities between religious inquiry and how these other spheres of inquiry would describe and analyze the content of demonic attitudes and behaviors. Conversely, the term "demonic" provides a descriptive and interpretive tool out of the religious resource, which can be applied to various cultural and behavioral phenomena even if they seem not to be overtly religious. "Demonic" points to a way of being in the world religiously, that is, in relation to objects and values to which ultimacy is attached. My argument here is that this way of being in the world religiously actually presents a second "option" in religious life. Demonic religion identifies a particular way people can choose to be religious.

Second, religion that goes demonic is powerful, dangerous, and commonplace. Powerful, the demonic can penetrate any religious barrier of creed, practice, or tradition. Dangerous, the demonic can attach to an absolutist vision

of ultimacy with consequences that are unmistakably destructive. Commonplace, the demonic can — and does —
attach to any way of life that is centered on ultimacy. The
demonic can appear in any relation with ultimacy, including
in any religious tradition, for any relation to ultimacy holds
the potential for overvaluation turning absolute.

Third, demonic religion distinguishes itself from its life-
affirming counterpart because of three distinct characteristics: its destructiveness in a context of ultimacy, its negation of freedom, and its denial of goodness through self-
deception.

Central Characteristics of the Demonic

As helpful as Tillich's insights are in explicating the demonic,
an even clearer analysis of the content of the demonic can
be derived from focusing on the three central characteristics
just mentioned.

Demonic Destructiveness in the Context of Ultimacy

Demonic religion, like religion in the life-affirming mode,
addresses persons in the freedom of the spiritual life. The
demonic attracts, allures, and seduces as it promises to satisfy the very same needs that life-affirming religion does:
the needs for belonging, meaning, and relation with ultimacy. But demonic religion does not promote goodness, nor
is it essentially concerned with advancing and preserving

[90]

life itself as a central value. In the face of ultimacy, the demonic denies the goods of life and even life itself status as intrinsically valuable goods, but renders them disposable.

In the demonic turn, ultimacy is dissociated from any central moral concern to protect, promote, and preserve goodness and the particular good of life itself. Furthermore, a characteristic of the demonic is that it inevitably elides ultimacy into ideas of absoluteness. The demonic, in other words, creates an intimate connection between ultimacy and absolute power and authority; those gripped by the demonic seek to act in conformity with the will of the absolute rather than in pursuit of goodness or its expression in the goods of life. Demonic ultimacy establishes the meaning of action on the basis of power rather than on the basis of goodness.

From the moral point of view, actions generated from demonic springs bear, in publicly observable ways, fruits of destruction. Reason itself is assaulted. Ultimacy claims power to overrule reason's restraints on action. Moral ideals grounded in goodness — such things as respect for persons and for the goods of life — are subordinated to the will of the absolute. The demonic gets to destruction through its avowal of absolutism, for absolutism silences debate and crushes opposition. The logic of the absolute is such that whatever opposes the onslaught of the absolutist perspective is rendered, in the eyes of the absolute itself, a kind of defiant "enemy" that has no role except to conform or face elimination. Absolutism requires a totalized response — for or against, included or excluded, even life or death. Religious communities gripped by absolutist views of ultimacy have been known to identify the deviant impure and then encourage decontamination by means of violent, total destruction — through religious wars, inquisitions, heresy trials, and execution. Political absolutism that eventuates in mass killing also demonstrates how this demonic dynamic of absolutism plays out. Whether the example is Hitler's Nazi regime or Pol Pot's Cambodia, demonic absolutism assumes power to identify political opponents and render them disposable according to some totalizing criteria of undefiled political community. Those people excluded and branded as enemies are deemed worthy of destruction.

The demonic sponsors and encourages attitudes that demean and harm others — racism, sexism, classism, ageism, nationalism, and any other form of exclusive group identity avowed as part and parcel of ultimacy itself. Attitudes that separate people and assign value to persons on the basis of difference reinforce the boundaries of community sanctioned in the demonic turn. Countering the threat posed by excluded and "demonized" outsiders becomes a primary preoccupation of community life as the demonic shuns inclusiveness and diversity.

The demonic reconfigures otherness by invoking a category familiar to religion: purity. But the demonic absolutizes purity and thereby sanctions a cleansing of all that is impure, defiled, or perverse — all that is other and excluded. The acts that accomplish this cleansing can burst any bond of restraint and run the gamut of human cruelty. The demonic turn from goodness opens up action possibilities that range from common acts of discrimination all the way to organized missions of terrorism, murder, war, crusade, genocide, and even omnicide. Demonic action related to the destruction of the demeaned and thus demonized outsider can include various rituals of purging or purification in religious or political community; the devising of rigid codes to identify and punish deviance, including formulas of condemnation and thought control; and even the vigilantism wherein a group claims an ultimate power over life and then exercises it as if it were absolute power.

Demonic acts, whatever they are in particular, inevitably inflict intentional harm on the outside other and thus merit description as acts of violence. The targets of destructive activity are always twofold: the autonomous human person who in freedom can challenge the demonic turn away from goodness, and the humane community that seeks to forge universal bonds of unity based on mutuality and respect. The systems of moral meaning generated out of the vision of goodness stand in vigilant opposition to absolutism and its demonic ethic of power. The demonic inevitably expresses contempt for moral critiques generated out of a vision of goodness.

The destructiveness of the demonic can take many particular forms, but it originates in the human desire to absolutize — or, to use Tillich's word, "divinize" — ultimacy itself. The demonic arises in the wake of an aspiration to claim, assert, and then exercise absolute power under the aegis of absolute authority. Tillich claimed that the demonic aspires to a divine greatness — "to be like God" — so that the demonic identifies the human grasp to take possession of an absolute ultimacy, even to claim it for oneself.[8] But in the human effort to absolutize ultimacy — that is, to claim ultimacy under the protective and all-encompassing cloak of absoluteness — the demonic turn necessarily begins to unravel in contradiction. Destructiveness follows this unraveling; the bonds of unity holding together the personality as well as communities, even nations, begin to loosen as personalities become internally conflicted and communities disintegrate. The destructiveness of the demonic follows in the wake of the demonic aspiration to absolute power, and it emerges in all that the demonic wills accomplished.

Human beings under sway of the demonic dissociate ultimacy from goodness and hand ultimacy itself over to an absolutized ultimacy that must, necessarily and eventually, contradict itself. Thus does the God avowed as good spawn contradiction when absolutized, for the absolute God inevitably assumes responsibility for destruction and even evil. The demonic, because it embraces the absolutism and thus follows the logic of absolutist thinking, becomes destructive by aspiring to absolute power and authority. The demonic inspires human beings to undertake projects consistent with absolutized aspirations, and the projects that the demonic sponsors yield an inevitable destructiveness.

This rather formal description of demonic absolutism is anything but abstract when examined empirically. Although the history of religion is replete with relevant examples of the destructive effects of demonic absolutism, the demonic is always at work in religious life, even casting its shadow on the front page of today's newspapers. The contemporary religious and political landscape is littered with examples of demonic violence as religion snakes its way into the motivations for various acts that demean, destroy, and oppress, even to the sanctioning of war. To the extent that religion plays a role in generating, at least in part, motivation for violence and destruction, the form of religion at issue may be identified as demonic.

Religion can be discerned functioning in a variety of particular situations, inspiring acts of destructive violence in some cases, in others condoning violence by not acting to restrain it. In the mix of demonically destructive acts, special notice must be taken of religiously inspired suicide, whether in a suicide terrorist attack or in mass acts of self-killing like those committed in ancient Masada;[9] or in Shinto-based kamikaze attacks during World War II; or, in more recent years, in the People's Temple in Jonestown, Guyana, or the Heaven's Gate community in California. The destructive power of religion is never stronger than when it empowers people to cast off prudential self-regard and self-kill in defiance of the moral prohibition on suicide. When so basic a natural and moral commitment as self-preservation is swept aside in the name of religion and in obedience to ultimacy and the divine will, demonic religion shows the terrible awesomeness of its power. Any power that can motivate persons to suicide is dangerous.

Violence supported, sanctioned, or even inspired by religion is not only familiar in the contemporary world, but such violence continues to manifest an attack on goodness and on the good of practical reasonableness that is part and parcel of rationality itself. Practical reason seeks to conform thought and action, and, in the name of goodness restrain, and hopefully eliminate, acts of violence and destruction.[10] When the demonic succeeds in attacking rationality and dissociating action from goodness, the avowal of certain highly cherished life-affirming values become subject to demonic alteration by those who may resort to speaking the language of mind-boggling contradiction. A highly visible example of this contradiction appears in the absolutizing of the value of life — "sanctity of life." Many people who use this phrase in a literal sense do so believing that the sanctity of life can only be upheld by killing those who practically violate or fall short of satisfying the absolutized standard this view imposes. Thus do many who support the death penalty hold that those who kill should themselves be killed in order to demonstrate that killing is wrong and that society values life highly. This idea is itself an expression of absolutist contradiction, although the contradiction is often missed or glossed over. The demonic not only makes contradiction inevitable but familiarizes contradiction, making it palatable as rational, although it must appeal to hidden, secretive, nonpublic meanings beyond the logic of language itself. Consider how easily graspable and nonproblematic Utah Senator Orrin Hatch's statement appears today: "Capital punishment is our society's recognition of the sanctity of human life."[11] That such a statement should appear noncontradictory when it takes form linguistically as a contradiction is the result of demonic absolutism casting its spell.

The "sanctity of life" issue provokes other behavioral contradictions. In America, domestic terrorists have appealed to ultimacy and even invoked a reverence-for-life ethic to justify assaulting and even murdering health-care professionals who perform abortions, holding the absolutist view that no abortion is or possibly can be morally jus-tified.[12] Accordingly, the absolutist logic in such killings must go something like this: because those who commit murder should themselves be killed, and because abortion is murder, abortion providers are thus murderers who de-serve death. Killing them is therefore permissible action. Absolutism drives the view that abortion is murder, which not only prevents any abortion from ever being consid-ered a justified killing, but also exempts the killer of the health-care professional from observing ordinary moral pro-hibitions on killing. The absolute drives the killer of the abortion provider not only to killing but to certainty that even such extreme action as killing is a permissible and laudable response.[13]

Homosexuality is yet another issue where absolutist views affect the determination of who should live and who should die. That many people oppose homosexuality for religious reasons is beyond dispute. Citing religious sources where homosexual activity is adjudged an abomination in the sight of God, some extremists have gone so far as to advocate death for homosexuals. Their justification rests in an inter-pretation of Leviticus 20:13, where the teaching declares quite plainly that those who engage in homosexual activ-ity should "be put to death." To hold this teaching as normative, persons must invest the sacred Scriptures with absolute authority to express the divine will in interpreting these acts and prescribing a response to them. The ab-solutist reading of the text yields the conclusion that the divine will is clearly revealed through the text and the divine will is that homosexual persons should be put to death.[14] This absolute meaning is grasped through an absolutist interpretive lens.

These responses to ultimacy are mired in absoluteness. They are thus turned away from goodness and turned toward life-denying projects that seek to harm, even kill others — even at the risk of self-sacrifice and the destruction of meaningful life in community. Demonic religion makes its appearance whenever and wherever religion honors ultimacy by fostering violent attitudes and inciting acts that lead to destruction.

From the moral point of view, the destructive and contradictory results of absolutist religion are apparent in the empirical results of demonic religious activity. By "empirical" I mean to point to such observable phenomena as these: Jim Jones and his Jonestown followers are dead. The Heaven's Gate membership rolls have been purged, with every member of the cell community dead. Middle Eastern suicide bombers wind up dead, having so objectified themselves under an absolutist ideology that they allow themselves to become transformed from persons into weapons. In the hands of a demonic concept of ultimacy, the body comes to have value as a tool of destruction as it fragments under explosive force and disintegrates into an unrecoverable corpse on the pretext of advancing justice. From the moral point of view, nothing life-affirming comes out of such actions. The suicide terrorist wreaks destruction and loss of life. The murderers of abortion providers face loss of freedom if caught, perhaps even loss of life if subject to execution. Advocates of execution of gay persons would, were they to create their ideal world, pile up literally millions of bodies, and they would do so on the grounds that such killing is a religious duty that expresses the divine will revealed as a divine command. Morality would condemn these actions, as would life-affirming religion. That persons actually do such things as an expression of their religious understanding is the consequence of religion having gone demonic.

Destruction flows from the absolute. Absoluteness, recall, encompasses everything and holds all the cards. It is not open to change; it is not open to debate; it will not be affected by contrary points of view or be persuaded to alter its ideas or redirect its proposed course of action by rational argument. Absolutism thus will not invite qualification on its absolute pronouncements or engage in reflective reconsideration of the actions it sponsors. An ultimacy construed to be absolute denies diversity in thought and perspective. It does not hear the plea for an exception. It seeks to suppress such exceptions and conform diverse and opposing perspectives under the unity of the absolute itself. In the logic of absolutist thinking, the absolute necessarily seeks the destruction and total elimination of whatever opposes it. Destruction is therefore the consequence of absolutist thinking. When transformed into action that seeks to conform to the divine or absolute will, demonic thought sponsors activity that seeks not only to serve the absolute but to oppose, destroy, and totally eliminate all that does not conform to that will.

The moral point of view, however, because it concerns fallible human beings in their condition of finitude and limitation, is no respecter of absolutism. The moral point of view subjects all human activity to scrutiny; it will insist that the consequences of absolutist thought when expressed in action, including religious activities, be critically engaged and analyzed. The moral point of view discerns that action sanctioned by an absolute will or manifesting an absolutist ethic will wind up in contradiction and thus defy practical reason itself. An absolutist ethic can offer no action guide except that which requires unquestioning obedience to the absolute and its representatives, who claim power to transmit infallibly the absolute will. The moral point of view, however, exposes the fallacies of absolutism and proposes that an absolutist ethic cannot be followed consistently, for it will contradict itself and push those who follow it into contradiction. Consider the bomber who, in order to save fetal life, plants explosives at a health center where abortions are performed by actually putting expectant mothers and their fetuses in danger of violent death.

People who preach an absolutist ethic inevitably fail to live up to it themselves. Nowhere has this been more amusingly exposed than in the cases of certain televangelists who have preached an absolutist ethic of sexual purity only to be caught themselves in situations defying the sexual exclusivity clauses one could assume were made in their own wedding vows. The strictest, most repressive proponents of a religion gone demonic preach a morality generated from the will of an absolutized ultimacy, yet they cannot themselves live consistently with their absolutist perspectives.

No one can. Practitioners of demonic religion must, under the cruel logic of absolutism, finally defy practical reason itself, turn their back on the goodness they assume to be attached to ultimacy, and contradict themselves. Action that follows on the heels of absolutist thinking inevitably subverts rationality and destroys, however unwittingly, reason itself.

The demonic pursues in single-minded fashion an overvalued interest in the "that which" of absolutist attraction. In so doing, the demonic, when expressed in communal life, tears away at the integrity of those structures that order society. The demonic also assaults the integrity and the autonomy of the individual personality. Absolutism seeks to destroy all that opposes it, including reason itself, which sees absolutism as contradictory and thus an enemy of rationality. The demonic seeks to destroy reason as reason confronts it critically with qualification, exceptions, a commitment to noncontradiction, and exemptions from absolutized principles.

Absolutism, because it is generated by power and not by goodness, inspires acts that serve absolute power by disempowering any and all who might oppose it. Those gripped by the demonic will engage all that does not conform to the will of the absolute as an enemy, as a perverse force that must be opposed, suppressed, and ultimately, in the name of ultimacy, destroyed. The demonic seeks no compromise with this opposition, for the absolute does not, by definition, compromise. The absolute seeks its way by destroying all that opposes it.

Demonic religion centers on an absolutized conception of ultimacy, and because of this intimate involvement with absolutism, demonic religion ends up being a destructive power. The evidence of this destructiveness is, as I said, empirical, a point essential for grasping the self-deception at the heart of the demonic enterprise (which I address below). To discern demonic religion, look for the destruction left in its wake. When a religion expresses itself in such a way that it tears down psychic or communal integrity, or objectifies persons so as to render them "other" — as impure, perverse, and inferior outsiders worthy of being hated and demeaned — "otherness" itself becomes disposable to an absolutist vision that seeks destruction of all not encompassed by the absolute. The absolute knows no other way. The logic of absolutism necessitates the destruction of all opposition, a simple dynamic discernible wherever absolutism appears, whether in politics or in certain psychological states, in morality or religion. Religion that centers ultimacy not on goodness but on absoluteness — with all that absolutism entails — exposes the core of demonic religion, and destructiveness is characteristic of religion gone demonic.

Having made the case that the demonic is destructive, I must now qualify this notion to say that destructiveness is not in itself sufficient for determining the presence of the demonic. Aside from the obvious fact that not all destruction invokes the spiritual category of ultimacy, even religion grounded in and shaped by the vision of goodness can call for a certain kind of tearing down, breaking apart, or clearing away in the creative process. Destruction qualified by inclusion into a greater, ultimately life-affirming creative process appears throughout religion. Even the Hebrew account of the creation of light in Genesis could be said to be destructive of the totalizing condition of darkness that preceded God's first creative act. In Hinduism, Shiva, the god of dance and music, destroys even as Brahma creates and Vishnu preserves, so that the destructiveness is not a totalizing view of divine power but a way of contextualizing, even relativizing, divine creativity. Jesus "cleanses" the temple of those who profane its holiness. The Muslim *umma* (the community of the faithful) calls to arms to preserve the life of the community in the face of those enemies who seek to destroy it. If the demonic is present in any of these religiously grounded activities — and it certainly could be — it nonetheless must be argued for, because these examples come to us out of their traditions as part of a more complex vision whereby the destructive activity is in a dialectical tension with, and subordinate to, a life-affirming creativity expressing a deeper vision of goodness.

Having said that, it is also the case that when the demonic appears, it is so turned toward power and away from goodness that it inevitably expresses itself in a dynamic of destructiveness. The demonic is destructive in such a way that it moves against creativity and toward death, opposing, even negating, freedom itself, which identifies the second distinctive characteristic of the demonic.

The Demonic Negation of Freedom

The "demonic," being a term derived from the religious context of human existence, expresses a spiritual possibility.

As spiritual, "demonic" takes on meaning in the context of freedom. Freedom identifies the essential presupposing concept required for thinking about people as spiritual beings. Freedom and spirit are, in fact, complementary and intermingling terms, and even casual employments of "spirituality" in ordinary discourse refer essentially to freedom. Spirituality is what people do with their freedom.

One of the things human beings do with their freedom, both individually and communally, is to limit it for such important interests as advancing the common good or even assuring survival. Human beings curtail freedom whenever they organize themselves into communities and structure social life through the creation of social, political, economic, and even religious institutions. These structures exist because human beings create them, and they require for their existence a restriction of freedom. The demonic turn does not identify an effort to restrict freedom for rational and life-affirming purposes such as survival or promoting the common good. In the demonic turn, humans beings use their freedom to renounce freedom. This negation of freedom is the second characteristic of the demonic.

The demonic marks a passionate pursuit of ultimacy but does so in opposition to goodness and at the expense of the good of freedom. The demonic appears whenever freedom is suppressed, opposed, denied, or renounced. In the political realm, the demonic appears in political and social repression and in the move toward an absolutist politics of concentrated power. Although the demonic can infect any form of societal or political organization, totalitarianism or despotism presents the demonic in its most dramatic form.

In the religious realm, the demonic appears as an unbending ideological stance that drives toward religious or moral absolutism, where free thought and inquiry are denigrated and even suppressed. The demonic is present anywhere power is exercised to suppress spiritual freedom and to counter all that would promote the goods of life. The demonic is present in forms and structures that drive toward absolutism, yet in that connection to the absolute itself are the seeds of the demonic's own undoing. Just as absolutism logically entails its own contradiction, the demonic move into absolutist expression results in the destruction of form and structure.

The demonic is easily discerned in religious life and history, but the power of demonic absolutism is even more evident in the political realm. The examples of freedom's extinguishment are to be found wherever political liberties are constricted in the face of a concentrating power. Human rights abusers exemplify political demonism.

Observers and analysts often comment on the role of the demonic in the political realm. By invoking the term "demonic," they indicate the spiritual dimension of those events and processes put into place to contract liberty and constrict the freedom of the human spirit. Gore Vidal is a noted writer who uses the language of demonization to just such a purpose.[15] And an example of one who used the term more analytically for such purposes was cultural anthropologist Ernest Becker. Becker quite often appealed to the category of the demonic to comment in his writings on the presence of evil. Becker seemed to equate the demonic with evil itself, something I am reluctant to do because such an equation misses the gradations of movement in the demonic turn and suggests that the demonic can only be present in a fully realized form. "Evil" may describe the demonic when fully realized, but the demonic is, as a term of spiritual life and possibility, a much more fluid and free-floating notion than Becker's equation suggests.

In any event, Becker argued that evil was made possible by human beings refusing to accept the burdens of spiritual — as well as political — freedom. He observed that human beings in freedom create their societies and establish institutions to run them. Power to run these institutions is entrusted to leaders, who, when they come under the influence of demonic impulses, feed their desire for more power by revoking political liberties and successfully urging people to renounce their freedom. This theory, Becker's theory of dynamic political demonism, harkens back to Hegel's master-slave relation and Marx's invocation of "false consciousness," for it is a theory of voluntary enslavement. Human beings create, out of their freedom and subjectivity, structures of governance that "objectify the human spirit"; paradoxically, by "unleashing maximum power only to enslave" themselves, they sound the death knell of political and spiritual evolution. For Becker this self-enslavement announced the political instantiation of the demonic.

Specifically [the demonic] comes into being when men [*sic*] fail to act individually and willfully, on the basis of their own personal, responsible powers. The Demonic refers specifically to the creation of power by

groups...who blindly follow authority and conven-
tion, power which then engulfs them and defeats them.
...The irony is that in the realm of aspiringly free
creatures, structures of power become enslaving over
the very individuals who contribute to their creation:
the group dominates the individual and the leaders
manipulate the groups.[16]

This analysis, however dated the language may seem at
the opening of the twenty-first century, does point to the
ever-relevant expansion and contraction dynamic of spirit
in the political realm. Becker's morally charged critique offers a viewpoint that posits freedom, responsibility, and the
individual at the center of power, but then points to the way
this power is voluntarily given over to structures of power
that then become entrenched and assume spiritual authority.
Power, in other words, is relinquished and freely renounced,
and it is given over to what Becker called "experts" — leaders who becomes specialized in the art of taking power by
means of manipulation and group domination.

For Becker, power accumulates only in the face of a
renunciation of freedom and responsibility, and this renunciation identifies the demonic at work in the political realm.
Becker's analysis may have continuing relevance when applied to economic globalization and to the corporatizing
powers that fuel it, as well as in the persistence of absolutizing tendencies attached to sovereignty, which include
such movements as nationalism, imperialism, support for
an execution power, suppression of human rights, and even
state-sponsored terrorism. The immediately relevant point,

however, is that an analysis like Becker's reinforces the idea that the demonic asserts itself in political processes and relationships. The demonic is present as a spiritual power and grows at the expense of freedom.

Kierkegaard suggested a reason that human beings renounce their freedom when he wrote that "anxiety announces freedom's possibilities."[17] As the essential condition for moral autonomy and for spiritual relations with the good of ultimacy, freedom places a burden on human beings: the burden to reflect and inquire, to question and challenge, to assess and evaluate, to fashion meaning and undertake projects expressing care and obligation toward self, others, and even ultimacy. Freedom imposes the burden of selfhood itself, for it presents the possibility that human persons can enter into relations with themselves, with others, and with ultimacy such that they not only avow an identity through these relationships but act in ways that are consistent with the choices they make to be persons of a certain sort. Undertaking this project of selfhood identifies the great spiritual challenge of human existence, and the freedom that makes it possible generates disquiet, apprehension, and anxiety. The essential reason people renounce their freedom, then, is that doing so effects a significant reduction of existential angst. The spiritual need persons have to reduce anxiety and overcome the "fear of everything"[18] — including the fear of death — provides a powerful motive for the renunciation of freedom. The turn to the demonic allows this to occur.

The demonic offers a totalized response to spiritual need, which is essential to its allure. The demonic fashions a spiritual-religious option that offers a unifying vision of a transcendent ultimacy, a vision that forges powerful bonds of community and personal identity in relationship to the object of ultimacy. People can turn to various structures of meaning to address their anxiety, but religion is a primary resource given that anxiety is a spiritual condition generated by freedom itself. The demonic offers certitude and a structure for understanding. It suppresses freedom's questions and uncertainties, addressing spiritual anxiety through rigid, authoritative structures and institutions that rid the world of ambiguity. Those gripped by an absolutist ultimacy come to a self-understanding where they view *nonabsolutism as itself irrational,* for the absolutist system claims to provide total understanding. Nothing escapes it; nothing can be left unresolved or ambiguous. Such an option for understanding is invariably attractive to human beings who seek meaning and purpose and who find insufferable the anxiety generated by freedom.

Human beings can exercise freedom to make choices that repudiate freedom. When freedom is renounced, human beings rid themselves of ambiguity and uncertainty, and choose structures and institutions that exercise choice for them. The surrender of freedom is always a sign of the demonic, which expresses itself in all the little indicators of freedom itself. The demonic is not playful. The demonic has no sense of humor and does not laugh. It exhibits no flexibility in interpretation or appreciation for the context of decision making in human existence, which is always, experientially, a context of ambiguity and epistemological uncertainty. The demonic celebrates the unambiguous pronouncement and the kind of power that can offer such pronouncement. The demonic always expresses itself through proclivities to establish control, constricting and constraining possibility. It fosters a harsh judgmentalism and even emotional rigidity. While alluring with its ability to meet people's spiritual needs, the demonic then meets those needs by reducing existential anxiety with the "value added" bonus of overvaluation and absolutist extremism. The demonic opposes freedom even while it feeds on freedom, and it acquires freedom only as human beings in freedom offer freedom up in order to meet their spiritual needs for meaning and for belonging, which the demonic addresses and even satisfies.

The demonic always offers the lure of power. It is present as the spiritual issue in any absolutizing of a political agenda; it manifests itself in the movement away from freedom toward oppression, destruction, and disintegration. The demonic comes to rest in the social and political world as totalitarian despotism. In the religious realm, it will show itself in the structures invested with the power to interpret ultimacy. The demonic establishes absolutist structures, either as institutions pronouncing absolutely (e.g., "outside the church no salvation") or by investing finite structures of interpretation with infinite and absolute significance, as is often the case in biblical and other religious forms of fundamentalism. The demonic appears wherever religious form and practice center on power and do so at the expense of freedom, and even of goodness itself.

The Demonic and Self-Deception:
The Denial of Goodness

The question arises: How can people gripped by the demonic persist in their movement down the path of demonic destruction? My answer to this question provokes what I take to be the third characteristic of the demonic: that the demonic is sustained by people deceiving themselves about the meaning of their actions.

Self-deception is a difficult psycho-behavioral notion to explore, and rather than offering a theory of self-deception here,[19] let me invoke the concept of self-deception and suggest that "self-deception" refers to a self-directed project people undertake for certain reasons to mislead themselves about the meaning of things they are doing or feeling. This way of looking at self-deception allows us to discern that self-deception is itself an action that yields a kind of "split" between an action and its meaning.

Appeal to the concept of self-deception is essential for understanding how it is that people choose the demonic option in the first place as well as for understanding how they are able to sustain commitment to this option as they see the destructive consequences of the demonic issue forth over time. I would never deny the possibility that some may choose the demonic option in a state of full awareness, like Edgar Allan Poe's narrator in his short story "The Black Cat," whose reason for committing a murder was "because he knew it was wrong." Such perversity is certainly possible in human experience.

Most people, though, who make choices that lead to such negative outcomes as the loss of freedom and the spread of destruction would not, in my view, do so under the harsh light of full awareness. The demonic places persons in opposition to freedom and in conflict with goodness itself, thus yielding the negativity of the demonic. But persons gripped by the demonic do not also simply understand themselves to be "demonic." In other words, people do not choose the demonic like they choose how to fill a plate when visiting the salad bar, having decided "tomatoes but no olives." In the demonic turn, individuals respond to spiritual need, but they do not see before them a positive and negative option, then proceed to pick the negative because it is the negative option. Rather they choose the negative option because it is attractive and promises to meet spiritual need. The allure of power at the heart of the demonic is compelling, even decisive, but in order to embrace it they have to construe and interpret the demonic possibility in such a way that its status as demonic is covered up. In other words, they embrace the demonic possibility but do so only after having convinced themselves that it is really consistent with life-affirming values and notions to which they are also committed. Self-deception accounts for this process and interpretive possibility.

The demonic is subtle and must be detected from behavioral evidence of contradiction; what can be detected in the demonic is a disconnect between action and its meaning, between how a person acts and how a person interprets that action. Rather than acknowledging itself as demonic, I suggest, the demonic relies on rationalization, excuses, and denials to square demonic actions with a nondemonic interpretation. Human beings are inspired to action by the lure of goodness, and the demonic does not present itself, when looked at unflinchingly, as goodness. The demonic is alluring and attractive, and what it offers as a way to meet spiritual need is, for some people, a preferable way. To make the demonic turn, however, requires that an interpretation cover the movement down the path of the demonic, and that that interpretation conform to life-affirming values centered in goodness, for this is the ordinary spring for action: We are moved to action by goodness and by preferences for what is good. Individuals move in the direction of the demonic because they want to and because that way is attractive and preferable to its alternative. Yet so committed are they to the alternative that they invoke life-affirming values grounded in a vision of goodness to justify and explain what they are doing, which is an action description of self-deception. This identifies the "split" between knowing and not knowing that self-deception as a concept invokes — that is, the idea that as self-deceiver, individuals can cover things up, yet, as self-deceived, they are the duped victims of a deceptive action.

In self-deception, people create this split by acting one way and interpreting another. They conform action and its meaning in such a way that the action comes to look like ordinary action, where we know what is good and then act in ways that conform to it. Self-deceivers, even demonic self-deceivers, are committed to a self-understanding generated around goodness. But they also want to do things and meet needs in ways that do not satisfy the demands of goodness, so they deceive themselves into explaining to themselves, and sometimes to others, that their destructive acts are not really destructive but good. They offer elaborate, even ingenious explanations to make their case.

That human beings can make such a move accounts for the fact that people can choose to turn in the direction of the demonic. They make that turn by covering up the meaning of that choice and conforming it to goodness, thus persuading themselves that what they are doing is good and consistent with life-affirming values. To be sure, they are expressing by this interpretive move that they are committed to a moral understanding of what they do as consistent with goodness. Only morally committed persons are candidates for self-deception.

Ideas of goodness, then, provide persons gripped by the demonic with their internal explanation for why they do what they do. But the demonic allure is deceptive and misleading, and persons who fall under its spell ordinarily continue to interpret their actions as being consistent with goodness even as their actions enmesh ever deeper in the demonic dynamic. Self-deception, then, once in place and functioning, explains how people can maintain a steady progress on a path that can lead, finally, to full realization in evil.

The self-deception issue is crucial for understanding how people who do terrible and destructive things can actually proceed to do them. They are able to do them, I suggest, because they are able to interpret their actions not as demonic or evil, but of a piece with goodness and an expression of life-affirming values. The terrorists who died on September 11, 2001, gripped by what appears to be a demonic religiosity, undertook horrendous acts that their own religion condemned. How could they square what they did with what their religion teaches, which they would have understood as good? We can assume that they interpreted their actions as thoroughly consistent with their religion, but, even more importantly, as conforming with the actual will of God. In other words, they engaged in various interpretive maneuvers that redrew the boundaries of meaning in order to open up the possibility for murderous and suicidal action. Perhaps they told themselves that their acts of killing were not unjustified murder at all but acts of justified war against a terrible enemy, and their prospective deaths were not suicides but an acceptable, even appreciated sacrifice in a war that Allah approved. In the face of such interpretations, one could certainly ask, "How could you say that those interpretations are not valid?"

This important question must refer us back to self-deception. The demonic, I have argued, grips persons in such a way that the undertaking of wrongful deeds is accompanied by a cover story of goodness to explain and justify harmful, destructive actions. The demonic covers demonically inspired action with a narrative that claims to support a vision of goodness, even as the actions themselves betray that vision. The actions themselves, however, are not luminous with respect to goodness, which is, I suggest, the case with the September 11, 2001, events. It is characteristic of the demonic, however, that even such destructive and murderous acts as those of September 11 will be present in the minds of those who undertake them as good, even life-affirming. Absolutism is what makes possible such a contradictory state of affairs in the ideologies of religion and politics. The terrorist who kills and is killed could easily seek a unity of thought and action under cover of a religious interpretation broad enough to square action and interpretation.

But psychologically, a "split" is discernible between the act and the best, most reasonable interpretation. Reason itself would discern as ordinarily beyond the reach of interpretation as good a destructive act that inflicts harm and suffering on persons. Paul Tillich, who opened up the demonic to interpretation as a form of self-deception, paid considerable attention to this split between thought and action, writing at one point, "a main characteristic of the demonic is the state of being split. ... The demonic self-elevation of particular forces in the centered personality and the claim of their absolute superiority leads to the reaction of other forces and to a split consciousness."[20]

This split in consciousness appeals to the concept of self-deception, and self-deception can be shown to be at work in service of the demonic, preventing the demonic from coming to light in the full realization of consciousness as demonic. In the disparity between action and interpretation, this demonic self-deception becomes publicly observable. Furthermore, when the demonic fosters self-deception, it makes possible destructive, even evil acts by persons who deceive themselves into believing the acts are not evil but good. The acts may be acknowledged as not obviously good, because even the September 11, 2001, terrorists would have understood that what they would do that day would not be perceived by Americans as good. But under the logic of the absolutism that steered them into destruction, the absolutism that encompasses all things and transforms evil acts into acts endorsed and sanctioned by the absolute ultimate (Allah in this case), murder and suicide were rendered "good." To imagine terrorists killing themselves and others as a conscious act of wrongdoing and evil, with no goodness attached, would be almost impossible. Much more imaginable is the idea that the goodness is there but hidden from the eyes of those who cannot see it. Even more imaginable still is that terrorists who die killing others do so not only thinking that their actions are justified, but that they are good, that they are even life-enhancing and ultimately promoting the value of life. In that contradiction we see the demonic dynamic and the contradictions that absolutism creates.

The demonic invites, even invokes, self-deception, which is perhaps the most overlooked and subtle characteristic of the demonic. Self-deception comes to the fore when we ask why a person would "choose" the demonic over the life-affirming option. The answer is that the allure of the demonic is strong, the response of the demonic to spiritual need is great, and the choice for the demonic is made possible by means of a self-deceptive act that keeps at bay all thought of the demonic. In other words, the demonic exercises its power as the demonic even as persons interpret their actions as being consistent with a vision of goodness. It would be rare to find individuals so perverse and alienated from the grip of goodness and life-affirming rationality that they would choose the demonic and choose it clearheadedly, as if they could perversely choose to do what is wrong for the simple reason that it is wrong.[21] Again, such a possibility is not unheard of, but this is not the usual way wrongdoing is accomplished. Self-deception is a key to the functioning of the demonic.

Features of the Demonic: A Summary

Having discussed the three central characteristics of the demonic, I wish to present several other summarizing features, some mentioned along the way, that fill out the picture of the demonic option. The following propositions clarify important aspects of the demonic.

The demonic is real religion. First of all, in presenting the demonic as a live option for the expression of human religiosity, I mean to affirm that demonic religion provides a valid way for human beings to enter into relationship with ultimacy and thus express themselves in ways that are authentically religious. Demonic religion is not false religion or perverse religion or untrue religion. It is real religion, and religion itself so encompasses the demonic that it understands it as a powerful and dangerous option for religious expression. When people adopt religion in its demonic forms, ultimacy can be discerned driving their activity and expression as they engage the world and others. The judgment that demonic religion yields harmful effects and is destructive of human purposes; that it subverts all that allows human beings to flourish; that it contradicts goodness or is unworthy of avowal by rational human beings; that it ought to be discouraged, opposed, suppressed, or even defeated — these judgments are all moral, not religious. The demonic is always a possibility in religious life. Demonic religion is real religion.

The demonic meets spiritual needs. Second, demonic religion in a formal way meets the same spiritual needs that life-affirming religion does. Human beings have a spiritual longing for understanding and meaning, and given the mystery of existence, that spiritual quest can only be fulfilled through some kind of relationship with ultimacy, whether or not that takes form as a "transcendent other." Religion — even demonic religion — has power to meet this need for meaning and transcendent relationship. In that such a relationship assists persons in understating and making peace with the unknowns of existence, religion — even of the demonic variety — instills a sense of power, mastery, and control over existence.

The demonic also meets the need of human beings to form bonds with one another in community: as life-affirming religion gives rise to communities of like-minded, so too does demonic religion. Thus the human need for belonging is met — in demonic form. The needs that demonic religion — or life-affirming religion for that matter — meet are psychological, political, philosophical, and existential. Religion provides people with an access to meaning and purpose in life that no other realm of existence satisfies, and demonic religion responds to the human needs for meaning and certainty, for power, for belonging. Demonic religion meets human spiritual need.

Demonic religion is attractive. Unquestionably the demonic is alluring and has power to become itself an object of human desire. Because demonic religion is real religion and meets real human spiritual needs, it presents itself in such a way that those who find their way into it come to express themselves in ways consistent with the particular vision of ultimacy at the heart of this religious form. People are not attracted to demonic religion because it is false or a perversion of religion; they are attracted by all it promises to do for them, and more often than not it delivers on its promise. Demonic religion satisfies the spiritual need for transcendent meaning, for understanding and certainty, for power, and for belonging.

People who find themselves gripped by demonic religion do not understand their religion to be demonic. They may in fact understand it to be the true essence of life-affirming religiosity; this peculiar phenomenon of demonic religion, discussed previously as related to self-deception, underscores that those attracted by the demonic option do so believing that they are serving rather than turning away from a vision of goodness. The demonic so presents itself that it can be interpreted as a good. The demonic sponsors actual forms of religious or political expression that promise to realize this good, so that people will be motivated to act consistently with demonic commands and aspirations since they come to be present to moral consciousness as good acts, worthy to perform. In presenting itself garbed in the appearance of goodness, and by addressing and meeting spiritual needs, the demonic is attractive and has an enormous power to allure and seduce.

The demonic is a live option. Fourth, the demonic presents itself as an option in religious life that can be chosen. The demonic presents itself in competition with another way to be religious, the life-affirming option, and it sometimes wins. It wins because it is present to the moral consciousness as a live option that addresses spiritual need and satisfies human longing for meaning, power, and belonging. Life-affirming religion makes the same appeal. For persons facing religious decision, whether that decision comes to consciousness explicitly or implicitly, the avowal of ultimacy presents itself calling for understanding, commitment, and a dedication to conform one's life with the values ingredient in the vision of ultimacy at the heart of the religious enterprise. Demonic religion calls for persons to conform their lives to a vision of life grounded in the particularities of demonically presented ultimacy, which, because it is religious, carries with it a demand for commitment, perhaps self-sacrifice, and for action in the realm of other-regardingness consistent with the values sponsored by ultimacy itself. The decisions people make are enacted and visible in public behavior. We can infer belief and disposition from what people do and how they act. Just as life-affirming religion is behaviorally manifest, so too is demonic religion.

How persons come to adopt and then express themselves through demonic religion is affected by many variables, including cultural context, family life, social or political situation, educational upbringing, personal psychology, and all that affects human beings in their individual lives and as persons who become morally formed by intersecting with others in a variety of communities. But at some point and on some level of awareness, human beings who are religious decide for one way of being religious rather than another; moreover, they seek to conform themselves to what they believe about ultimacy and what they believe they will derive as benefit from the particular form of ultimacy they avow as true and meaningful for them. The decision to opt for demonic religion is not made in a vacuum; it is a constrained choice, as most human choices are. Opting for demonic religion is contingent and affected by many factors, but the fact is that when religious people become religious they express themselves behaviorally and enact a religious vision that turns in one of two basic directions: that of the life-affirming or that of the demonic. To have turned religiously in one of these directions is always the result of having opted — for complex individual, social, and cultural reasons — to be religious one way rather than another. That other way — the way not chosen — is always available and always present itself to religious consciousness as a possibility in the realm of spirit. It may be present to consciousness as a temptation or as fallacy, but it presents itself as an option human persons have the capacity to accept or reject. Demonic religion, then, is an option, one people actually choose.

The demonic indicates a direction. Fifth, and finally, the idea of the "demonic turn" is meant to hold up the subtlety of religious life and the fact that a turn in one direction rather than another ought not to be equated with the full realization of a religious possibility. That most religious people are "turned" in the direction of a religious possibility expressive of goodness does not mean that every one so turned has fully realized the possibility of goodness and thus merits description as a saint. Similarly, a demonic turn does not mean that individuals have come to a full realization of evil.

The demonic turn is a spiritual possibility that finds expression in different ways and to different degrees, and the critical issue concerns the decision to turn one way rather than another. In that turn, steps are taken down a path, and every step taken moves one further toward the end of fully realizing the end of actual evil. The idea of a "turn" suggests a kind of gradualism and relativity, but also a clear directionality. Helpful in thinking about this is the notion so central in Eastern religions, most notably Hinduism and Buddhism, of karma. Karma is a law of cause and effect that creates a moral universe. In that moral universe, everything one does affects everything else one does, but often overlooked is how every consequence of every action so affects the next action that it restricts maneuverability and freedom to act. The pathway before one narrows, however slightly, with every step taken down it. So, for example, people who develop drinking problems may affect their ability to respond to those problems by making decisions about who they will socialize with and how they will integrate alcohol into their lives; with steps taken in the direction of confirming ever greater importance for the role of alcohol, the options to change course become more difficult. The pathway starts to close in, and eventually, maneuverability is affected to the point that freedom itself can be lost. People seriously afflicted with an alcohol "problem" have lost the freedom to make decisions about the role of alcohol in their lives, even as they relied upon freedom to move as they did. The term "demonic" can be understood as karmic in this way: every act that is destructive of relationships leads to others, until soon the destructiveness comes to have what appears to be a life of its own. On the other hand, every individual, even those far down whichever road they have chosen, can have experiences and changes of heart that allow them to turn toward the other option. That the demonic appears in the folds of religious communities is no mistake but a clear consequence of self-deception entering to affect understandings of acts as good.

No religious community or tradition is exempt from the effects of the demonic. Although many Americans today look at Islam as having sponsored demonic forms, the fact is that when Paul Tillich examined the demonic, he saw it everywhere: in capitalism,[22] fascism,[23] and even science itself[24] — all in their distorted claims to ultimacy. When he turned to religion, Tillich concerned himself with his own Christian tradition, identifying the demonic in everything from formulas of condemnation, the inquisition, the tyranny of Protestant orthodoxy, and the fanaticism of its sects, "the stubbornness of fundamentalism, to the declaration of the infallibility of the pope."[25]

No religious community — no community — and no religious tradition can avoid involvement with the demonic, because this spiritual possibility is ever present and ever alluring, and the burdens of anxiety created by freedom can be onerous and difficult to carry.

Life-affirming religion, as well as demonic religion, presents a long road, a continuum of sorts, where at any given moment individuals are at different points along the way. Perhaps the point where life-affirming religion is fully realized is what we mean when we identify someone as a "saint." Perhaps the point where demonic religion is fully realized is what we mean when we identify someone as consumed by the condition of malefaction we call "evil."

But the complexity of religious life is such that we must recognize that saints were not always saints, and evil persons were not always embodiments of evil. People are in different places along the way, with very few cases of "full realization" available for our inspection. So full realization is not of concern here, but the turn people can make freely in one direction rather than another. Even there, people can be turned one way one day, another way another day. The demonic has an everyday ordinariness that is not hidden from view. All persons have known the demonic in different ways and to different degrees in their own experiences, even as they have known life-affirming forms the same way. This concept is important, because the idea that one of these ways of being religious is preferable to another — a case I shall make in these pages — depends upon an ability to recognize that the capacity for being religious either way is within our grasp. The moral chore of religious life is to choose the life-affirming form of religion in full view of the demonic option that never idles and never withdraws from view as an alluring enticement for how to "do" the human relationship with ultimacy.

Demonic religion, then ought not to be identified with evil, but only with a turn toward a way of being religious that emphasizes certain things that life-affirming religion does not, and that evil is only an appropriate term when this way of being religious finds itself more completely realized. Demonic religion is headed toward evil, but the demonic ought to be thought of as a particular way of being religious and as an orientation toward certain characteristics of religious expression rather than as a synonym for evil. Demonic religion is complex and fluid and ought not to be uncritically equated with a full realization of evil.

Discerning the Demonic and the Domination Ethic

Demonically directed individuals express an unchallengeable certainty about religious and moral meaning; they absolutize symbols and thus refuse to recognize symbols as symbols, especially the symbols of words themselves; and they don the armor of moral superiority. Thus armed they sally forth to enforce that certainty in the face of opposition to it, resorting to such power-laden and freedom-denying acts as religious intolerance, political and economic oppression, and the creation of restrictive, even oppressive, social, political, and religious structures.

People gripped by the demonic constrict and self-enclose, for the tone of the demonic is nonexpansive and inward-looking. This is not the inwardness we associate with life-affirming spiritual cultivation, which issues in an increased awareness of interconnectedness and sensitivity to others; it is, rather, the concentrating effort of the ego to marshal its resources in a grasp at power. Demonic negativity expresses itself not only through overt action but through affect. The demonic concentrates in such powerful but negative emotions as resentment, frustration, fear, antagonism, contempt, revenge or retaliation, even malice. If the shoeless wanderings of St. Francis illustrate the freedom and light touch of a life-affirming spiritual adventurer, the heavily garbed and humorless Inquisitioner, institutionally vested with judgmental authority over life and death, illustrates the ponderous malevolence of a demonically realized spirituality.

From an ethical point of view, the demonic cannot be said to foster the kind of fellow-feeling where persons encounter each other with respect and mutuality. The demonic, rather, distorts visions of equality and resists the building up of community based on mutual respect. The demonic forges strong bonds of unity, but it does so around the egoistic desire for power. The demonic fosters a grasp at the power of domination over others, creating bonds of both individual and group identity and a sense of belonging "over against" others and "at the expense" of others. The demonic raises its head whenever the expansive vision of "we" is reduced into an objectifying pronouncement of an "us" against "them." The demonic appeal to an absolutized ultimacy creates the sense of an unquestionable objective reality delivered up with certitude. Certain not only of truth but of the moral superiority it bestows, those gripped by the demonic enter the moral sphere of self-other relations as moralizing absolutists. They "demonize" others, denying those with whom they are in opposition the human dignity and the protections, even that of life itself, that they should be able to claim as persons.[26]

[127]

Part II

RELIGION AND THE RESTRAINT OF VIOLENCE

MORAL REFLECTION inquires into the meaning of action. Religion is not morality, but moral reflection subjects religion to scrutiny as it asks why people enact their religious beliefs and commitments the way they do and why they do so one way rather than another. The moral point of view attends to reasons for action, and religious action is always subject to moral interpretation and evaluation.

The life-affirming/demonic distinction has been offered as a way to help conceptualize the moral option that presents itself whenever people act religiously. Thus far, we have considered both modes as valid forms of religious expression and have acknowledged how a turn in either direction can meet spiritual needs. Moral inquiry, however, asks more of us. In the preface of this book, I presented a statement from Swami Vivekananda who, at the turn of the twentieth century, showed deep appreciation for this life-affirming/demonic option in religion. But reflecting on the moral meaning of this option, Vivekananda went on to advocate for one way of being religious over another, thereby addressing the moral question to be found at the heart of all action and behavior framed by religion in the context of the human relationship to ultimacy. As this book now moves into a second phase of its moral argument, I want to do the same thing — advocate for one option over another.

As a function of the demonic is to express itself destructively through acts of religiously inspired violence, a function of life-affirming religion is to oppose violence and respond to violence in ways that assert life-affirming values. The moral point of view endorses opposition to violence and does so on the grounds that such action conforms to the vision of goodness that undergirds the moral life itself. Holding to the descriptive point that religion has in the past and will continue in the future to involve itself with violence and the use of force, I want now to advance, even defend, the life-affirming religious option. This end can be accomplished by seeking to expose the ways religion provides resources for responding to violence and doing so in ways that resist the demonic.

That religious people in the name of their religion and under its authority need not pursue the life-affirming option is obvious enough. Religion can incite and sustain violence, doing so through its power to authorize and legitimate uses of force in the name of ultimacy itself; historically, religion has provided the spark for innumerable conflicts, many of them violent. How can religion create a possibility for responding to the problem of violence in such a way that life-affirming religion is preserved and not sacrificed? How does religion support and endorse life-affirming values in the face of conflict and threats to the goods of life, even goodness itself? These questions are at issue in the second part of this book.

In the pages that follow, pacifism, holy war, and the idea of just war are subjected to moral inquiry and evaluated in light of the life-affirming/demonic distinction. As action responses to violence that may express religious ideas and commitments, each of the three responses is nevertheless a mode of action that serves a moral possibility, either expressing a life-affirming vision of goodness or, conversely, turning in the direction of the demonic. We begin with an examination of these possibilities as they are present in the responses to violence housed under the general heading of pacifism.

Chapter Four

The Pacifist Option

PACIFISM IS A PHILOSOPHY directly related to the activity of settling conflicts, and many who avow a pacifistic philosophical stance do so in the context of religious faith. In broad, general terms, pacifism identifies a philosophy that says disputes should be resolved peaceably and nonviolently. The principle of pacifism is that violence should not be met with violence, that peaceful means (e.g., arbitration, surrender, migration) should be employed to settle conflicts between nations and even between individuals. We associate pacifism with such luminaries as George Fox, Tolstoy, Gandhi, and Einstein. Even Jesus has been presented as a pacifist, and there is ample evidence in the Christian Scriptures to support such an inference.

The term "pacifism" invokes a core meaning related to nonviolence, but in actual usage the term covers a wide range of meanings related to war, killing, violence, and uses of force. Although pacifists are usually identified as those who would deny the moral legitimacy of war and thus withhold moral justification for uses of force, some flexibility and nuance are necessary when invoking the term "pacifist." Some self-identified pacifists would deny that any use of force is justifiable between nations, yet they would allow a use of force by police. Nuclear pacifists oppose any use of nuclear weapons but not use of conventional weapons; others identify themselves as pacifists on the grounds that they oppose a use of force against any noncombatant; still others identify pacifism as a moral prohibition on all forms of killing, including killing in the name of self-defense. These notions are obviously not all equivalent.

Pacifism provokes reflection on the good of life and the protection, preservation, and promotion of that good by nonviolent means. Pacifism is committed to shunning violence and uses of force harmful to the goods of life, including that of life itself, so that the nonviolent commitment at the heart of pacifism can easily be interpreted as presumptively a life-affirming response to violence. But because religion has assumed a major role in advancing pacifism and has thus connected the commitment to nonviolence with ultimacy itself, that commitment is subject to the distorting effects of the demonic. Even a supposedly life-affirming pacifism, when sponsored by religion and grounded in ultimacy, can be subject to the distorting effects of the demonic. Any form of religiously grounded pacifism that allows the ethic of nonviolence sponsored by ultimacy to be transformed into an absolutist ethic can be expected to reveal all the moves that take place in the demonic turn. The commitment to nonviolence, once absolutized, can be expected to yield contradiction as all forms of absolutism do;

even religiously grounded pacifism, if absolutized, can come to express the demonic. I shall now discuss this form of pacifism further and provide an example of an absolutist pacifism that exemplifies exactly that demonic move toward self-contradiction.

Absolutist Pacifism

Ethicists sometimes draw distinctions between various forms of pacifism that are reason based. Appealing to reason rather than religion, the case is sometimes made that reason itself is sufficient to justify a response to conflict that refrains from aggression and refuses to rely on use of physical force. One form of reason-based pacifism, deontological pacifism (Greek: *deont-*, "that which is obligatory" or "duty"), holds that nonviolence is itself a practical duty that reason commands and thus bids be observed as a duty. From this duty-based ethic it is a short leap to the idea that the duty to act nonviolently in the face of conflict is itself a standard that brooks no exceptions and holds without qualification. Such a form of pacifism would not look to consequences but only to the reason-based injunction that a use of force to oppose force is itself a violation of reason's command.

A quite different mode of moral reasoning is advanced in utilitarianism or consequentialism. Consequentialist pacifists of the rule-utilitarian stripe[1] would not see any intrinsic evil in aggressive actions or uses of force, but would, rather, ground their pacifism in the idea that war and violence always lead to negative consequences for the greatest number. Consequentialists would articulate an ethic based on the negative utility of resorting to force, and this would suffice to justify a pacifistic stance. Holding that right action, even goodness itself, is determined by maximizing the greatest aggregate good for the greatest number, utilitarians (or consequentialists) so inclined to devise rules as general action guides could conclude that pacifism maximizes utility, minimizes disutility, and thus leads to the most desirable and "good" result, so that rules supporting this general conclusion may be devised and then employed to endorse the positive restraint of a pacifistic stance in the face of war, violence, and aggression. A consequentialist, therefore, could support pacifism as a rule-bound means for maximizing goodness or happiness (or whatever one establishes as the content of utility), and thereby hold that this end is only accomplished if everyone follows this rule.[2]

This philosophical understanding of pacifism may or may not yield an absolutist stance. Consequentialism, for example, is not usually thought about in terms of establishing principles or guidelines that are exceptionless and absolute; deontological perspectives, while tending more toward absolutist thinking, provoke controversy around the issue of philosophical rigidity. Although some deontologists do seem to wind up advocating moral absolutism, this is itself not a necessary conclusion to reason-based, duty-based moral thinking. The connection between deontological ethics and moral absolutism is not necessary, even if many who support the deontological approach to ethics actually wind up advocating moral absolutism. But when absolutism appears, the problems distinctive to all forms of absolutist thinking also appear. A deontological or duty-bound absolutism provokes contradiction, which appears as the human agent is commandeered by absolute duty and is thus robbed of agency and transformed from autonomous to automaton. Denied a freedom to discern moral ambiguity and evaluate moral meaning, the freedom to choose would itself be undermined, which in turn would deny the moral agent autonomy. Because the moral life requires human beings to assume the status of free agent, the loss of this status would undermine the possibility of the freedom and decision-making autonomy necessary in the moral realm of self-other relations. Moral absolutism, then, would actually suppress the conditions of moral existence and thus eviscerate human existence of moral meaning. Moral absolutism of a deontological stripe would shipwreck on contradiction and subvert the foundations of practical reason itself, all the while advancing an ethic as absolute and absolutely binding, about which there could be no question, no uncertainty — but also no freedom.

Such contradictoriness in formal ethical theories need concern us no further, although it is appropriate to note that the loss of freedom attendant to absolutist thinking destroys the very context for formulating any sense of goodness as well as meaningful decision making. The contradictoriness that inevitably inheres in absolutism subverts practical reason itself, and we can meaningfully ascribe "demonic" to this state of moral topsy-turviness, even though the action guides we would be dealing with present themselves as rigidly clear moral guidelines or principles. But as absolute, they are too rigid and too clear, so much so that they undermine the context of freedom and lead inevitably to contradiction and thus self-destruction.

Turning attention to the religious realm of relationship and meaning, let us be reminded that religious thinking is always framed by a concern for ultimacy and that ultimacy is susceptible to interpretation as absolute. Absolutist thinking in the religious realm affects how ultimacy itself is conceived and avowed, but more than this, it affects behavior in the realm of action. Absolutism, when it infects religion, necessarily affects how persons express themselves behaviorally in the moral realm of self-other relations. The specific issue at hand is how pacifism might be, when examined in the context of religious thought, so constructed as to preserve ultimacy while promoting a vision of goodness, the hallmark of life-affirming religion. How, in other words, can a pacifism grounded in religion support and promote life-affirming religion and avoid the pitfalls of demonic religion? For those who never even think of pacifism as a potentially "demonic" undertaking, is there any sense to be made of the idea that pacifism could be meaningfully deemed "demonic"? Is there a demonic pacifism?

There is of course a quick and formal answer to these questions: A pacifism grounded in religion is life-affirming to the extent that it expresses and embodies a vision of goodness that in turn avoids the snares of a contradictory, freedom-denying, and destructive absolutism. Yes, a demonic pacifism is possible. Any perspective, when it is absolutized, be it religious or philosophical or ethical, invokes the demonic to the extent that it invokes absolutist thought. Absolutism is the hallmark of the demonic, and demonic destructiveness need not issue in so dramatic an expression as terrorist murder. Conceding that there may be "gentler" forms of the demonic, I wish to acknowledge that pacifists who give way to absolutism are individuals seeking to protect and promote the good of life by an extraordinary commitment to nonviolence. Yet, because this commitment is conceived as absolute, contradictoriness will nonetheless appear, and the nonviolence will eventually and inevitably subvert the goods of life, and even the good of life itself.

That said, demonic pacifism would be that form of pacifism grounded in a religious understanding of ultimacy absolutized around such principles as "life is sacrosanct" or "no killing can ever be morally or religiously justified" or "the use of force must never be used in any circumstance." The absolutism shows itself in the "never" and "always" language. As absolutist, the perspective is exceptionless and uncompromising; as a religious perspective, this form of pacifism settles in an absolutized ultimacy, most likely manifest in an appeal to divine authority and "the will of God."

When people invoke God's will as their reason for acting, they appeal to a logic that is at least tight, even if not sound. Grounding the meaning of action in the divine will removes moral ambiguity, because no uncertainty attends a command to act issued from an all-knowing and absolutized arbiter of moral meaning. More than that, appeal to the divine will allows individual persons to act as if they were actual agents of the divine, so that any call for flexibility in applying nonviolent principles or calling for an exception in the face of a peculiar circumstance would be to raise a dispute with the divine will itself. The absolute pacifist would not, as an absolutist, entertain the thought of such a dispute. Neither would such an absolutist acknowledge room for reflecting on a variety of action possibilities sensitive to difficult situations and complex circumstances. Moral reflection in the context of freedom would insist on such reflection in the face of ambiguity and uncertainty; absolutism imposes itself by command and simply requires obedience.

Religiously grounded absolutist pacifism provides one resource for responding to violence. Its prescription to nonviolence expresses commitment to an absolute principle of nonviolence, and that absolutism is derived from the divine will, which such pacifists accept as having been revealed with absolute clarity. What makes this perspective less than tenable from the moral point of view is its status as absolute. As absolute, this form of pacifism will necessarily turn on itself in contradiction and assault the goods of life by eroding freedom and even agency itself. How does this occur?

To answer this question, let me offer the example of the distinct form of religiously grounded absolutist pacifism associated with Christian "nonresistance."

The nonresistance perspective takes its source authority from New Testament Scriptures and is believed by those who hold it not only to be the literal words of Jesus but a direct, clear, unambiguous, and authoritative revelation of the will of God. This grounding of the command to nonresistance in the will of God allows us to associate nonresistance with a religiously absolute pacifism.

The actual source authority for the perspective is a verse in the Gospel of Matthew (5:39), where, in his Sermon on the Mount, Jesus said, "Resist not evil," or, as other translations put it in English, "Do not resist those who wrong you."

This particular idea is enunciated in the context of Jesus' words of instruction to his followers regarding how they should act in the world if they are to act as God wants them to act. Ideas about action that have long been deemed distinctively Christian emerge from these passages in Matthew, and the "resist not evil" instruction is put forward in the context of other action guides, such as the call for followers to love not only the neighbor, with whom one may be at peace and who is therefore not difficult to love, but to love one's enemies and pray for one's persecutors. In all of these sayings, Jesus advanced a perspective of ethical extravagance that claims "there must be no limit to your goodness" (Matt. 5:48). This last verse appeals obviously to goodness, but the "no limit" qualification associates prescribed action with an absolutism that is itself grounded in the divine will. The association of goodness with unlimited goodness and then with the divine will is actually made explicit in Matthew 5:48: "There must be no limit to your goodness, as your heavenly Father's goodness knows no bounds" (REB).

A literal interpretation of these passages yields an ethic that prohibits a use of force — any use of force — to restrain or resist evil. So encompassing is this command given its status as an expression of the divine will that running

[142]

the risk of death would be preferable to violating it. Non-resistance is so extensive a notion that it will not sanction any exertion of effort designed to blunt threats to one's own well-being. Thus does nonresistance deny any right of self-defense. St. Augustine, an early proponent of just war theory, held that Christians are called to insert themselves between combatants and risk endangerment, because by so doing self-defense was eliminated as a motive for action and the intent of the Matthean nonresistance clause could be honored.

If nonresistance to evil is an absolutist perspective, as I am claiming, is this kind of thinking abusive of human freedom, contradictory, and destructive so that we would be justified in calling it demonic? My answer is "Yes." I can illustrate my reasons for this answer through the example of an absolute pacifist, one of the outstanding nonresisters of the modern era, Russian novelist and religious thinker, Leo Tolstoy.

The Nonresistance of Leo Tolstoy

Tolstoy, as is well known, was one of the profoundly significant writers of the late nineteenth and early twentieth centuries, an accomplished novelist and cultural force who was loved by common folk as well as critics. "During the last twenty years of his life he was the best-known citizen in the world of thought [and] when he died in 1910 no writer remained whose fame could even be distantly compared with his own."[3] But Tolstoy was also a person who

[143]

went through a profound spiritual crisis, which then led him to undertake an utterly fascinating spiritual journey.

Although feted in the highest cultural centers of Russia and possessing the stature of world citizen, Tolstoy nonetheless experienced a deep spiritual discontent, which he reflected on in his extraordinary memoir, *My Confession.* Tolstoy reveals that with all he had accomplished he could not find happiness. He looked around and wondered why some of the peasants who labored in the fields, whose lives were hard and without luxury, seemed not to suffer his spiritual afflictions. Tolstoy came to envy them their simpler life and the faith that made it possible, and as he applied his enormous critical powers to the problem of spiritual simplicity, he finally endorsed a Christian faith that included at its core an affirmation of Jesus' teaching as recorded in the Gospels. Looking for what was distinctive in Jesus' teaching, Tolstoy found his answer in the Sermon on the Mount and in the ethical injunctions it provided for how human beings should live if they wish to live in accordance with God's will. Tolstoy wound up endorsing the "nonresistance to evil" doctrine enunciated in Matthew, making nonresistance the very heart of his religiously based ethic, and his nonresistance clearly was framed in terms of absolutism.

Tolstoy made the details of his journey of faith, so important to his biography, available in his various religious and ethical writings. He devoted considerable attention to such matters especially in his later years. These are extraordinary writings, moving and spiritually discerning. Despite all I am about to say about them, I continue to value them highly. But the critical question at the moment is this: is the pacifism advanced in these writings demonic?

The idea that absolutist thought could yield contradiction and lead to destruction was certainly not beyond Tolstoy's critical grasp. In an essay entitled "What Is Religion and of What Does Its Essence Consist?" Tolstoy wrote the following critique of the nonradical, traditional Christianity of his day:

> Christ reproached the scribes and Pharisees because they took the keys to the kingdom of heaven, but neither entered themselves, nor permitted others to.
>
> The learned scribes of today do the same thing: they have taken the keys, not to the kingdom of heaven, but to enlightenment, but neither enter themselves, nor allow others to. Using any manner of deceit and hypnotic power, the priests and clergy have instilled in people the idea that Christianity is not a religion proclaiming the equality of all men, and therefore destructive to the whole of today's pagan structure of life, but that on the contrary, it supports this structure and instructs us to differentiate between people, as we would differentiate between one star and another. It bids us to acknowledge that all power is derived from God and to obey it absolutely. It suggests that in general terms their position is ordained by God and they should bear it meekly and humbly, and submit to their oppressors. These oppressors need not be meek and humble but, as emperors, kings, bishops and secular and spiritual authorities of any kind, they must correct others

by teaching and punishing them while themselves living in splendor and luxury, the provision of which is an
obligation of those they subject.... Those who behave
in this way are the very hypocrites Christ condemned
so strongly — indeed the only people he condemned.
And he condemned them because no other monsters or
evil doers have ever brought so much evil into human
life as these people have.[4]

This extraordinary passage connects several ideas that
have been central to the argument of this essay. First, Tolstoy acknowledges the incredible power and the incredible
danger that religion wields. What is the danger? The danger
is that those responsible for advancing religion are in fact
its greatest corrupters — hypocrites who wield the power
of religion for unworthy ends. How does this come about?
I would suggest that Tolstoy appeals in the above passage
to absolutism. The religious appeal made to the masses is
that the way the church conducts its affairs is consistent
with the will of God and therefore people are obligated to
support that interpretation of the will of God through contemporary religious structures. They are to do so, Tolstoy
says, "absolutely," which corresponds to the religious leaders of Tolstoy's day laying claim to a power from God that
obliges people, as Tolstoy says, "to obey it absolutely." And
they do, which is the significant point. The fact that final
appeal is made to absolutism allows absolutism to entail its
own contradiction. Tolstoy observes the contradictions of
this absolutism, then offers the moral judgment that they
amount to hypocrisy. The religion of equality and freedom

has become a religion of power differentiation that finally suppresses freedom. In the name of absolute obedience, individual believers finally accede to their own oppression.

This passage exposes Tolstoy's own sensitivity to the ideas about absolutism that have been so much at the heart of the present discussion. Tolstoy acknowledges that religion is powerful and dangerous, that it can work against freedom. He associates absolutism in religion with contradictions that are themselves made possible by the appeal to absolute authority. Tolstoy, then, knows about that form of religion I have chosen to call in these pages "demonic." The attack Tolstoy launches in the above passage could be said to be an attack on demonic religion.

But what is Tolstoy's alternative? By extracting the essential teachings of Jesus from the Gospels and thus evading corrupt Church structures, Tolstoy found what he believed was Christianity in its purest form. From the Gospels he derived what he interpreted as the authentic Christian way of life, and it was a radical alternative to the institutionalized faith he found so corrupt and disheartening in his own time. Part and parcel of this new Christianity was a pacifism built on a nonresistance to evil doctrine. Tolstoy's interpretation of the doctrine was simple. Nonresistance held that "no physical force must be used to compel any man to do what he does not want to do, or to make him desist from doing what he likes."[5] Is the force of that "no" in "no physical force" an exceptionless and absolute "no"? Is this the speech of an absolutist who recognizes the contradictions of the demonic institutionalized religion of his day yet who responds with another form of absolutism, a pacifism that itself represents a turn toward the demonic?

If Tolstoy's nonresistance is itself going to qualify as a demonic alternative to the demonic absolutism he clearly saw in the Church of his day, we would have to establish that Tolstoy's nonresistance notion is itself absolute, that it is opposed in some fundamental ways to freedom and the goods of life, and that it is actually contradictory and destructive. I think all of these things can be shown from Tolstoy's own writings.

First, Tolstoy doubtlessly understood his alternative religious vision, which entails nonresistance to evil, to be noncompromising, admitting of no exceptions — absolute. As Tolstoy writes in "The Law of Love and the Law of Violence,"

> The true meaning of Christ's teaching consists in the recognition of love as the *supreme law* (Tolstoy's italics), and therefore not admitting of exceptions. . . . Christianity (i.e., the law of love not admitting any exceptions) that does permit the use of violence in the name of other laws, presents an inner contradiction resembling cold fire or hot ice.[6]

The radical Christian command to love and "resist not evil" Tolstoy clearly accepted as ultimate (i.e., "supreme") and absolute, as is made clear by invoking the idea of "not admitting of exceptions," which is one way to define something as "absolute."

So, against the false Christianity that is kept in place by appeal to absolute power and authority, Tolstoy offers a true version that is, as absolute religion, governed by the law of love that does not admit of exceptions. There is no doubt that Tolstoy's radical alternative religion is also absolutist, and as such it would, if followed, completely transform society: "The precise and definite meaning given to the doctrine of love and the guidance resulting from it inevitably involves a complete transformation of the established structure of life, not only among Christian nations, but among all the nations of the world."[7] Tolstoy writes on the issue of violence in particular:

> As soon as the law of love ceased to be the highest, immutable law of human life, all its beneficence disappeared, and the teaching of love was reduced to eloquent homilies and words which were nonobligatory and left the whole way of the life of the nations as it was before the doctrine of love appeared: that is based on violence alone. But the Christian teaching in its true meaning, recognizing the law of love as supreme, and permitting no exceptions in its application to life, ruled out any form of violence and consequently could not but condemn the whole structure of the world founded on violence.[8]

The transformation Tolstoy envisions goes beyond that of a social reformer who wants to correct injustices. Tolstoy wants a yin society in contradistinction to the yang society of his day. His envisioned alternative is not a reform but a complete replacement in opposition to all the details of the social, political, and economic world as it is presently constructed, for the law of love utterly and completely condemns the present order based as it is on violence. What this means in concrete detail is spelled out in *My Religion:*

> This faith has changed my estimate of what is good and what is bad and low. All that formerly seemed to me good and high — riches, property of every sort, honor, the consciousness of one's own dignity and rights — all this now has become bad and low; and all that seemed to be bad and low — work for others, poverty, humiliation, renunciation of all property and all rights — has become good and high in my eyes. If now in a moment of forgetfulness I may be so far carried away as to use violence for the defense of myself or others or of my own property or that of others, I can no longer calmly and consciously serve that temptation, which destroys myself and other men. I cannot acquire property; I cannot use violence of any sort against any manner of man, with the exception of a child, and then only to save him from some evil that hangs over him; I cannot take part in any activity of the authorities having as its aim the defense of men and their property by violence; I can neither be a judge nor one sharing in court duties; I cannot be an executive or one sharing an executive position; I cannot contribute to having others take part in courts and executive positions.[9]

Tolstoy's absolutist nonresistance expressed itself in a radical opposition to nationalism and to the militarism of the czarist state, as well as to the Orthodox Christian Church, which excommunicated him in 1901. In a short space it

[150]

is impossible to do justice to Tolstoy's religious and moral views, and clearly one could look to Tolstoy as a prophet pointing out the insidious dynamics of the very militarism that would eventuate in the First World War. At present, I wish to do nothing more than to say that this critic of Orthodox Christian Church absolutism does not seek to reform that institution but to assert in opposition to it another form of absolutism, namely, that associated with a nonresistant pacifism; in that affirmation, he expressed the contradictions that absolutist thought necessarily entails. His religious faith, in other words, which at first appears so life-affirming in its intended aim of bringing about peace in a world ruled by a law of love rather than a law of violence, fails in the end to yield that life-affirming stance. Tolstoy, critic of the absolutism he sees around him, is advocate of another form of absolutism, which will itself prove destructive. Tolstoy's law of love, because it was absolutist, eventually turns on itself and saves humanity the way absolutism always does: by destroying it.

Tolstoy's nonresistance appears at first glance to be life-affirming in its uncompromising affirmation of nonviolence and its advocacy of a rule of life based on the law of love; yet if the movement of this thought is demonic and thus not life-affirming, contradiction will arise — necessarily and inevitably. The demonic is to be discerned not in Tolstoy's affirmation of nonviolence but in his ideological absolutism.

Tolstoy, in my view, does provide us with an extraordinary example of a pacifism gone demonic. The demonic nature of it is exposed by several contradictions. First is the enunciation of a life-affirming pacifism opposed to war and

violence. Tolstoy's conception of nonresistance was not offered as a technique for opposing injustice. It was, rather, a
religiously conceived way of life authorized and sanctioned
by an absolutized ultimacy. In a sense, so overpowering was
this vertical relation to ultimacy, expressed in an absolute
requirement of nonresistance, that Tolstoy finally abandons
the horizontal moral realm of self-other relations altogether.
This abandonment is evident by his refusal to acknowledge
the legitimacy of social organization and institutional structures which can, admittedly, themselves fall into demonic
modes and destroy the goods of life and subvert goodness
itself. But those structures and institutions also serve to preserve and promote and advance the goods of life and protect
the good of life itself; nonresistance to evil thus expresses an
opting out of the moral realm of relations where evil is confronted and injustice resisted. Tolstoy, however, abandons
engagements with evil. His perspective does not allow him
to advocate the protection of life when life itself is threatened with injustice and possible destruction. By refusing
to resist those social and political forces that subvert the
goods of life and even threaten life itself, Tolstoy positions
himself outside the sphere of moral relatedness where he
could oppose their advance. Because he cannot resist evil
nor encourage others to do so, Tolstoy commits himself to
condoning the advance of evil. The moral point of view
can interpret this religious commitment no other way: the
practical effect of Tolstoy's religious commitment is that evil
proceeds and goodness itself is subverted by that advance.
By actively refusing to oppose evil, Tolstoy abandons moral

engagements and thus opts out of the moral life. Transcending the moral realm of self-other relations, Tolstoy opts to live out of a pure, absolutized religiosity, something noted by one of his biographers, who commented, "Tolstoy has rightly and sincerely gone into partnership with the Deity to make smooth the rough places of the earth, but he is so over-strenuous that he does not leave his partner a fair share of the work."[10] That nonresistance to evil should eventuate in condoning evil's advance is more than ironic — it is contradictory, at least from the moral point of view. That the quest for a spirituality designed to serve the law of love should abandon the moral realm and all that attends that realm by way of moral relations whereby each assumes a responsibility for the welfare of all, and all for each one, is likewise a consequence of nonresistance that the moral point of view would necessarily reject as lacking compassion and sensitivity to others — as failing to express love in action.

Tolstoy's nonresistance philosophy works counter to the idea that the good of life, like any good, should be protected and promoted. Nonresistance, as Tolstoy absolutized it, constructed an ideological barrier to any action designed to protect life from a threat of harm; then he provided a spiritual context for supporting and sustaining this ideological stance. Tolstoy enfolded nonresistance with a spiritual practice regimen, which was a program of asceticism; in relation to this development in Tolstoy's own thinking we discern most clearly how Tolstoy's nonresistance comes to serve a demonic vision of a pacifism that not only leads to contradiction, but eventuates in the destruction of the human race.

Tolstoy's Demonic Pacifism

At this point, let me provide more detail about the conceptual moves Tolstoy made, which present, I believe, a fascinating portrayal of pacifism gone demonic. Destructiveness, for example, a hallmark of the demonic turn, is easily extracted from Tolstoy's presentation of nonresistance, for nonresistance is premised on the idea that the very basic structures of society must be overturned and destroyed. These structures, which reasonable people could discern as having evolved for the specific purpose of preserving, protecting, and promoting life — in everything from family structures to police functions — are, as Tolstoy makes clear, compromises with the law of violence. Under the new social order created by the law of love, they are to be uprooted and demolished. The social order is not to be reformed, but destroyed and re-created on a basis totally opposed to that which passes away. Tolstoy understood the call for a new order to be totalizing in its effect, absolute and uncompromising in its vision.

Tolstoy's aim was to evolve individuals rather than societies, so he did not advocate working with existing social structures to alleviate various social problems. Tolstoy, a great admirer of Rousseau, faced a dilemma that Rousseau faced when theorizing how to construct an ideal community. The problem, as it confronted Rousseau, was how to conjoin Christianity and its ideals of love with the harsh reality of worldly power as it finds expression in the structures of states and in loyalties such as patriotism. Rousseau's solution was to admit the incompatibility of Christianity and the state, and then eliminate Christianity. Rousseau, then, banished Christianity from the state while trying to organize the state so that it might serve justice. Tolstoy, the religious absolutist, rejected this solution and took the other path. He eliminated the state.[11] Thus Tolstoy identifies a rather imposing list of dispensable items that will necessarily disappear as the structures of statehood collapse under the weight of the law of love: governments and public authorities are eliminated; property is abolished, along with taxes; also gone are those things that taxes would support but which Tolstoy believed existed only in relation to the continuing influence of the law of violence, such things as aid to the impoverished, police protection, a military, and anything that might place social constraint on a person. Since all of these social and political structures were created by the law of violence, eliminating them is a logical consequence of eliminating the law of violence. Tolstoy, then, is not concerned with reform or with justice, but with absolute fidelity to a religious ideal. "It is impossible," he writes, "for men not to feel that the admission of non-resistance to evil ruins their lives as they are now, and exacts of them something new, unknown, which terrifies them."[12]

Tolstoy, ever reflective and discerning, admitted that this idealized, absolutized vision of a new order was beyond his personal grasp, and in the face of it he would admit to failure. But he did not compromise the ideal. The idea was not conceived to be pliable and justice-related; it was, rather, absolute in its demand and effect, so that once the law of love was realized, concerns for justice and rectifying injustice in social systems would drop out of consideration as irrelevant. The law of love subsumes justice and in a practical sense evacuates it of meaning.

Yet Tolstoy himself is not impervious to concerns for justice, and he would act in ways that manifest a continuing regard for life-affirming values. The Tolstoy biography presents evidence of continued moral engagement, but the problem is that Tolstoy is quite aware that continued moral engagements represent a failure, in Tolstoy's own eyes, to live the life of perfection he believed God required of him and all persons. For example, consider Tolstoy's actions and reactions to a natural crisis.

In 1891, a severe drought afflicted central Russia. Tolstoy was aware of the suffering and the threat to life that this event posed, and he was deeply affected. Struggling against himself, he responded to the crisis by writing and then publishing articles that detailed the depth of the suffering and the Russian people's need for food, and he did not restrain himself in criticizing what he thought were serious governmental failures that had the effect of making everything worse. So Tolstoy, despiser of money, took to the world stage to appeal for money to help alleviate the sufferings and soon "Tolstoy, the anarchistic scorner of cooperation, found himself at the head of a tolerably large philanthropic organization."[13] As a result of Tolstoy's ability to command world attention, funding from international sources to help alleviate the problems brought on by the drought started to flow into central Russia. By all accounts Tolstoy organized the philanthropic effort well and clearly made a difference.

Although feeding the hungry might be thought to exemplify the law of love in action, Tolstoy would understand all that he did to alleviate the suffering of his fellows as anything but exemplary. He would write that the work of feeding the hungry was oppressive to him: "I feel nothing except the deepest oppression.... The oppression is not in the toil... and not in an occupation for which I feel no heart, but in a constant inward consciousness of being ashamed of myself."[14] Tolstoy distinguished between feeding the hungry and organizing persons and working structures in society to accomplish that end. Tolstoy's nonresistance negated any positive purpose for societal structures, and raising money and organizing (including trying to put pressure on the government to work more effectively to help) clearly caused Tolstoy mental conflict and spiritual distress. This is the kind of contradictoriness to which his absolutism led him.

Caught as he was in the grip of absolutism, Tolstoy could understand his own actions as violations of the absolute tenets of nonresistance, which required that he not participate *in any way* in the structure of the social and political order based on violence. He fed the hungry yet wound up a hypocrite in his own eyes, hence the distress. The irony — the contradiction — goes to freedom itself. Tolstoy's philanthropic and compassionate act, which could reasonably be said to conform to the law of love and the ethic of Jesus, violated the inflexible, absolutist nonresistance program and thus gives rise to guilt and inner torment. Tolstoy spoke of experiencing the "deepest oppression" in performing what reasonable persons could deem a charitable and compassionate act, yet he was plagued by conscience for failing to live purely and above the corruption of the world; in this inner torment Tolstoy's absolutism showed itself strangling spiritual freedom.

Just as life-affirming religion would freely express itself in acts of compassion aimed at the luminously good end of bringing food to the hungry, demonic religion would pervert the meaning of this act with a contrary interpretation that was destructive of goodness and ultimately destructive of freedom itself. Thus we see Tolstoy, a good man having done a good deed, plagued by inner demons. Those demons were created by his absolutist beliefs. We also see Tolstoy in contradiction, even self-deceived from a moral point of view, having done a good thing he did not really think was good; the "constant" pressure of this internal torment led him to express a sense of "oppression." That is a fascinating word for him to use, given that oppression identifies loss of freedom. Yet the irony is that Tolstoy felt this oppression from having freely acted — against his philosophy — to advance the good of life by feeding the hungry. Tolstoy felt what he did because he wanted to relinquish his freedom to a purified absolutism, and he knew that he had failed to do so.

My general claim is that religiously conceived pacifism, when it takes an absolutist form as did Tolstoy's nonresistance, actively opposes life-affirming values. Religiously conceived pacifism, when absolutized, proves to be life-denying and life-destroying — demonic — rather than life-affirming. The following discussion is meant to present how this particular form of nonresistant pacifism winds up actually destroying life and doing so rather completely — absolutely.

Tolstoy's Nonresistance as Life-Denying

The details of Tolstoy's life after conversion to the law of love reveal many contradictions. Conversion to the law of love did not translate into inner peace, as the feeding of the hungry example illustrates. Neither did it lead to relational harmony. Tolstoy's life was riddled with conflicts, including marital strife, but further attention to such matters is, while not necessarily irrelevant to exposing the dynamics of absolutism, simply ungenerous. Curiously, the most destructive contradiction to emerge from Tolstoy's absolutism arose in regard to the ascetic practices that Tolstoy believed that nonresistance necessitated.

The asceticism I am about to describe is a most peculiar asceticism, and my reader may find the move I am about to make bizarre and demanding of more of an explanation than I shall offer. But given that my point is that contradictions emerge from absolutist perspectives, then I make that point by teasing out a description of an actual move made in Tolstoy's thought. Explanations for the contradiction would lead us into psycho-biography and interpretive work beyond the scope of the present discussion, but I offer that we gain access to the logic of absolutism by seeing how Tolstoy, as an absolutist, developed his nonresistance philosophy. In the end, we can see how even a pacifist, when gripped by absolutism, can wind up with a perspective that is life-denying and "demonic" rather than life-promoting.

We get at this deepest of contradictions by taking seriously all that Tolstoy did in his thinking and in his life to show that nonresistance was not only an antiwar, antiviolence perspective, but that it was the object of ultimacy and as such was authoritative over the affairs of life. Tolstoy was a Christian, but he had rejected the divinity of Christ as the true core or source of ultimacy in his revised version of Christianity. Tolstoy posited ultimacy in nonresistance itself. Nonresistance, then, not Christ or Christianity, was the true center of Tolstoy's absolutism, the core of his religion, the actual object of his "ultimate concern" from which all other things religious and ethical flowed. Nonresistance, then, was offered as an idea of ultimate value that should affect every aspect of life.

As Tolstoy became ever more radical and consumed by nonresistance, he adopted an ever more extreme asceticism. Asceticism for Tolstoy was the spiritual activity that enabled human persons to distance the body and all things animal (e.g., the animal personality) from spiritual and ethical striving. Readers of Tolstoy's fiction are of course aware that his novels show him a deep admirer of beauty and physical strength, but his religious conversion changed these attitudes. As his nonresistance absolutized and took over more and more of Tolstoy's understanding of how to live, he came to associate nonresistance with a broader ethic of conduct. That ethic of nonresistance was sustained by a spirituality that valued self-sacrifice, self-abnegation, and renunciation. Tolstoy's nonresistance, then, finally expressed itself in a condemnation of material progress, which in turn came to require an ever more radical ascetic practice, since by such practice nonresistance in action could better conform to nonresistance in thought. To enact nonresistance in his personal life, Tolstoy undertook to forsake his ways as a leader of high material and intellectual culture, preferring to labor with the peasants. He even left his wife and took up the cobbler's trade. Seeking spiritual and ethical simplicity and honest directness, Tolstoy tied nonresistance to renunciation of what he called "the life of personality," by which he meant something like the egocentric life of animal impulses. He entered onto a spiritual pathway of asceticism, denying the body and seeking to dissociate spiritual progress from anything material. He sought to put the life of the body and its impulses into what he called "forgetfulness." [15]

This renunciation of body has some rather profound consequences. Tolstoy would claim that the only pathway to goodness was through renouncing those things that have come to express the law of violence at work in social structures and violence-related forms of life — such things as property and money. By such renunciation were thus removed obstacles to living the life of spiritual perfection. Tolstoy held that giving to the poor was an act conformed to such spiritual perfection, for the giver of alms demonstrates love for humanity and in that love finds true happiness. Renunciation, then, is the route to happiness. The entire Tolstoy nonresistance program sought in similar ways to identify the obstacles to spiritual progress, do away with them, and present an idealized alternative life of simplicity. This alternative life could be realized by means of what is in effect a personal ascetic regimen. Tolstoy thus extracts as a logical consequence of nonresistance a spirituality of renunciation and an ethic based on asceticism.

This ascetic move affects Tolstoy's understanding of marriage and sex. In 1886, Tolstoy wrote a panegyric to motherhood in *What Shall We Do Then?*[16] Three years later, however, as his thought continued to radicalize (absolutize), he abandoned such an idealized view and turned in an opposing direction. He hinted at the sexual implications of his ascetic ethic in the controversial novella, *The Kreutzer Sonata*. In this work, Tolstoy adopted the view that the ideal life of virtue requires absolute celibacy. Thus in a fictional form, Tolstoy conveyed a movement of thought concerning the life of absolutized nonresistance, connecting nonresistance to sexual abstinence. This is the critically important move that Tolstoy makes that presents evidence that nonresistance turns, finally, in a life-denying, demonic direction.

Tolstoy would assert explicitly that nonresistance necessitates through its ascetic program a cessation of human reproduction. In a letter from August 7, 1886, Tolstoy writes the following: "Read about suffering and the antiseptic method for dressing stations and birthing houses. They arrange battles and birthing houses, then they arrange methods to make them harmless." Commenting on this passage, Daniel Rancour-Laferriere writes: "Here Tolstoy is expressing his ironic attitude toward two forms of physical violence — war and giving birth. In another notebook from the same period, the message is more direct: 'The antiseptic method is chiefly good for war and for birthing houses, that is *for what should not exist.*'" Rancour-Laferriere again:

"The comparison is interesting and would lead to a consideration of Tolstoy's famous pacifism and his theory of nonresistance.... [T]he negation of birth is what is relevant here. To say 'should not exist' is to assert that birth should not exist."[17]

Tolstoy in these letters ties nonresistance to a moral prescription of ascetic celibacy that then logically entails the absolutist view that, as Rancour-Laferriere says, "birth should not exist." Tolstoy associated human reproduction with that part of the animal nature of personality that he also sought to renounce and "forget." The significance of this renunciation must not be missed. It is life-denying. Nonresistance, which aspires to a world of radical equality and aims at the life-affirming ends of peace and nonviolence, turns on itself in this ascetic move of renunciation. Tolstoy pushed nonresistance so far as to require for its achievement the renunciation of that animal aspect of human existence — sex and reproduction — without which the life of the human species would necessarily cease. This asceticism is nihilistic, life-denying, and destructive, given that an end to human reproduction would destroy human life as surely — certainly more completely — than any form of war Tolstoy himself would have known. In the asceticism, then, Tolstoy's religious absolutism turns on its own life-avowing ideals of peace, undoes itself in contradiction, and leaves us with a religious perspective that exemplifies the destructive, contradictory, and life-defying character of the demonic.

Tolstoy's nonresistance is a religiously grounded pacifism that becomes absolutized and eventually life-denying. Tolstoy did not start off to be life-denying. He affirmed the need for human beings to live together in peace and radical equality and saw the law of love as the guidepost for realizing this possibility. Nonresistance set forth the program of action and the actual requirements for achieving this end, and the program was presented as uncompromising, exceptionless, and commanding in an absolute way. Tolstoy's religious vision held that people must unite by love, and this must certainly be judged a positive, life-affirming notion.

But the absolutism of Tolstoy's perspective led to collapse and contradiction; such is the logic of absolutist perspectives. In Tolstoy's case that turn to contradiction occurs when nonresistance creates an asceticism for the virtuous that so purifies that it eventually does away with sexual temptation and the biblical idea of "adultery in the heart." But it accomplishes this spiritual purification by doing away with the means of human reproduction. Tolstoy's avowal of the good of sexual asceticism became snagged in the absolutism of nonresistance and so pushed to the extreme that virtue finally attaches to the ascetic renunciation of sexual relations. With this comes the end of human reproduction, which signals the end of human life. The profound irony is that Tolstoy's religiously grounded pacifism does finally bring peace, but it is the peace of species extinction. Tolstoy's nonresistance finally destroys human life and any future for human beings.

Tolstoy's absolutism transforms the ascetic ideal of nonresistance into a practical renunciation of sexuality so extreme that it does away with sexual desire and sexual intercourse and thus birthing. My claim is that such a perspective is not life-affirming and does not express the luminosity of goodness. In the sexual arena, Tolstoy's pacifism turned extreme and the absolutism of the perspective unraveled, showing itself in contradiction. Tolstoy aimed absolutist pacifism at the life-affirming goal of ending war and violence, yet absolutism led to an asceticism that turned on these life-affirming values and created the conditions for demonic destructiveness.

What can be more indicative of demonic destructiveness than ending the human race? Tolstoy of course did not rely on means that were violent, yet his peace ideology advocated an extremism that led, eventually, to a prohibition on sexual relations. What is so curious is that the consequences of Tolstoy's antiwar, antiviolence pacifism yield the same result as warfare itself: the destruction of human life. The absolutism of the perspective, in fact, would push matters such that the destruction of life would transcend that caused by warfare and eliminate the species — peacefully of course. Thus absolutism can transform life-affirming religious affirmations into vehicles of destruction. The nonsexual loving demanded by Tolstoy's absolutist pacifism in the end destroys the human race. I say that this expression of religious faith and action is not based in life-affirming religion but demonstrates the functioning of its opposite: demonic religion.

A Moral Critique of Absolutist Pacifism

The criticism often leveled at nonresisters is that they condone evil by refusing to oppose it. This criticism is not a religious criticism but emerges from a moral critique of the practical consequences of nonresistance behaviors. From the moral point of view, the case can be made, persuasively I think, that nonresistance is a form of action that expresses, at least behaviorally, a *practical* indifference to injustice. Not only is the nonresister responsible for acting in ways consistent with the philosophy of nonresistance, but those actions themselves yield results that are, from a moral point of view, equivalent to participating in the evil, which will continue and perhaps even expand if not opposed.

This criticism does not and cannot arise from a religious point of view because the appropriate religious response to such a form of ultimacy is to adopt nonresistance as a necessary aspect of religious faith. Judgments can then be made in a religious context about who is faithful to this religious vision and who is not, and how well it is realized in one community as opposed to another. But a moral critique evaluates the meaning of nonresistance actions, and the criticism that nonresistance condones evil is, from a moral point of view, inescapable. This criticism can be directed at an absolute nonresister like Leo Tolstoy.

The moral point of view would criticize the nonresister's repudiation of self-defense, deeming it practically unreasonable. More importantly, however, it would condemn the effort to make nonresistance a more general universalizable ethic, for here is where the idea of condoning or participating in evil actually comes to light. For not only do nonresisters offer no opposition to the continued progress of evil when it presents itself, but they endorse this mode of action, advocating nonresistance to others as a commendable ethic. To the extent the evil or injustice continues and spreads, it does so because it is not stopped and resisted; and nonresisters commit themselves to a policy of noninterference — they do nothing to stop the forward progress of evil. Practically speaking, this action condones evil and its growth and expansion, and the moral point of view would find this approach objectionable. Such intentional nonresistant inaction in the face of evil could hardly be said to be luminous with respect to goodness.

The moral point of view is not the same thing as the religious point of view, and it is important to realize and accept the sincerity of a nonresister's religious self-understanding. Religiously grounded nonresisters would not understand themselves as acting to condone evil — not because they do not see the evil effects of those undertaking acts of injustice and violence, but because, religiously, nonresisters do not understand themselves to be in relation to the perpetrators of injustice and violence. They are in relation and accountable to the ultimate authority — God — and the divine directive is clear in support of nonresistance. So nonresisters would not agree that they are condoning the violence of evil persons but, rather, acting as they understand God wants them to act. By this religious claim grounded in ultimacy, they assert that their primary relation is to God and they would judge their actions by consistency with the divine will. They would not view their actions from the moral sphere of self-other relations, where a moral critique would rightly say these individuals are condoning violence and its possible increase.

A moral critique of nonresistance also invites consideration of a self-deception dynamic. Nonresisters would of course deny that they are condoning evil or injustice, or that by their nonviolence they are participating in violence. But a moral critique would examine the nonresister in the sphere of self-other relations and adjudge the meaning of their acts as exactly that — as refusals to resist evil that increase destruction at least in part by the nonresister's refusal to resist. Self-deceivers, recall, express self-deception by denial and by rationalizations that do not square with the best, most rational explanation of an action. A moral critique would claim to have access to the best, most reasonable interpretation of action. For a nonresister to face the deaths of innocents by evil and injustice and say that such evil ought not to be resisted because nonresistance is actually God's will in the matter or somehow satisfies heaven's mysterious plan ought not, from a moral point of view, to go unchallenged. Such an explanation invites consideration of self-deception — of course, from the moral point of view.

The self-deception lies in nonresisters refusing to see the moral meaning of their acts. That is, they refuse to acknowledge the consequences of nonresistance in the moral sphere of relations, opting instead for an interpretation grounded in the self-relation to God that conflicts with what morality would claim as consistent with advancing the goods of life and the vision of good. From a moral point of view, the nonresister is self-deceived. From a moral point of view, any religious perspective that endorses peace and nonviolence but then functions to increase suffering and destruction is contradictory and an indication of the religion having made a turn towards the demonic. Absolutized pacifism yields such a contradictory and destructive result.

Human beings cannot by an act of will extricate themselves from their life situations. The moral point of view refuses to acknowledge that human persons can ever disengage from relationship with others. But the nonresister can deny the significance of moral, self-other relations, and, as absolutists, understand that by following the ideals of nonresistance, they transcend and marginalize moral relations, subordinating them to their relation to ultimacy. The ultimacy at the heart of religion trumps all other concerns, including moral concerns. Nonresisters can understand themselves as being related solely to ultimacy, and not, then, to the perpetrator of evil, the wrongdoer. From a moral point of view, however, such an understanding of human relations is itself the product of self-deception. To the extent that nonresisters are so engaged with others that they recognize others being harmed by violence and destruction, they acknowledge practical relation to these victims of harm and violence. Moreover, to the extent that nonresisters respond to those they understand to be perpetrating evil and wrongdoing, they acknowledge that they are in relation with the wrongdoers themselves. Nonresisters may not see this or acknowledge this relationality from their religious perspective, but it is clearly discernible morally. We are, from a moral point of view, always in relationship with those who would harm us or kill us. To say otherwise is morally grounded self-deception, even if one creates a religious explanation that refuses to acknowledge the moral meaning of the wrongdoing or injustice coming one's way.

From a moral point of view, not to resist the wrongdoer is to condone the wrongdoing. Not to oppose the wrongdoing but to let it move by unchallenged is then morally equivalent to participating in it. Thus does the act of wrongdoing come full circle and include the nonresister.

Tolstoy, ironically but perhaps inevitably, broke the circle by feeding the hungry rather than refusing on principle to get involved with money or institutional power structures. In that act of compassion he exemplified goodness at the very moment his absolutism forced him into self-loathing. But any nonresister who refuses to oppose evil eventually participates in that evil by assisting the perpetrator. Nonresisters of course deny any such participation, and they judge their actions in light of divine perfection; they are seeking to live *purely,* not morally. Participation in evil, however, can be discerned in their actions; and that participation contradicts the idea that one can live purely, divorced from involvement with others in the moral sphere of self-other relations. This contradiction is necessitated by the logic of the absolute idea itself. From a religious point of view, the engagement with evil at the very moment one is denying any such involvement reflects the presence of self-deception. From the moral point of view, such religiously framed self-deception provides evidence of the demonic turn.

Nonviolent Resistance to Evil

Having overviewed Tolstoy's nonresistance as an example of an absolute pacifism that is life-denying and demonic, I would now consider briefly a form of nonviolence engagement that is, when religiously grounded, life-affirming.

I refer to nonviolent resistance. Interpreting nonviolent resistance as an authentic expression of "pacifist" sentiment
and orientation is commonplace, and it is often identified by those who avow it, and even by many who do
not, as appropriately fitting under the linguistic rubric of
"pacifism." A Tolstoyan absolutist, of course, would not
find such a perspective a sufficiently pure form of pacifism.
Whereas Tolstoy objected to government and even the rule
of law, a nonviolent resister could be expected to accept the
legitimacy of certain forms of government. A nonviolent resister, however, would be critically engaged with political
authority and oppose and resist particular laws and practices deemed to be unjust. Nonviolent resisters do not seek
to destroy the social and political order. Their more life-
affirming aim, rather, is to reform government and society
and conform them to notions of justice.

Nonviolent resistance presents a stark contrast to the
nonresistance perspective, for nonresistance is not active
in opposing and resisting injustice, wrongdoing, and evil.
Those who endorse nonviolent resistance, however, engage
nonviolence as the means of action — the technique, if you
will — to bring about a peaceful and just social, economic,
and political order.

Nonviolent resistance expresses a commitment to moral
engagement that seeks to resist evil and injustice by means of
nonviolent methods. Nonviolent resistance may spring from
religious, philosophical, or even practical political commitments, but it is always subservient to the larger issues of
justice and peace, which are themselves framed in the sphere

of moral relations. As a moral and social philosophy, non-violent resistance provides the means for organizing and bringing to bear a consistent program of action that aims at confronting, opposing, and undoing injustice. Nonviolent resistance seeks to check injustice; it does not advocate or value nonviolence except in relation to opposing injustice and resisting its forward movement.

Although it may seem simplistic to say that nonviolent resistance is more like a preferred technique and less like the kind of all-encompassing absolutist philosophy Tolstoy advanced, there is nonetheless truth in making such a distinction. Tolstoyan nonresistance affected every aspect of life, including, as Tolstoy understood, the taking of oaths, the abolition of property and taxes, disparagement of money, disengagement from social and governmental life. It even eventuated in a life-denying asceticism that in Tolstoy's case led to the call for an end to sexual relations and propagation of the species. For the pacifist absolutist like Tolstoy, the world is not a site of injustice, but of impurity and corruption. Nonviolent resistance, however, is premised on the idea that the world is imperfect and filled with injustice, violence, and human wrongdoing. It formulates itself in relation to a vision of goodness that seeks to advance goodness in the face of violence and injustice, acknowledging that goodness is to be pursued in the world, which thus requires that obstacles to goodness must be opposed. Nonviolent resisters adopt nonviolence, then, as the preferred technique most effective in opposing injustice, for nonviolence provides a means of resistance to injustice that does not, as a technique, contribute to an increase in injustice and suffering. As a technique, then, the commitment to nonviolence expresses a mode of action itself conformed to a life-affirming vision of goodness. It does not shy away from injustice but confronts it with the power of nonviolence, which effects opposition to injustice by means designed to lessen suffering and destruction. Nonviolent resisters, then, actively oppose injustice. They do so by means that aim at preventing an increase in the suffering of others. The methods of opposition and resistance are designed to make sure that any increase in suffering that does occur as a result of the resistance falls not on those the resisters oppose or on any who could possibly be affected negatively by acts of resistance, but on themselves. Nonviolent resisters risk receiving harm as they act nonviolently to prevent harm. Assuming moral responsibility for their acts of resistance, advocates of nonviolent resistance seek to avoid producing any harmful effects from their acts of resistance, but acknowledging that such consequences are possible, they act nonviolently in order to direct any increase in harm or suffering to themselves and not to others, which includes even those who would, from positions of power, seek to quash their opposition.

Nonviolence identifies a program of opposition, a technique if you will, that expresses in publicly observable ways a grounding in goodness. Goodness is luminous in the effort to oppose injustice by means that themselves seek to preserve and even enhance the goods of life. Nonviolent resistance is action that, when considered religiously, is essentially life-affirming, because it seeks to preserve and defend life even as it opposes the injustices that pose threats to life. Nonviolent resistance aims at realizing the life-affirming goods of peace and justice, and it offers a technique designed to oppose and undo injustice while minimizing suffering, injury, and destruction.

Nonviolent resistance may reflect values associated with certain visions of ultimacy and thus can be deemed an essential mode of action that various religious systems can endorse. Yet nonviolent resistance is not itself the full expression of ultimacy. It is always a means for realizing some good end, that end being best served by a technique of engagement that itself embodies goodness. As a means for realizing the ends of justice and peace, nonviolent resistance escapes being so valued that it comes to stand as the object of central religious affirmation, as if this technique were ultimacy itself rather than action that ultimacy might endorse. Religious people who opt for nonviolent resistance do so believing that this mode of operation is consistent with the larger values they affirm in their religious systems, so that the techniques of nonviolent resistance become ways of enacting a deeper commitment to a vision of ultimacy and even of goodness itself.

For nonviolent resistance to become the object of ultimacy rather than one of its modes of expression would be an odd development religiously. Tolstoy's nonresistance, as I argued earlier, actually became the object of ultimacy itself. Not attaching divinity to Christ, Tolstoy did seem to attach divinity to nonresistance, having gone, as one critic has suggested, "beyond Jesus himself. The spectacle of the later Tolstoy is often a noble one, but it could justly be said that on occasion he forgot that even Christianity at its most extreme called only for the imitation of Christ, and not for his supersession."[18]

Nonviolent resistance, however, does not play into absolutist thought so easily. As a mode of enacting a vision of goodness, it is always parasitic on a philosophical or religious viewpoint, which is to say it is always a means to some end, the end being justice or peace or goodness or some notion of ultimacy. We see nonviolent resistance advocated by persons grounded in various religious, philosophical, and political visions; it may emerge as a derivative expression of ultimacy. By that I mean that a religious person could assert that nonviolence provides the authentic means for engaging the world, opposing injustice, and doing so in ways consistent with the life-affirming values believed to be expressive of ultimacy itself. So Christians, Jews, Native Americans, Buddhists, Hindus, and Muslims could all advocate nonviolence as a means of responding to evil and injustice, but nonviolence would not rise to the level of itself being an absolute. It is always a derivative expression of how people choose to enact their religious commitment in the world.

The program of nonviolent resistance is closely associated with Martin Luther King Jr., who committed himself to nonviolence in the American civil rights movement. King understood nonviolence to be a technique of moral and spiritual engagement, and he explicitly tied this technique directly to Jesus-inspired ideas of Christian nonviolent action. Gandhi and Thoreau were also important to his thinking about the role of nonviolence.

Arguably, the clearest exposition of nonviolent resistance as a religiously grounded response to evil is found in Gandhi, who inspired King. What Gandhi produced in his thinking about nonviolent resistance was an action program grounded in a spiritual core. Centered in the idea of *satyagraha,* or "truth force," nonviolence was deemed the mode of action authorized by, and consistent with, the life-affirming values of the spiritual ideal. Gandhi, in other words, advanced nonviolence as a consistent and powerful expression of life-affirming religious commitment. As a form of pacifism, Gandhian satyagraha escapes the clutches of the demonic in ways that Tolstoy's absolutist pacifism could not.

A brief examination of central features of satyagraha shows how it forms a nonabsolutist, life-affirming expression of a religiously grounded pacifism.

First, Gandhi conceived of satyagraha or nonviolent resistance as a power or force — "truth force." "Truth," Gandhi wrote, "is soul or spirit. It is, therefore, known as soul force. It excludes the use of violence because man [sic] is not capable of knowing the absolute truth and, therefore, not competent to punish."[19] Gandhi, then, distances his religious conceiving from any claim of epistemological absolutism, and in this he is quite different from Tolstoy, who believed that the divine truth of nonresistance was clearly knowable as a direct expression of the divine will.

Gandhi also conceived of satyagraha as a form of self-sacrifice. The logic of self-sacrifice was based on the idea that because absolute certainty is not available, individuals who make mistakes should not make others pay for them but take on themselves any suffering caused by mistakes:

> Everyone admits that sacrifice of self is infinitely superior to sacrifice of others. Moreover, if this kind of force is used in a cause that is unjust, only the person using it suffers. He does not make others suffer for his mistakes. Men [*sic*] have before now done many things which were subsequently found to have been wrong. No man can claim that he is absolutely in the right or that a particular thing is wrong because he thinks so, but it is wrong for him so long as that is his deliberate judgment. It is therefore meet that he should not do that which he knows to be wrong, and suffer whatever it may be. This is the key to the use of soul force.[20]

Gandhi was aware that the power of religion can turn in destructive directions: "Your belief that there is no connection between the means and the end is a great mistake. Through that mistake even men [*sic*] who have been considered religious have committed grievous crimes.... We reap exactly what we sow."[21] Gandhi was thus clearly aware of religion's potential to serve as a demonic force, and he sought to act religiously in such a way that he would avoid the demonic and the karmic consequences of religious destructiveness.

Additionally, Gandhi's avoidance of absolutism is demonstrated by his constant appeals to reason. Never does he deny a natural right to self-defense: "I believe that every man and woman should learn the art of self-defense in this age"; and to this reasonable appeal he then adds that "Satyagraha is always superior to armed resistance. . . . It is a weapon that adorns the strong. It can never adorn the weak."[22]

Gandhi conceived of satyagraha as nonvindictive and nonretaliatory, so it does not produce or operate out of negative, destructive emotional energy; never does Gandhi distance himself from his opponent, with whom he is always in relation. Gandhi asserts as a basic understanding that the person of violence whom he might oppose remains a brother or sister: "Humankind," he writes, "is one big family. And if the love expressed is intense enough it must apply to all mankind."[23] This is undoubtedly a religious vision, but it also represents a movement into the sphere of moral relations, where religious value is extended to conform to an even more basic moral vision of goodness and human relationality.

The force that is brought to bear out of the law of love and which underwrites satyagraha is based on the "implicit belief that the sight of suffering on the part of the multitudes will melt the heart of the aggressor and induce him to desist from his course of violence," and Gandhi states that the basic assumption of satyagraha is "complete unity of the people in their desire and demand for freedom."[24] This freedom is political as well as spiritual.

Satyagraha, then, is conceived apart from any claim to absolutism; it is a mode of operation that seeks to win over opponents by a mode of engagement that presents no harm to the opponent; it does not seek to divide but to unify people, oppressors with oppressed; it brings a force to bear not to harm but to effect a change in the direction of freedom and justice; it is based on the reasonable idea that returning blow for blow as in retaliation is finally an ineffective way to deal with political conflict and problems involving power in the moral sphere of relations (one need only glance in the direction of the Middle East to witness the force of that insight); and it seeks not to destroy but to enter into moral relationship with others. Even the single *Satyagrahi* will "not find himself single-handed for long," Gandhi writes: "The village will unconsciously follow him."[25] The use of soul force aims to effect what Gandhi calls a "change of heart."[26]

Satyagraha is a distinctive form of pacifism. It is pacifistic in its commitment to nonviolence, but Gandhi understood satyagraha to be a powerful force, an alternative spiritual and moral force that effectively opposes injustice and effects change in the direction of peace through the means sanctioned by satyagraha itself: nonviolent resistance. Gandhi understood that satyagraha had the power to effect a change in the human heart and turn it away from violence, which, for Gandhi, included "corruption, falsehood, hypocrisy, deceit and the like."[27] Such behaviors were clearly contrary to the vision of goodness conceived through satyagraha. Moreover, Gandhi understood that satyagraha had power to effect a change in society, transforming it from oppression and violence, and doing so by sponsoring a nonviolent means of confrontation that aims at earning the respect of the oppressor to whom the nonviolent resister presents humility and self-restraint.

Gandhi's aversion to demonic destructiveness can even be seen in his refusal to seek a Tolstoyan demolition of the state. The former lawyer would write,

Our civil disobedience, therefore, must not be carried beyond the point of breaking the unmoral laws of the country ... and to be avoided is action that precipitates chaos and anarchy. A civil resister is, if one may be permitted such a claim for him, a philanthropist and a friend of the State. An anarchist is an enemy of the State and is therefore a misanthrope.[28]

Gandhi dissociates himself from the kind of extremism that shuns any hope for reform of society. He abhors anything that would express misanthropy, the kind one could associate with Tolstoy's vision of a pacifism that puts an end to the human race.

In all that he would attribute to the power of satyagraha, Gandhi can be seen working to advance human freedom and doing so universally, for his nonviolent pacifism was not only aimed at the victims of oppression but at the oppressors themselves. He sought to enact a vision of justice that would change the dynamics of power and human relations, satyagraha being a means that expresses goodness and brings practical benefit to both oppressor and oppressed. Furthermore, he sought through his spiritual vision to resist violence, oppression, and injustice with the most effective practical tool he believed to be available. Satyagraha was always directed toward action and making practical decisions, and Gandhi presented it as such.

For all that he did to connect his program of nonviolent resistance to ultimacy and religious authorization, Gandhi never allowed his actual response to violence to ignore or forget the body and the ethical space wherein human beings are in relationship with one another seeking to promote the goods of life. He made a moral appeal to all persons advocating mutual respect, so that however important the God-relation of religion is, it never so dominated the sphere of action that the practitioner of satyagraha moved out of the moral realm of self-other relations. Gandhi's response to violence through a pacifism of religiously grounded nonviolent resistance appealed to rationality and practicality at every turn, and it abhorred absolutism the way nature abhors a vacuum. Gandhi's vision does not fall into contradiction or absolutism.

As a nonabsolutist form of nonviolent but morally engaged pacifism, satyagraha serves to expand the goods of life, promote the good of life, and enact a vision of goodness. Satyagraha sponsors a technique for engaging the world with a force meant to confront and oppose injustice morally, and the technique of resisting injustice by the power of nonviolence in action and attitude was itself meant to exemplify goodness. As Tolstoy's absolute nonresistance illustrates a demonic form of pacifism, Gandhi's pacifism provides a religious response to violence and oppression that is, from a moral point of view, undeniably life-affirming.

Chapter Five

The Case of Holy War

I N WESTERN MONOTHEISM, religious people have sometimes justified a use of force by appealing to the idea
of holy war. Those who engage in holy war do so on the
certain belief that they are doing the will of God as God,
the infallible arbiter of moral meaning, has revealed that
will. Specific instances of holy war seem always to reflect
absolutist thinking, although in a generic sense, holy war
refers simply to any use of force justified by appeal to divine
authority.

Holy war constitutes religiously framed action that is subject to moral critique. The moral point of view discerns in
holy war action that assaults the goods of life in destructive,
even murderous ways. From the moral point of view, generic
holy war ought to be considered presumptively demonic.
The question, in fact, is whether any life-affirming exceptions can be found to the rule that holy war is absolutist
and thus of a piece with demonic religion.

That religious people and communities can appeal to an ultimate authority to justify uses of force, either for aggressive or defensive purposes, is a datum of human experience beyond dispute. This phenomenon of religious life is known throughout history, and examples of such appeals can be found in all the Western monotheistic traditions. But the appeal to ultimacy can easily turn into an expression of absolute faith, which then can refuse the restraining influence of reason and moral reflection. When religious absolutism is invoked to motivate violence and warfare, the results can be horrendous: indiscriminate slaughter, suicide, and a defiant refusal to submit to morality's restraint on violence and war.

The general question under consideration is how religious people can respond to violence and injustice in ways that are life-affirming. The specific question at issue in this chapter is whether holy war can in any way be life-affirming. To answer this question I consider briefly how holy war expresses ways of thinking and being religious in the Western historical religious traditions of ancient Israel, Christianity, and Islam. Is there any evidence that these traditions endorse the idea of holy war, and if they do, is there any evidence that holy war can be on the life-affirming, rather than on the demonic, side of the religious option?

Ancient Israel

My remarks here are not designed to address the religious tradition of Judaism but only to look back to the Hebrew Scriptures to see the demonic and life-affirming possibilities of holy war. I would note at the outset that in ancient Israel, generic holy war is clearly seen in the divinely authorized and directed notion of *hērem,* or "ban," which refers to the idea that something is set apart for divine use and is to be used by Yahweh and not by Israelites.[1] *Hērem,* from a moral point of view, is a demonic religious notion whereby God directs a total obliteration of the enemy, sometimes with rationalization, sometimes without.

In the realm of action, *hērem* refers to a divinely sanctioned use of force and violence for ends willed by God, so that *hērem* satisfies the formal criteria for invoking generic holy war. *Hērem* is divinely directed, and the Hebrew Scriptures set forth the details of Yahweh's expectations. In the *hērem,* Yahweh seeks general destruction, as in the conquest of Canaan (Josh. 6:17–18), or even total annihilation, as in God's command to King Saul to include in the slaughter of Israel's enemies "man and woman, child and infant, ox and sheep, camel and donkey" (1 Sam. 15:3; 22:19). God's desire to see this chain of life obliterated is to be taken seriously and literally. Yahweh commands Saul to inflict *hērem* on the Amalekites and King Agag, whom he has defeated, yet Saul spares the king (1 Sam. 15:9). In addition, the Scriptures record that Saul preserves "the best of the sheep and of the oxen and of the fatlings, and the lambs, and all that was good, and [Saul] would not utterly destroy them"; to which Yahweh responded with this lament: "I repent that I have made Saul king; for he has turned back from following me, and has not performed my commandments" (1 Sam. 15:10).

Hērem thus presents one version of a divinely commanded "holy war" in ancient Israel. *Hērem* is obliteration bordering on omnicide, and when commanded by God, the faithful were to respond to the command of God with absolute fealty. God's involvement in the actual destruction and the divine desire for the annihilation of enemies is unambiguous.[2] Yet Saul, in the *hērem* stories of 1 Samuel, is shown resisting the divine will and refusing to obey the command to undertake total destruction. He is thereby shown acting in restraint of Yahweh's destructive power, wanting not to be God's agent of total annihilation. Although traditional religious interpretation has pointed to Saul's disobedience, a moral interpretation of Saul's actions would note Saul's exercise of moral agency as he resisted the divine command for absolute destruction, the consequence of which is that Yahweh laments his choice of Saul as king. *Hērem* provides an exceedingly clear example of absolutist holy war, with Yahweh appearing in the *hērem* texts as a demonic force set on total destruction. One could only hope that were Saul sufficiently conformed to the moral point of view he might have seen the *hērem* command as unworthy of a life-affirming God.

Although appeal is made to the idea of generic holy war and reference to the "wars of Yahweh" can be found in 1 Samuel 18:17, 25, 28 and Numbers 21:14, the term "holy war" is never used in the Hebrew Bible. Use of the term "holy war" to describe Israel's involvement in and understanding of its own wars can be traced to Friedrich Schwally, who used the expression in a 1901 monograph. Among other scholars who used the term were Max Weber and, later, the scriptural scholar Gerhard von Rad, who explored the issue in depth in his book *Holy War in Ancient Israel*.[3]

Weber had thought of holy war as topological, and he identified three pure instances of holy war: the war of Deborah and Barak in Judges 5; the war of the tribes against Benjamin in Judges 20; and Saul's war against the Ammonites in 1 Samuel 11.[4] For Weber, holy war was the result of the binding of the tribes of Israel in confederacy. When a tribe broke the obligation to preserve the binding confederate relationships, holy war ensued, and its purpose was to uphold the mutually binding obligation to defend the confederacy of tribes.

Von Rad's theory of holy war is more complex. His claim was that holy war is an actual institution bound up in cultic tradition. Holy war, then, depended upon a cultic organization and tradition working together, which occurred most clearly in Israel's history during the period of the judges. Knowing nothing of cultic worship in the time of the Exodus and the settlement, Von Rad excluded these periods from holy war eligibility. Von Rad argued that the idea of holy war became dissociated from worship and cultic practice, then was caught up in the larger narrative history of Israel and eventually spiritualized. Accordingly, it was transformed from a cultic practice of worship and institutional life into the literature of Israel, where it was "used to serve ends quite different from those it served in its original cultic settings."[5] Von Rad separated holy war in the period of the judges from later prophetic developments, arguing that the eighth century (B.C.E.) prophet Isaiah was unique among the prophets in standing in the tradition of ancient cultic-institutional holy war. This claim is controversial, however, one that other scholars have questioned.[6]

[186]

Drawing on Von Rad's further claim that "holy wars" or "wars of Yahweh" were instruments of prophetic criticism against the royal court, scholar Peter Weimar has examined four narratives to see if they present a picture of Yahweh acting to achieve victory, which was the central part of the holy war tradition. Weimar examines Exodus 14, Joshua 10, Judges 4, and Samuel 7. The common structure of these four narratives show the following:

1. An enemy takes action against Israel.
2. Israel becomes discouraged.
3. A prophet urges confidence and faith in Yahweh.
4. Yahweh intervenes and puts the enemy to rout.
5. Israel's only action is to pursue the routed enemy.[7]

These narratives, however, are advanced against the background of the contemporary political situation and involve holy war as a tool to criticize the Davidic court. The narratives use holy war to point out a contrast with the "Political policies that locate sovereignty elsewhere" than in Yahweh alone.[8]

There is no question that a holy war tradition exists in ancient Israel and that it is a faith-related concept in which Yahweh is warrior and defender of Israel. A busy scholarship exists on the question of holy war in ancient Israel, and although it shows a diversity of religious meanings for the idea of holy war, our purpose is to clarify the moral meaning of holy war. Given that from the moral point of view holy war must be considered presumptively demonic, the question of moral importance turns to the other religious option. That is, does the moral option at issue in these pages extend even to holy war, so that we might actually find a life-affirming example?

An extraordinary example of a life-affirming holy war in the story of ancient Israel is told, I believe, in Exodus 14, and then 15, this latter considered to be the oldest text in the Hebrew Bible. The Exodus 15 narrative, the Song of Moses, follows on the story of the deliverance of the people of Israel from bondage in Egypt and the destruction of the Pharaoh's pursuing army in the Red Sea. The story reconnects the covenant of Yahweh and Israel, with Yahweh promising to heal the people of Israel and provide for them if they keep the commandments and do what is "right in God's eyes."

Examined from an ethical point of view, the prospect of a life-affirming holy war in ancient Israel would be turned away from all that characterizes demonic holy war. So a life-affirming example would have to be one in which the human beings involved in very practical ways repudiated violence and aimed their efforts not at destruction but at life, and not at suppressing their enemies, but only at realizing freedom. Given that the people of Israel were a religiously bound and covenanted faith community, a life-affirming holy war would have to somehow spring from faith and rest in the life-affirming power of trust, as if God would protect and deliver them and not ask them to assume a destructive power as agents of the divine will.

We see such a notion of holy war in the Exodus story texts. Yahweh is Israel's protector. Yahweh is the warrior. Because of trust in Yahweh, Israel has no need of a military hierarchy to plan maneuvers of aggression or defense.

Israel does not participate as an engaged combatant seeking the destruction of the enemy. Israel is seeking freedom from oppression, not retaliation or revenge. The battle with the Egyptians that ensues is, I would argue, holy war. It is not holy war because human beings claim it is a war God wills be fought; it is, rather, a holy war because it is a war that Yahweh, the Holy One, actually fights.

In the examples of holy war identified by Weber, Yahweh enlists the people of Israel to do the divine bidding in defeating the enemies of Israel. There is massive slaughter and tactical mistakes are made, and the moral point of view could not evaluate these holy wars as life-affirming, divinely sanctioned though they be. In the Exodus story, however, we have a holy war that is essentially life-affirming. The people of Israel flee Egypt and seek freedom. They do not seek to fight but to emigrate, which is a nonviolent response to oppression. When "war" breaks out and the pursuing Egyptian armies seek to destroy the Israelites, the people of Israel do not respond with violence. Yahweh is trusted; Yahweh is the warrior, the champion of Israel; and God does all the fighting. The role of the people is to trust in God's protection, to do what is right in God's eyes (which is to trust Yahweh), and to seek freedom and life beyond slavery and oppression. The destruction of Israel's enemies and pursuers is left to God and God alone. There is no human participation in killing Israel's enemies. Neither does God enlist the people of Israel to kill those whom God evidently wants killed in order to protect his people. Yahweh's actions against the armies of the pharaoh are in defense of the people of Israel and aimed at freedom from bondage.

The people of Israel are not active combatants except in that they place their trust in a champion warrior to defend their cause. The war, therefore, is God's war; the violence afflicted is defensive and noninvolving of humans in killing or destruction.

This seems to me to be the archetypal example of a life-affirming holy war considered from a moral point of view, and it would seem to reflect a nonviolent engagement, even a pacifism of sorts on the part of the people of Israel.

Demonic religion, recall, yields an inevitable destructiveness and a loss of freedom; and the goods of life, including the good of life itself, are compromised and finally subverted. Goodness itself is undermined and made nonluminous. In the story of the liberation of the people of Israel from bondage in Egypt, the relation of the people of Israel to their pursuers is nonbelligerent, nonvindictive, and nonretaliatory. They seek the life-affirming end of freedom and choose the nonviolent means of peaceable emigration. They do not take up arms or devolve into fighting or plot out revenge for all the wrongs they have suffered. They seek life in community with Yahweh, their protector and defender.

If ever there was an example of holy war that avoids the demonic and the inevitable destructiveness of demonic religion, this story in the book of Exodus is that story. This is an example of life-affirming holy war. Destruction and violence occur, and clearly the power of God is invoked for protection. Although God acts as God will act, the human beings do not understand that their role is to be agents of a destructiveness that God wills. Rather, they form community in trust, and in faith they allow themselves to be protected by Yahweh. The people are directed by a vision of goodness toward freedom and new life, and they engage in life-affirming nonviolence. This is, to my mind, a rare example of a life-affirming holy war.

Israel would not always maintain the relationship of trust with Yahweh that it had when the people of Israel fled bondage in Egypt. When their relationship to Yahweh shifts, when reliance is not put on Yahweh for protection but in a military hierarchy and a kingship, Israeli's story undergoes dramatic change. The Exodus notion of holy war is lost in the political and military machinations of the new kingdom. With Israel's kings flawed and unable to provide protection and victory against enemies, Israel experiences, under military organization and kingship, devastating defeats, culminating in invasion and captivity.

Von Rad was right about Isaiah. When Isaiah holds up a mirror to Israel and says, "For thus said the Lord GOD, the Holy One of Israel, 'In returning and rest you shall be saved; in quietness and in trust shall be your strength' " (Isa. 30:15), he invokes the memory of the Exodus holy war tradition. He reminds the people of Israel that their sole weapon against oppression had been trust in Yahweh. Isaiah reminded a captive people of that life-affirming holy war where deliverance was accomplished by Yahweh's actions of defense and protection. For Isaiah, that holy war exemplified the covenantal dynamics that set the standard against which every other conflict and call to arms in the story of the people of Israel would have to be measured — and found wanting.

[191]

Other stories in the Hebrew Bible might also make a claim to holy war, such as the war with Jericho, where the weapons employed were trumpets. No narrative, however, so well exemplifies a life-affirming picture of holy war as that told in the Exodus story.

Christianity

I am simply unaware of any notion of holy war authorized by the major sources of Christian understanding, by which I mean the Gospel stories of Jesus and his teachings, and Paul's writings. The claim that Jesus might have been a revolutionary who was advocating active resistance to the Romans has a certain plausibility to my mind, for such an interpretation at least would clarify why Jesus of Nazareth was found guilty and executed for the crime of sedition. A remnant of historical memory of Jesus using force or advocating it might be attached in some way to the story of the temple cleansing, when Jesus is said to have "driven" out the moneychangers and overturned tables (Mark 11:15). But with these things unknown and the tradition being so deeply obscure if not lost altogether, I would assert that no holy war tradition is authorized in the sources or exemplified in the narratives.

Wars and destructive uses of force in acts of aggression undertaken to spread or defend the Christian faith should be considered, from the moral point of view, to be presumptively demonic. Appeals to crusades are a clear case in point. As the historical crusades of medieval Europe demonstrated, "crusades" refer to divinely authorized wars of aggression;

an appeal to divine sanction and authorization hovers over "crusade" even when today political figures employ the term to rally support for uses of force against enemies. The effort to justify a crusade by invoking God as the sanctioning power for violence and war exemplifies religion in the demonic turn, an interpretation that various Christian modes of analysis would support. Whether talking about the historical crusades of medieval Europe against Islam or more ordinary language appeals to the idea of a religiously legitimated crusade, the idea of an aggressive war of crusade is simply warfare that appeals for authorization to the divine and ought to be analyzed within the Christian tradition as an exemplification of religion in the demonic turn.

Islam

Any examination of the notion of holy war in Islam must begin by reminding Americans, who may not know much about Islam, that despite its connections to Western religion and its status as an Abrahamic tradition, Islam developed with clear notions about the fusion of religion and politics. Islam has historically intermingled religion and politics in ways that cannot help but seem unusual to Americans. The constitutional principle of church-state separation so integral to the formulation of freedom of religion and the religious pluralism experiment in the United States is in no way a norm for historical Islam.[9] Islam reminds us that developments such as the American legal principle we shorthand as "separation of church and state" results from the contingencies of history and the relativities of culture.[10]

Historically, Islam has claimed authority in all spheres of life, including politics, so that Islam could be said to have created forms of societal organization and political governance that conform to religious ideals, tenets, and instructions. Islam affected society and government in those countries where Islam became the dominant religion, and it did so in ways that are distinctive from the American system, especially with regard to political liberties involving separation of church and state. (Islam as a religion of toleration would, in general, find the "free exercise of religion" clause of the First Amendment more amenable to its values than the "establishment" clause that gives America its doctrine of church-state separation.) How this fusion of religion and politics was effected can be traced to the distinctive cultural, political, and historical situation out of which Islam grew.[11]

The issue that this background poses for an understanding of the idea of holy war in Islam, then, comes to the fore in the following issues. Islam was born in a world of power politics and conflict. Military force was integrated into Islamic thought not only as an aspect of community defense but as theological doctrine. Appeals to holy war arise in Islamic history, even in the Qur'anic call to a jihad of the sword. The Islamic community does not speak with one voice, and no one is authorized to speak for all Muslims. A holy war or jihad — more about the relationship of these two distinct notions momentarily — called by some Muslims will be disputed, even dismissed, by other Muslims. Rarely is a jihad called that commands widespread support. The Christian crusades in the Levant, curiously, were never seen as posing a threat to the Muslim community sufficient to warrant a jihad or holy war in opposition to them. The last jihad to seriously threaten Christendom occurred in 1683, when the Polish army broke the siege of the Ottoman Empire in Vienna. (The date of the siege collapse was, incidentally, September 11.)

Jihad, which literally means "struggle" or "striving," is not the conceptual equivalent of holy war but is rather a fluid, complex notion that I shall discuss in more detail shortly. That care must be used in employing the term was brought home in the aftermath of the September 2001 attacks when Muslims were the first to remind us that Islamic extremists may undertake generic holy war by appealing to jihad to justify murder and suicide under the sanction of the will of Allah, but that does not mean such an appeal has standing beyond the community of the extremists themselves.[12] Osama bin Laden no more speaks for the Muslim world than Leo Tolstoy speaks for the Christian world. That religious people can take the demonic turn by invoking holy war is a familiar feature of all of the monotheistic traditions of the West; some further consideration of generic holy war as a religious possibility in Islam is in order.

Islam and Generic Holy War

Muslims justify a use of force when either defending Islam or pursuing objectives relevant to conforming the world to the will of Allah. In situations relevant to these two purposes, Muslims can invoke the idea of holy war. In Islam, a use of force that might be morally justifiable — say, in terms of a concern for justice or self-defense (i.e., just war) — would not be presented as morally justified action but as religiously meaningful, religiously authorized and sanctioned action. The realm of the moral is subordinated and lifted up into religious categories of meaning, with religion providing the context for moral life and interpretation. For all the value and justification that could be gleaned by a moral analysis of some Islamic tradition or rule of conduct, its ultimate meaning for Muslims would not be framed in a universal moral appeal but through a religious appeal to the will of Allah. This is the case even as Islamic attention to moral ideals and practices provides a major preoccupation of the Qur'an, the *hadith,* and the legal traditions that develop in Islam. On the question of using force, a war deemed justified by appeal to the will of Allah would have in that appeal a reason sufficient to justify a call to battle — even if there could be other, morally independent reasons for justifying a use of force.

Islamic monotheism refers all things to God, so that a call to arms is morally justified because it conforms to the divine will, which suffices to provide absolute justification. Moreover, this circular justification process imposes on the faithful Muslim a duty to take up arms and enter the conflict, provided, of course, that the Muslim accepts the divine sanctioning for a prospective use of force. Muslims debate and even disavow the legitimacy of calls to holy war by other Muslims, as is well known from the worldwide Muslim repudiation of the September 11, 2001, attacks. But a Muslim who undertakes a use of force — and this is the focus — inevitably legitimizes that action by means of appeal to the will of God. That move to invoke the will of God in moral matters — in the debatable and contingent affairs of human beings who are acting in the moral realm of self-other relatedness — invites absolutism into the processes of moral deliberation and evaluation.

Appealing to the divine will as authorization for action can easily dispense with moral reflection and deliberation, because moral meaning vaults into a one-dimensional command-obedience dynamic, so devoid of freedom, uncertainty, and decision as hardly to deserve description as an ethic. But a justification for action that rests in the explanation, "I do what I do because God told me to," powerful though that position be, can be invoked to support all kinds of morally dubious acts as the appeal to ultimacy puts a stop to quibbling about moral meaning. On this model of moral reasoning, if God approves an act or if an act is believed to be consistent with God's will, then the appeal to God suffices as justification. Moral objections at that point can be turned away by the word of the divine, "Your ways are not my ways." God's ways, in other words, are not to be reduced to moral problematics. When this kind of absolutism takes over the justification process, talk about a regrettable use of force, even a limited use of force, becomes difficult if not impossible.

The overpowering and dangerous invocation of holy war stifles deliberation about how to conform a use of force to a reasoned theory of justice — or even express a life-affirming religious stance. In that Islam requires that all things — all human action and intentionality — submit to God, all things moral are subjected to redescription through religion. Distinguishing a justifiable from an unjustifiable war cannot be accomplished if, in fact, religion has already pronounced on the issue of taking up arms and found such action consistent with religious reasons for action. Moral meaning will thus be flattened and serve not as an independent philosophical point of analysis and evaluation, but as an addendum to religious legitimation. A religiously justified use of force might very well claim, almost as an afterthought, to be a right use of force or a good thing to do. But from a moral point of view, a divine command ethic that is in play directing all action back to the will of an absolute God necessarily discounts and subordinates any contributions from practical or moral reasoning. Moral reasoning, however, considers suppression of its activity the stuff of which fanaticism is made and would offer that whenever religion insists on this suppression of the moral point of view, religion itself has turned demonic.

Religion that advocates the collapsing of religion and politics has appeared throughout the history of religions and particularly in monotheistic forms; it has historically played a crucial role in the development of an idea of Islamic civilization. Although Islam refers an action like a use of force to religious justification, examining Islamic life and practice and discerning moral meaning is still possible. Let me illustrate the difficulty of discerning moral meaning in military conflicts in Islam by looking quickly at two classic battles.

The first major battle in the history of Islam was the Battle of Badr, which occurred in 624 C.E. or year 2 following the *hijra*. One of the world's outstanding contemporary scholars of Islam, himself a Muslim, Seyyed Hossein Nasr, writes that the Battle of Badr "has become enshrined in the minds and hearts of Muslims to this day as the most crucial battle and 'holy war' (jihad) involving the very existence of the Islamic community. . . . The victory was a direct sign from heaven for the young Islamic order and enabled the Blessed Prophet to sign the treaties of alliance with some of the tribes around Medina and to fortify his position in that region."[13]

Nasr describes this battle then in two ways, one religious, one moral. First, it is described as a holy war, and holy war is explicitly associated with jihad. But Nasr also indicates that this battle was defensive and it preserved the Islamic community from extinction.[14] Nasr thus makes an implicit appeal to a moral theory justifying use of force, such a theory being understandable outside the confines of Islam by reasonable people who deem self-defense a morally legitimate reason for using force. Scholars have long noted that a theory of just war seems reflected in Islamic teaching about using force, given that force is always constrained and familiar features of traditional just war thinking in the West, such as noncombatant immunity, are observed. Professor Nasr, very much a philosopher cognizant of Enlightenment modes of thinking, justifies use of force in this battle by appealing to an implicit theory of justice associated with a morally justified use of force in a particular conflict situation.

Yet Professor Nasr also understands how this conflict was enshrined with religious significance for Muslims, who, even today, see in the Badr victory a "direct sign from heaven." I would argue that this way of thinking about moral issues and problems is quite foreign to modern Christians and Jews whose ethical grounding, despite the role of religion, is fundamentally reason-based and the product of Enlightenment era values. I return to this comment momentarily. At issue now is the moral meaning of the Battle of Badr.

That the Battle of Badr was morally justified is debatable as the moral meaning of all forcible action is at least debatable. Ethics is not the realm of absolutes but of discernment of meaning in the midst of self-other relations. Moral meaning is embedded in contingency and ambiguity, and moral discernment occurs in the context of conflict, even conflicts of interpretation. To justify the Battle of Badr by appealing to self-defense is not the same thing as saying that victory was "sent from heaven." Arguing that use of force in the Battle of Badr was justified in order to preserve the Islamic community makes a rational appeal, an appeal quite at odds with the explicitly religious understanding offered in the comment that the victory was "sent from heaven." This comment is not only unnecessary from a moral point of view, but it has the practical effect of subordinating the rational appeal to moral meaning. Nasr makes an appeal to moral justification, but that is not all. He also presents the Islamic understanding of ultimacy, in relationship to which the Battle of Badr is interpreted as a holy war undertaken in conformity to the will of God.[15] When Muslims make that move, Badr becomes holy war beyond — despite — any moral critique. It is a holy war and justifiable as such for those who hold that the will of God was the core justification for the fight.

An ethicist not committed to a Muslim self-understanding would offer independently of any appeal to the will of Allah the moral insight that the use of force in this particular battle, being an extreme emergency fought defensively to save a community, could be morally justified. Theories of justice and arguments to support a claim of justice could be enlisted — and debated. But from a religious point of view, only the justification grounded in the will of Allah matters, for in that will is authorization for holy war. These two justifications cancel each other out. The religious does not need the moral; the moral does not need the religious. The religious could easily conclude that the independent reasoning of moral reflection is blasphemous; the moral could easily conclude that the religious construction of meaning is grounded in the assurance of absolute faith, which is, from the point of reason, an expression of fanaticism or religion going — or gone — demonic.

Professor Nasr's short book *Muhammad: Man of God*[16] tells the story of the Battle of Badr, but it does not tell the story of the Jews of Qurayzah. This second battle is a story of an unfortunate ending to a conflict between Muslims and Jews, and it is told in many other biographies of Muhammad.

In the post-*hijra* consolidation of power in Arabia, Muhammad turned his attention back to Mecca, where opposition to his religious message had earlier spurred his decision to emigrate from Mecca to Medina. As Muhammad's power grew, he set his sights militarily on Mecca, and when he did so, he garnered the support of the Jews of a small town, Qurayzah, for they had given signs of wanting to side with Muhammad. But then, a powerful confederacy formed to oppose Muhammad's advance. Believing that Muhammad was vulnerable and facing defeat, the Jews of Qurayzah joined the confederacy based in Mecca. The Jews of Qurayzah then came to pose an additional military threat to Muhammad's forces, and clearly intrigue and treachery were involved in the clan's activities and leadership. Islamic scholar W. Montgomery Watt says of the Jewish leadership,

> They had thus been guilty of treasonable activities against the Medinan community. Muhammad, realizing that after the failure of the Meccans his position was very much stronger, was not prepared to tolerate such conduct, and determined to remove this source of weakness from Medina and to teach a lesson to the enemies and potential enemies.[17]

Muhammad laid siege to Qurayzah, and after twenty-five days the Jewish community surrendered unconditionally.

Pleas for mercy were delivered to Muhammad, and Muhammad responded by asking if the offending Jews would accept a decision about their fate from one of their own leading allies, Sa'd ibn Mu'adh, and to this offer the Jewish community agreed. As Karen Armstrong tells the story: "Sa'd judged that all the 700 men should be killed, their wives and children sold into slavery and their property divided among the Muslims. Muhammad cried aloud, 'You have judged according to the very sentence of al-Llah above the seven skies.'"[18] The next day, the men were tied together in groups and beheaded.

Given the context of warfare and conflict, certain kinds of practical justifications might be offered for Muhammad's actions in this situation. Armstrong herself offers a contextualized explanation:

> The umma [Muslim religious community] had narrowly escaped extermination at the siege and emotions were naturally running high. [The Jews of] Qurayzah had nearly destroyed Medina. If Muhammad had let them go they would at once have swelled the Jewish opposition.... The summary executions would have impressed Muhammad's enemies ... and the Qurayzah themselves seem to have accepted its inevitability.... This was a primitive society — far more primitive than the Jewish society in which Jesus had lived.... Some scholars [like W. Montgomery Watt, see below] have argued that it is not correct to judge the incident by twentieth century standards.[19]

What Islamic scholar W. Montgomery Watt had written about this incident is this:

> Some European writers have criticized this sentence for what they call its savage and inhuman character. It has to be remembered, however, that in the Arabia of that day when tribes were at war with one another or simply had no agreement, they had no obligations towards one another, not even of what we call common decency. ... What surprised Muhammad's contemporaries at the executions of all the males of Qurayzah was that he was not afraid of the consequences of his act ... what

was uppermost in [the minds of Muslims] was whether allegiance to the Islamic community was to be set above and before all other alliances and attachments.[20]

But Karen Armstrong herself, reflecting on the moral meaning of this slaughter, offers this telling comment: "It is probably impossible for us to dissociate this story from Nazi atrocities and it will inevitably alienate many people irrevocably from Muhammad."[21]

How is the execution of the Jews of Qurayzah to be evaluated? On the moral front, a utilitarian case could be made that enough positive consequences flowed from this mass execution that the important work of bonding a community of faithful above clan and tribal loyalties was sealed by this dramatic and powerful act. In other words, the executions helped forge the bond that would unify Arabia. So someone arguing from a "realpolitik" perspective and invoking a utilitarian-consequentialist ethic could interpret this action as a morally justified military step due to the positive consequences that flowed from it.

On the other hand, a surrendered people, treacherous though they may have been, were slaughtered in a way that Karen Armstrong compares, I think rightly, to a Nazi atrocity. From a moral point of view, this response seems more than excessive; it seems murderous. The suggestion that it is unfair to impose a contemporary standard of morality on this event hardly relieves the pressure of moral interpretation given that the contemporary world has known genocidal acts and extermination of communities no one in Muhammad's day could have ever envisioned; in fact, were we to use twentieth- or twenty-first-century moral standards we might not take much notice of this event, so much would it appear but a fly in the ointment compared to more contemporary acts of mass military slaughter.

Not a twentieth- or twenty-first-century standard, but the moral point of view should be invoked to evaluate the meaning of the slaughter of the Jews of Qurayzah. And it is clearly a shameful, horrendous event in Muslim history, and abiding respect for the moral point of view would, I humbly suggest, prevent so eminent a scholar as Professor Nasr from even mentioning this incident in his biography of Muhammad. Yet this massacre, from a Muslim point of view, was justified action as much as the Battle of Badr. It was an act of warfare justified because it was clearly framed as an act of generic holy war. It was an act justified at the time by an appeal to God, and the executions were actions believed to be consistent with God's will. Armstrong relates how Muhammad endorsed the decision for slaughter and then called for Allah's approval, so that this call for divine sanction and authorization is much the same as interpreting victory at Badr as "a direct sign from heaven." However much moral reflection would distinguish these two military events, the appeal to the will of God for justification renders these two events moral equivalents, because moral meaning has been subordinated to religious interpretation and the authorization for the acts rests in approval by God.

To be Muslim and to understand that all action ought to be undertaken in conformity to the will of Allah means that moral meaning is subservient to religious meaning. The decimation of the Jews of Qurayzah is God-authorized and

God-approved action. From a moral point of view, however, this slaughter is repugnant. This event, as Armstrong rightly points out, cannot help but remind us of more contemporary acts of military slaughter, including those in the twentieth century visited specifically on European Jews.

Ethical reasoning grounded in life-affirming visions of goodness would be hard-pressed to offer, much less accept, any moral justification of the Qurayzah executions. So despite the fact that it is possible to argue a rational realpolitik defense of this massacre based on significant and even, for some, positive consequences, this act of war is subject to serious moral debate, and it can certainly be condemned as an unjustifiable slaughter. But a debate over moral meaning is not possible if, as Muhammad is alleged to have said, the judgment to kill these enemies of Islam is "the very sentence of Allah." By that claim these executions, then, are justified — ultimately justified — as acts of generic holy war. Questioning how these executions would enhance a vision of goodness and promote the goods of life is suspended in the face of a nondebatable legitimation based in ultimacy — ultimacy gone absolutist beyond morality.

The point could be made, and fairly so: Have not Jews and Christians done similar things? Have not Jews and Christians, fellow "people of the book," also appealed to "heaven" to sanction morally dubious acts? The answer to this is, "Yes, of course." But the fact is that the Western Enlightenment so affected the relationship of religion to culture, including the insertion of reason into the foundations of moral thinking, that religious communities were themselves affected by the cultural shifts. So it is in the scheme of things today for Christians and Jews to live in their religious worlds yet also adopt the moral point of view as they live in a secular context. Many contemporary Jews and Christians make moral judgments based on Enlightenment ethical programs of analysis, then conform those analyses to their religious affirmations. The effort expended to prioritize life in a pluralistic and diverse community around moral rather than religious affirmations has allowed for a rethinking of religion so that a certain dissociation of moral commitment to religion is widely accepted, at least in America, as not incompatible with religion. Few Christians in America greeted the September 11, 2001, attacks with Jesus' words, "Turn the other check" and "Resist not evil."

Religious ideals of conduct have been altered by modes of ethical analysis and reasoning that do not, in the first instance, but only secondarily and contingently, appeal to religious ideals for authorization and legitimation; in the case of Christianity, many American Christians would simply hold that Jesus' ideals of action as enunciated in the Sermon on the Mount are impractical and are not normative except as religious ideals. But they are not treated as practical action guides, and practical reason does not function to engage those ideals in the course of daily life as people decide what to do and how to act. These observations of course do not apply to all Christians, but they do apply to many if not most American Christians. The First Amendment, one of the finest products of Enlightenment thinking, enshrined a legal guide that has functioned to advance the idea that the good of the polis is promoted by keeping government independent of religion and religion independent of governmental policy. Centuries of devastating religious wars in Europe had finally brought home the wisdom of a reasoned toleration for varieties of religion in an ethnically and religiously diverse polis.

Religious wars and political conflict centered on religion were in large part responsible for creating the conditions where what we call the Enlightenment redrew the relation between religion and politics. Islamic cultures, on the other hand, have not experienced so deep a transformative split between religion and politics. Despite the fact that in Islamic societies cultural practices are much more flexible than doctrinal demands, and European law and secularizing distinctions have influenced contemporary societal norms, value shifts in Islam have not transformed the "religion-politics" dynamic in a way comparable to the dramatic changes that occurred in Europe in the post-Reformation, post–"Age of Faith" era of the Enlightenment.[22]

Islam has a proud history of learning and even interpretive innovation. Islam, as no schoolchild should be unaware, preserved the ancient classical works of Greece and Rome and transmitted them on to the West when the West, during the Dark Ages, simply abandoned the classical traditions. Islam, in a very real sense, through its encounters with the West and its openness to learning and scholarship, made possible the European Renaissance which, in turn, also contributed to creating the conditions for the emergence of modern science and the Enlightenment shift to reason-based, rather than revelation-based, moral thinking.

Moreover, Islamic tradition was "enlightenment bound," so to speak, because it held core positions against anyone monopolizing interpretation or serving as Islam's official spokesperson. That Islam never developed a clergy is not insignificant. To keep interpretation open in moral matters, Islam affirmed a four-tiered structure that included appeal to the Qur'an, appeal to the traditions of Muhammad in the *hadith* of the *Sunnah* or "custom" of Muhammad, consensus in the community (*ijma'*), and the use of analogy (*qiyas*) for updating the applicability of Muslim ethical teaching to contemporary circumstance.[23] Openness to innovation in interpretation of Islamic teaching was nowhere better seen than in the affirmation of the *Ijtihad. Ijtihad,* which is of a piece with intellectual jihad, is the doctrine that a person who knows Arabic, understands the issue at hand, and knows as well the *hadith* and other sources of interpretation, could interpret the Qur'an and the *Sunnah.* As a process of interpretation, *Ijtihad* allowed that any adequately qualified person can study the text and derive a *Hukum,* or rule, for interpreting the issue under consideration. This allowed for interpretive innovation and reflected a liberalized stance toward the sacred texts. When *Ijtihad* was in effect, the authority for interpretation rested not so much in scholars as in individuals and their offering of particular readings of the texts. Scholars of early Islam taught that if interpretations came along better than their own, the stronger opinion should be accepted. *Ijtihad* fostered intellectual growth and broadened understanding; it, too, was an "enlightenment bound" notion inherent to the Islamic tradition.

But by the fourth century after the *hijra* (i.e., the tenth century C.E.), a change in direction was under way. Arabic had fallen into neglect, and, even more significantly, the culture of interpretation had been affected by the increasing authority of scholars as Muslims began to attach themselves to interpreters rather than texts.[24] A Fatwa, attributed to al-Qaffal, was called to "close the door of *Ijtihad*." Although the *Ijtihad* did not disappear, it did go into decline; as Europe groped slowly toward the Enlightenment with its reassertion of reason and emphasis on interpretive innovation in the area of sacred texts, the Islamic move as a culture seemed to progress even more slowly, even at times formally resisting such innovation.[25]

Contemporary Americans live in the wake of the Enlightenment. The Enlightenment affected the relation of religion and politics as well as repositioned moral thinking so that it would rest not on divine authority but on reason itself. Islamic civilization moved toward modernity under an entirely different set of cultural assumptions and historical circumstances than did Western Europe and the United States. During the Enlightenment, as Western Europe and, later, America, moved toward democracy and a separation of religion from political life, Islamic civilization reasserted the dominant power of the Islamic faith in all affairs of life, including the social, the political, and even the ethical. In a sense, Islamic civilization resisted many of the influences that in Western Europe led to the Enlightenment and the separation of the religious and the political spheres of power.

Yet the question is legitimately asked, "Have not Christians and Jews appealed to divine authority to legitimate action in the moral realm just as Muslims do?" and we answer, "Yes, of course." But that "yes" must be qualified.

History and cultural developments have affected how, say, a Muslim in Iran and a Christian in the United States would go about justifying an action as morally appropriate. I have offered one possible way to account for the differences in two arcs of history, one being the European with its Enlightenment emphasis on reason and the separation of the religious and political realms, the other being a reaffirmation of the centrality of Islamic religion in dominating interpretation of thought and action. These two arcs of historical movement represent distinct historical and cultural developments. With this sense of cultural difference in hand, let us reconsider a question about generic holy war: Is holy war in Islam ever life-affirming?

If we use the concept of holy war in the generic sense to identify a use of force legitimated by ultimate, divine authority, then we can easily conclude that holy war is a part of the history of Islam just as it is a part of Hebrew and Christian religion. But a problem arises because the Battle of Badr is, from the Islamic point of view, morally equivalent to the massacre of the Jews of Qurayzah, for both are ultimately interpretable as holy wars justified by appeal to the will of God. Independent, reason-based moral critique cannot edge its way in, because moral meaning is subsumed under the appeal to heaven. Muhammad himself announced divine approval for beheading seven hundred tied-up prisoners. Karen Armstrong mentions almost causally how this massacre of Jews by Muslims is akin to Nazi atrocity, but then she understandably backs off. No moral language of atrocity is available when God authorizes such a killing and

God is the absolute arbiter of moral meaning, whose judgment is not to be questioned and whose blessing on the event is not to be doubted. What God determines to be permissible is good to do because God willed it. In this religious perspective, there is no critical reason-based moral reflection at work evaluating action and discerning moral meaning independently of what it is believed God wills.

When we ask whether religion provides a life-affirming response to violence via holy war, I think the general answer is that it might in a rare instance, and I have argued that the Exodus is just such a life-affirming example. But holy war is presumptively demonic, and it is a moral critique that exposes the appeal to divine authority for justification of war and uses of force as demonic. For the moral point of view critiques actions in light of a vision of goodness and asks why God should want to use human beings as the agents to perform the acts of violence or killing God wants. Why does God, whom many monotheists avow as all-powerful, not do the killing directly out of the divine resource? Why should God require agents to enact a divinely willed destruction, unless God is not sufficiently powerful to enact the divine will that is God's own?

The Exodus story shows human beings practicing life-affirming religion even as God is acting as warrior and doing away with Israel's enemies, and this is what life-affirming religion would look like in holy war. When human beings have political, military, and territorial objectives, not to mention personal ambitions for glory, and they then invoke holy war as if God is authorizing destructive acts of killing, a moral critique would suggest that human beings, not God, are acting for mundane purposes that are easily and reasonably discernible as mundane. A moral critique would insist that the actions and reasons for them be evaluated as such. Generic holy war, then, ought to be evaluated as human action, despite the fact that a peculiar religious justification attaches to it; whether the holy war action is, morally speaking, justifiable or not justifiable, the appeal to religion for justification is always, from a moral point of view, a disavowal of human responsibility and an appeal to religion in its demonic turn. The exception would be a war God wants and God fights, so that God, not human beings, is the agent of the divine will.

Religion that turns demonic expresses itself through violence and killing. Human beings who opt to be religious in the demonic mode pursue destructive ends under the self-deceptive ruse that they are enacting God's will and doing good by such acts, and of this they are certain. People who are religious in the demonic mode maintain this belief in the goodness and divine sanction for what they do even as their acts fail to manifest the luminosity of goodness, even as moral critique condemns their acts as unworthy of free persons acting in relationships of respect with others.

Morally speaking, the Battle of Badr could possibly be interpreted as life-affirming, but this conclusion could be drawn only after considering the details of the battle and only after subjecting the actual uses of force to moral critique. It is certainly possible that moral critique would show what Professor Nasr indicates in the first instance of his "Enlightenment mode" analysis, namely, that the war was defensive and restrained and also necessary for the survival of the community. But then we must say that when that moral interpretation is subordinated to the Muslim under-standing of moral meaning, which is equivalent to religious meaning — it is a battle where heaven acted to give the vic-tory — Badr is constructed for analysis as a holy war. This religious interpretation has the practical effect of canceling any appeal to moral meaning. As holy war, the use of force at Badr, as any other similarly justified use of force, must be assumed to be invoking religion turned toward the de-monic. To claim that Badr was life-affirming religion would require an in-depth explanation that demonstrated that this battle was akin to the Exodus liberation, that paradigm of life-affirming holy war in which God acts as the agent for the war. Such a claim does not rely on humans to interpret the divine will — always a problematic, even self-deception-prone business — or otherwise to do what God should be powerful enough to do directly. To make the case that the Battle of Badr is, from the moral point of view, life-affirming would require the kind of justification hinted at by Pro-fessor Nasr, which could be deemed moral critique that stands apart from any religious justification for holy war. Those indicators of life-affirming religion — the promotion of the value of life, acting in the interests of serving a vision of goodness, the luminosity of goodness in the acts them-selves — would identify the criteria needed to argue for such an interpretation, and they would have to be demonstrated and withstand critical moral scrutiny.

To establish the positive, life-promoting meaning of the Battle of Badr would not then depend upon an appeal to religious authority or absolutism of any kind, but only to a vision of goodness. Professor Nasr deemed the Battle of Badr in a very practical sense luminous with respect to goodness; the critical moral question that would have to be asked is whether the goodness is truly luminous, that is, is it there for all reasonable persons to see, or is it only there to be seen by a faithful Muslim? The luminosity of goodness must not and cannot be hidden.

Muslims and religious people of all types and varieties can conceivably justify a use of force in certain conflict situations, and they can do so with moral — as opposed to strictly religious — legitimacy. A moral analysis would guide the way to establishing legitimate and permissible uses of force. The problem for religion, however, is that employing a moral critique inevitably exposes impermissible uses of force as well as permissible ones. A moral analysis would undoubtedly condemn the slaughter of the Jews of Qurayzah, as Karen Armstrong suggested by her invocation of comparison with Nazi atrocities; this moral critique would hold even though, as Armstrong reported, Muhammad is the one justifying the executions and doing so by an appeal to the will of Allah.

To undertake a moral analysis of Muslim actions justified religiously, one must step out of Islam and the essential perspective of faith that sees all action as referable to the will of Allah. The problem is that this move toward rational critique is essentially what Islam forbids. So there are holy wars in Islam in the generic sense I have been using the term. Are some of them life-affirming? Perhaps, but to say that in the affirmative is to also say that that conclusion cannot be reached by the only method Islam endorses for judging such things, which is a religious justification. Only a moral critique can determine the life-affirming, as opposed to a demonic, character of a religiously sanctioned use of force. Only a moral critique would care about making such a distinction.

Monotheistic religions in general have held that it is inappropriate to hold God up to the standards of moral meaning as human persons understand them and use them; given the way cultural contingency and relativism affect moral thinking, this claim is not an unreasonable one for religious people to make. But if goodness itself is the standard, then even divine action can be held up against that standard, and the moral meaning of actions attributable to God can be evaluated accordingly. That is what moral critique does: it evaluates the meaning of action in light of a vision of goodness. Human actions, even if believed to be divinely authorized, are subject to moral critique; if God so acts as to authorize an action that defies goodness, then the moral critique must hold firm to its assessment of the meaning of the action and then go so far as to suggest that the human agent is self-deceived in presuming God is endorsing an evil act, since God is good. The more uncomfortable move would be to allow religious persons their claim of divine authorization for human action and then refer evil acts to a God fallen into evil or madness. But a God acting to defy goodness is a God unleashing the power of the demonic. Saul, who refused to submit to the absolute destructiveness of the *hērem* demanded by God, stood before God as a moral man disobedient to the call for absolutism and God's unreasonable desire for wrathful judgment. Saul stood, at least a bit, on

the side of moral discernment, endorsing the moral requirement that goodness always call for the restraint of violence,
not for its unrestricted unleashing. Saul stood before a deity that was itself portrayed as gripped with demonic desire.
Saul refuses the temptation of absolutism and does not do
what God clearly wants. His story could be read as a refusal
to accede to the totalized destruction that is a consequence
of a demonic absolutism.

Moral consciousness shaped by the Western Enlightenment can certainly evaluate and interpret the moral meaning
of Islamic uses of force, including those appeals to divine
justification that emerge in generic holy war. In this perspective, Islam can be subjected to moral critique as can
any religion that authorizes uses of force in the name of an
ultimate reality that has gone absolute and thus turned toward the demonic. A moral critique can even go so far as to
say that the slaughter of the Jews of Qurayzah was a contemptible event from a moral point of view, and that story
illustrates how religion can be used destructively, murder-
ously, demonically. But these interpretations and critiques
meet with resistance from religious people, so long as the
kind of Enlightenment attitude that makes this kind of
moral critique possible does not come into play in the mainstream of religious thought itself. Thus, being sensitive to
the Islamic invocation of the divine will is difficult in matters where force is used, as is thinking about the kind of
distinction we have been dealing with, namely, that of the
life-affirming and the demonic. That distinction does not
itself work in the consciousness of a Muslim — or any other
religious person — who holds that the meaning of all things

is divinely determined and goodness is equated with the will of God. The life-affirming/demonic distinction, however, remains valid and useful for moral and religious critique, although I must qualify this statement by saying, "from the moral point of view."

Jihad

Jihad is a layered notion in Islamic tradition, and it has unfortunately entered the mainstream American consciousness as an idea of holy war associated with the fanatical irrationality and violence of Middle Eastern terrorism. The association of jihad with holy war, then, has perversely denied Americans access to the conceptual richness of the concept as well as distorted important aspects of Islam itself. Americans who follow the Middle East are aware of a terrorist organization, Islamic Jihad; even more dramatically, Osama bin Laden explicitly referred to the September 11, 2001, attacks on America as issuing from jihad. The terrorist context makes the Islamic notion of jihad difficult to present and understand, even for the kind of limited issue I wish to pursue here, which is to ask whether Islam has life-affirming ways of responding to violence that are distinct from the absolutism of demonic holy war.

I have chosen to present separately two ideas relevant to the idea of a justified use of force in Islam, ideas that lay the groundwork for discerning when Islam provides a response to violence that is essentially life-affirming. So I distinguish the generic idea of holy war from jihad. Holy war, whenever employed in any religious tradition, lends itself to absolutist thinking in that it is employed to establish divine warrants for a human use of force beyond any reasonable appeal to ethical justification. Holy war, I have argued, is therefore presumptively demonic even if independent moral warrants can be found to justify a particular use of force in a conflict religious people would interpret as holy war. The fact that holy war appeals for justification beyond the realm of moral reflection and human moral relatedness and rests on a divine authorization that always — absolutely — trumps moral appeals yields this conclusion. Jihad, on the other hand, is a more complex notion.

Jihad is invoked in various ways and at differing times to mean different things for Muslims, and a moral analysis must attend to these particularities of usage. "Jihad" can indicate a life-affirming doctrine that is nonabsolutist. Yet jihad has also been used as a synonym for generic holy war, which would then lend support to the idea that "jihad" can itself be of a piece with religion gone demonic. Apologists for Islam sometimes disavow the aggressive, militant, and demonic uses of jihad in Islamic history to emphasize the spiritual, life-affirming meanings associated with the term. Critics of Islam sometimes do just the opposite by ignoring the life-affirming employments of jihad and employing jihad as a holy war signifier. It is simply a fact of history and of linguistic usage that the term "jihad" has invoked these destructive meanings, even being used in justifications of terrorist acts.

In opening a discussion of jihad, I want to be clear that both of these perspectives came front and center following the attacks of September 11, 2001; both are in part right, and both are in part wrong. Scholarship on the issue of jihad makes clear that jihad does make a spiritual appeal, and there are even uses of the term that clearly do not envision anything but defensive, morally justifiable uses of restrained force. But jihad has been associated with generic holy war, and Muslims themselves quite commonly acknowledge this conceptual appeal. Even so great a scholar as Seyyed Hossein Nasr associates holy war with jihad in his description of the Battle of Badr, noted previously. But to equate jihad with generic holy war misrepresents the complexity of the term and threatens to suppress the life-affirming, as opposed to demonic, possibilities of meaning.

In what follows I outline the life-affirming interpretation of jihad. My purpose in doing so is to demonstrate that jihad provides the possibility for a life-affirming response to violence, one very much at odds with the holy war meaning for the term.

The meaning of "jihad" emerges from the religious context of Islam, which, as we have argued, subordinates moral meaning to religious interpretation. Despite the serious attention Islam gives to action and its normative regulation through law, the fact is that "the real basis on which rests this whole structure [of Islamic law] is religious, the idea that God is sovereign and 'the Ordainer Whose Will is Law.' Man [*sic*] must discover, formulate and execute that Will of which the final index is the Qur'an and Muhammad the most perfect commentator."[26] So on the issue of the use of force Rudolph Peters writes that Islam "does not distinguish between holy and secular wars."[27]

Placing Islamic moral concerns, including those that would govern a use of force, in their proper religious context allows us to discern the sense it makes to say that in Islam jihad must not, in the first instance, be made a conceptual equivalent of holy war.[28]

In two important senses jihad does not refer to holy war.[29] One sense is theological. It could be argued that jihad cannot refer to holy war because Islam does not acknowledge anything as "holy" except God. Muslims do not refer even to the Qur'an, the uncreated Word of God "akin to Christ in Christianity," as "holy." "Holy" belongs to God alone. Accordingly, it is simply a conceptual mistake to think of a war — any war, or anything else actually — as holy, for the only thing that merits qualification as "holy" is Allah. The idea of Islam endorsing the idea of a holy war represents a fundamental misunderstanding of basic theological tenets. On the basis of this central idea alone, one could rightly conclude that there is not and never could be in Islam a notion of "holy war."

The second appeal one could make to dismiss any association of jihad with holy war concerns the linguistic term "jihad" itself. Jihad is often translated as "holy war," but if we account the meaning of words and concepts to be in any way important, respect for linguistic integrity would have us note that the Arabic word transliterated "jihad" does not, as a matter of definition, mean "holy war." Jihad is best translated "struggle" or "striving." A second reason for dismissing the idea of holy war from the conceptual apparatus of Islam, therefore, is linguistic: the word "jihad" does not mean "holy war," and so to translate it is a linguistic mistake.

The idea of jihad relates to a striving, exertion, or the sincere effort to attain a praiseworthy aim, a spiritual good. As the Qur'an presents it, jihad aims at effecting change in one's self and calls at times for sacrifice as Muslims exert themselves for the betterment of Islamic society. So Islam recognizes jihads of the tongue and jihads of the pen, intellectual jihads like *Ijtihad* and even educational jihads.[30] The Prophet Muhammad drew a distinction between a greater and a lesser jihad. In an important saying or *hadith* traditionally, though not uncontroversially, attributed to the prophet — one major compilation of Muhammad's sayings does not include it — the prophet is reported to have said upon returning from a raiding party, "We now have returned from the Smaller Jihad to the Greater Jihad." When asked what this Greater Jihad was, he answered, "The jihad against oneself."[31]

The meaning of jihad is grounded in a spiritual, thus peaceful, notion concerning the struggle of the self against temptation. Getting out of bed and striving to be a good Muslim in the course of a day is jihad in this spiritualized sense. This spiritualized notion of jihad was prominent in early Islam, and this meaning of interior struggle is clearly at issue in uses of the jihad notion in the early parts of the Qur'an where the word appears infrequently. The verb *jahada* and its derivatives occur hardly at all in the "Meccan" parts of the Qur'an, that is, in those years of Qur'anic composition that occurred before the *hijra*. After leaving Mecca in the *hijra* ("migration") and moving to Medina,

Muhammad's leadership role becomes increasingly involved with military actions, and the meaning of jihad shifts as the term appears in the sacred text with more frequency. But in early Islam, when Muhammad is still in Mecca, jihad enjoins Muslims patiently to bear the aggressive behaviors of unbelievers.

After the *hijra,* Muhammad's role as a community leader changes as does Muhammad's vision for Islam, which becomes pan-Arabic as Muhammad envisions Islam as a cultural bond of such power that it is deemed capable of uniting all Arabs. After the *hijra,* the nature of the struggle that Islam experiences changed. As that struggle — that jihad — became more militaristic and more involving of uses of force in battles against enemies who posed threats to the Islamic community, the Qur'an reflected some alterations in the meaning of jihad. These meanings "abound in the Medinese chapters, set down after the fighting between Muslims and their Meccan adversaries had broken out."[32]

Islam has never lost sight of the spiritualized notion of jihad, but even these spiritualized renderings of jihad have undergone alterations as the Muslim understanding of its own struggle changed. Thus jihad comes to signify a corporate struggle of the entire Muslim community against decadence and corruption.[33] Jihad in this sense refers to the struggle all Muslims undergo as they "work with all their intellectual and material abilities for the realization of justice and equality between people and for spreading of security and human understanding, both among individuals and groups."[34]

These distinctive spiritualized uses of "jihad," uses that have never disappeared but are affirmed in the Muslim self-understanding, indicate that "jihad" lends itself to employments that are directed toward the interior life. These uses are undeniably peaceful. They aim at improving life, advancing life, and pursuing the goods of justice and equality. Jihad in this sense is clearly life-affirming, and at this point I think it safe to conclude that, yes, jihad can be a life-affirming notion.

But jihad was a fluid and adaptable notion historically, and a meaning developed that eventually lent itself to interpretation as "generic holy war." This jihad of physical force is the "lesser" jihad of the sword. Two-thirds of the uses of "jihad" or its linguistic derivatives in the Qur'an denote warfare and use of arms in military battle. "Jihad" came to reflect the struggle of the Muslim community for survival, thus attaching "jihad" to uses of force, especially military force. This particular use of physical jihad comes to prominence in those portions of the Qur'an set down in Medina, when Muhammad was attacked militarily and Muslims in Arabia were in a consolidation mode. But jihad in these uses is always defensive. Not only does "jihad" *not* endorse acts of military aggression, but "jihad" is invoked in Qur'anic passages to indicate how uses of force are always subject to restraint and qualification. The claim that Islam supports a just war theory can be extracted from references to the jihad of the sword. Classical Islam associates jihad with fighting against unbelievers, a category that does not ordinarily include Christians and Jews; with defending the community of believers; and with resisting evil and any threat to the continued existence of the community of the faithful. Women, children, and noncombatants are to be protected and rendered immune from conflict. Jihad — the jihad of the sword — emphasizes defensive justifications for uses of force. Shi'ite Islam requires an imam or an authorized substitute to be present for the launching of a jihad of the sword, but in the event of an attack the duty falls to all Muslims to defend a country and its people.[35]

Jihad has two functions, one being the propagation of Islam, the other being defense of the community (*umma*). Jihad is dealt with in law as a kind of theory of just war, which establishes rules for engaging in a war "comparable to *jus ad bellum*" as well as for the conduct of war according to rules "comparable to *jus in bello*." The cause of the war must be "in the way of God" and ordinarily not directed against another Islamic state.[36]

The idea of propagating Islam does not necessitate aggression, especially armed aggression, for the motive behind expanding Islam is to oppose false gods and to strengthen monotheism. As a proselytizing and expanding faith, Islam has throughout history come to oppressed peoples and been received as an attractive religious change; for it offered an understandable religion; it was committed to fighting for religious freedom; and it opposed any persecution that would interfere with people converting to Islam. The Qur'an (2:256) insists that there is "never to be compulsion in religion," and in the legal traditions jihad recognizes noncombatant immunity forbidding the killing of women, children, and aged people, even if they are unbelievers.[37]

In short, the meaning of "jihad" is not fixed but reflects a rich and complex history of usage. That history runs the gamut of meaning from an idea of interior struggle to be confronted as a spiritual challenge to contemporary uses that associate jihad with justification for political terror. "Jihad" has invoked meanings that appeal to religious absolutism, especially in all that is related to the idea of struggling against unbelievers, and such meanings are not beyond the conceptual reach of those who would interpret "jihad" as an equivalent for holy war. Some of the associations with holy war evolved from developments in Islamic law, which expanded the meaning of "jihad" to convey more and more of the aggressive jihad that seeks to subdue and conquer. But the origins of jihad had nothing to do with the absolutism of generic — and demonic — holy war tendencies. Writes scholar Rudolph Peters:

> Careful reading of the Qur'anic passages on jihad suggest that Muhammad regarded the command to fight the unbelievers not as absolute, but as conditional upon provocation from them, for in many places this command is justified by aggression or perfidy on the part of the non-Muslims. "And fight in the way of God with those who fight with you, but aggress not: God loves not the aggressors" (2:190) and "But if they break their oaths after their covenant and thrust at your religion, then fight the leaders of unbelief" (9:13) Authoritative Muslim opinion, however, went in a different direction. Noticing that the Qur'anic verses on the relationship between Muslims and non-Muslims

give evidence of a clear evolution from peacefulness to enmity and warfare, Muslim scholars have argued that this evolution culminated in an unconditional command to fight the unbelievers, as embodied in verses such as 5:9 ("Then when the sacred months are drawn away, slay the idolaters wherever you find them, and take them, and confine them, and lie in wait for them at every place of ambush"). These "sword verses" are considered to have repealed all other verses concerning the intercourse with non-Muslims.[38]

"Jihad," then, has been nonabsolutist in its meaning, and certain formulations of the jihad of the sword, especially earlier ones, conveyed meaning directed toward life-affirming, violence-restraining, nondemonic ends. But as the Muslim community grew and faced challenges, even threats to its continued existence, the jihad notion adapted and transformed. The Muslim community as a linguistic community loosened "jihad" from its original mooring site, where it was a defensive notion, and they set it free in the world of political and religious and cultural struggle where it developed into a true generic holy war notion. This transformation of meaning was confirmed by legal interpretations that reinforced the unconditioned or absolute nature of the jihad command while requiring that previous interpretations be superseded. Muslims have themselves absolutized the jihad notion and used the term as a way of indicating a distinctively Islamic notion of holy war. All of these uses, from the spiritual to the self-defensive to the aggressive and destructive, can convey meanings recognized as legitimate and authoritative uses of "jihad" by Muslims in the practice of their religion.

These different meanings, however, are not all equivalent from a moral point of view. The shifting of meaning exposes a movement from life-affirming religion to moral interpretation to demonic religion. "Jihad" as a linguistic signifier does not stipulate meaning but sets movable boundaries for meaning that Muslim people — and others — can use for a variety of purposes. Understanding "jihad" does not depend upon looking at a word and defining it, but at the person using the word, who appeals to the concept and employs the term to perform various meaning tasks. For some, the invocation of jihad points to the need for spiritual development. For others it signifies a holy war notion justifying — with God's sanction — aggressive acts of destruction, even the terrorist killings of innocents.

Therefore, when we ask whether jihad can be "life-affirming," we must look to those Muslims who are life-affirming in their religion; for we shall find in them a usage that points to an affirmative answer. Jihad can be life-affirming. It can serve as an implement to cultivate spiritual growth and support morally justifiable efforts in defense of life-affirming values. To the extent that jihad points to defensive action and appeals to a view of justice to restrain violence, there could easily be jihads that would, like just wars — which I shall discuss in the next chapter — prove essentially life-affirming. But this view of jihad opens jihad up to case-by-case critique, so that a moral evaluation of various jihad-sponsored uses of force would then be required. But this then requires us to move out of the religious realm of discourse where jihad has meaning for Muslims and assess jihad actions from a moral point of view. But because the moral point of view can find life-affirming connotations and uses for the jihad notion, responsible people ought not to define jihad in terms of holy war, for to do so would be to deny those life-affirming possibilities while giving into a demonic mode of thought that would subordinate the moral point of view to a demonic absolutism.

Conclusion

Generic holy war can arise in Islam just as it can arise in Israelite religion or in Christianity, and violent or destructive acts undertaken as expressions of the divine inevitably provide evidence of the demonic turn. Whether Islam could advance the possibility of a holy war that is nondemonic and life-affirming must be subjected to moral critique independent of any appeal for justification to heaven (ultimacy itself), but Islam itself does not sanction such a move.

Jihad, on the other hand, can more easily be seen as expressing a life-affirming idea of spiritual struggle, the end sought being spiritual purification and even the expansion of justice itself. The lesser jihad of physical force must be subjected to moral testing to see if the kind of just war restrictions it presents as a moral theory of defense and propagation of Islam restrains violence and otherwise serves a vision of goodness through its demands for justice. In a given situation where force is used and jihad is invoked, does the use of force preserve and promote the goods of life, and does it seek the end of restoring peace? Jihad has typically condemned reasons for using force that would fail to meet the test of "life-affirming," excluding actions such as fighting for territorial expansion, for vengeance or booty, or compelling others to accept Islam. So it would seem that an affirmative answer is at least possible when asking whether an external jihad can manifest life-affirming religious values. To the extent that defensive action is taken, or humanitarian intervention occurs to preserve the lives of oppressed and endangered people, it seems that no formal impediment exists to the idea of a life-affirming physical or external jihad.

But moral determinations must be offered, as I have argued, on a case-by-case basis. The September 11, 2001, attacks were jihad in the minds of those Muslims who undertook the destructive activities of that day, and such jihad as their actions represented was, morally speaking, beyond any bar of defense moral reason could recognize and affirm. And that is what must be said: not that jihad cannot mean what it meant to those who killed and committed suicide, but that such usage of the idea of jihad fails to enact a vision of goodness and is certainly not luminous with respect to goodness. It is not the religious test of allowable action that fails, for religion obviously played a part, and an appeal to ultimacy played a role in motivating those individuals to sacrifice their own lives while killing innocent persons. Those demonic acts of destruction were legitimate and authentic expressions of religion, although it is to be noted that the religion of Islam, in Qur'anic teaching, specifically forbids such actions. The critical issue to be faced around the question of holy war and religion is not whether religion can incite violence and demonic destruction by a holy war justification, for clearly religion can do that. The critical question pertains to the moral decision people confront about how they are going to express themselves religiously. The September 11, 2001, attackers, as Muslims, may have acted believing that they were doing the will of Allah, that they would be rewarded, and that those attacked were enemies and not innocents. Exposing the demonic nature of the religion that may have fed this understanding comes not by asking whether the religion involved was true religion or false religion but by asking the moral question: "Was goodness luminous in what they did?"

Islam, like other religious traditions, accommodates a response to violence that seeks to restrain and justify uses of force. Like other religious traditions, Islam can include people who seek divine authorization for uses of force that violate the moral vision whereby goodness is promoted and life is preserved. Muslims, like Christians or Jews or Hindus or Buddhists, can express themselves religiously in ways that reflect the demonic option, and the markers of demonic destructiveness and repression can show up in Islam just as they do in any other form of religious expression. When the demonic appears, as it does in holy war, it will subvert the goods of life and tear at life-affirming values. When human beings in the name of God and under sanction of divine authority engage in violence as an expression of their religious faith, they unleash the destructive potential of religion. Holy war exposes how explosive and dangerous religion can be when human beings choose to express themselves religiously through the demonic turn.

The demonic dynamic presents to moral consciousness possibilities for action that are simply not luminous with respect to goodness. Holy war, which attributes justification for human violence to the divine will, not only expresses this dynamic but exposes the divine will itself to moral critique. Moral critique guided by a vision of goodness would inevitably offer a conclusion that religious people engaged in holy war would find difficult to process and accept; for the moral meaning of holy war finally turns to ultimacy itself and offers that the divine will that would authorize such destructive action as takes place in holy war is itself demonic and unworthy of moral assent.

Chapter Six

The Case of Just War

RELIGION CAN INCITE VIOLENCE; it can serve as a force to resist and constrain violence. Having considered both life-affirming and demonic versions of two religious engagements with and responses to violence — pacifism and holy war — I now turn my attention to a third alternative — just war. Although just war is more appropriately a moral rather than a religiously grounded notion, religion has played an important part in receiving, developing, modifying, and transmitting just war thinking over the centuries in various religious traditions. Central aspects of just war thinking are today resident in the moral frameworks of Christian, Jewish, and Muslim moral reflection.

Just war presumes the good of peace, as I shall show, while aiming always at the end of peace. It sponsors a model of moral engagement committed to resisting violence and injustice, yet doing so by means that are restrained by concerns for justice. As a moral response to violence and conflict, just war refuses to indulge the extremism of moral

[233]

and religious absolutism while resisting evil in ways that always seek to upholding life-affirming values. Although just war is not always presented in the context of a life-affirming perspective — and critics of just war have with perspicuity observed how it can fall into demonic use — I endorse a version of just war that resists evil, addresses injustice, and seeks in means and ends to express a life-affirming vision of goodness. Just war, as I shall argue, structures a model for nonabsolutist moral thinking of wide applicability. Just war, as I shall present it, takes into account moral ambiguity and attends to human imperfection and limitation in structuring the process of moral assessment and decision making. Although it allows force to be included in the options of response to certain acts of violence, injustice, or evil, it will insist on a rational justification for any use of force and restrain such uses consistent with the requirements of justice and proportionality.

Just war models an approach to moderate moral reflection that can have wide applicability, and in other writings I have demonstrated how this model can be applied to elucidate the moral meaning of other troubling issues, including abortion and the death penalty. But just war theory was originally formulated as a way to consider the moral issues involved with war and use of force, and as a theory addressing these issues it has a long history in Western culture. Just war appeals have been so often invoked by those who authorize force that many critically minded people have become suspicious of just war itself. Many today hold, not unreasonably, that appeals to just war amount to little more than a predictable ploy that politicians and military people use to establish moral cover for the purpose of gaining support for a decision to use force or go to war.

But just war theory, in my view, identifies an ethic that not only restrains force even when a use of force is justified, but that offers a way to critique and oppose uses of force that fail to meet the stringent requirements of justice. Furthermore, philosophical coherence for the idea of a theory of just war — a justified use of force — can only be claimed if account is taken of the presumption that gives rise to the theory in the first place, which is the presumption that force ought not to be used to settle conflicts. Just war is not typically presented in such a way that the presumption against using force is made clear, but without this presumption just war is difficult to associate with a life-affirming action, and it is exactly that possibility that I want to argue for below. My argument is that just war theory can be presented as a coherent moral perspective that models a nonabsolutist approach to ethical thinking, and that when so presented it will function to resist violence, advance the goods of life, and pursue ends that are luminous with respect to goodness.

Just War in Historical Perspective

In his treatise *On Duties (De Officiis)*, Cicero wrote that "although reason is characteristic of men and force of beasts, you must resort to force if there is no opportunity to employ reason. Therefore, wars should be undertaken only so that one may live in peace without wrongdoing."[1] Cicero held that the end of war must be a just peace, that a justified use of force must rest on legitimate cause, and that "no war is just unless it is waged after the government has demanded restitution or unless the war is previously announced and declared."[2]

The origins of just war theory lie in these reflections of Cicero, who, as a Roman patriot, understood Roman law to embody natural law. Thus he formulated the rudiments of a comprehensive theory that could apply to all wars and govern all uses of force; what he included were rules to judge the justifiability of resorting to war (*jus ad bellum*) as well as rules to judge the morality of specific practices in the war (*jus in bello*). These rules were designed to restrain the use of force, and Cicero held that these rules expressed reason's recognition of a natural law notion of justice itself. Cicero understood war to be a matter of honor, though he tied honor to reason; his developed view was that natural reason should lead reasonable people to submit to Roman law without use of force.

But Cicero was also a critic of war. He deplored Roman cruelty to the point of holding Rome accountable for crimes, such as the sack of Corinth. As one commentator has written, "Cicero clearly states that evil should never be done, even to save one's country. The gods, or, natural law are above the state."[3]

Ciceronian just war theory was picked up and developed by St. Augustine, who hated war and doubted that any war could bring a lasting peace. It was Augustine who refused, for the first time in the West, to associate war with honor. From its inception with Augustine and then as it was transmitted through the moral teachings of the Roman Catholic Church, the just war idea has been based on the idea that public authorities have a duty to pursue justice, even at risk to their personal safety. The idea of justice advanced through the Church included the idea that charity and love of neighbor were integral to the notion of justice; such ideas very much affected how just war developed in Western Christendom over the centuries. In the twelfth century, Gratian's *Decretals* advanced a just war theory around the idea that just war can avenge wrongs and coerce the Church's enemies. Then Raymond of Pennaforte in the thirteenth century formalized Augustine's theory, regarding war as what we would today term a prima facie, or presumed, evil. Thomas Aquinas (1225–74) adopted Augustine's just war idea that a use of force required right authority, just cause, and right intention, but he also moved beyond Augustine, adding a self-defense feature that would later be formalized in the idea of a "just cause" criterion. A twofold or "double effect" idea came into play, namely, the idea that individual Christians subjected to unjust aggression could with legitimate justification kill their attackers so long as such killing occurred as an unintended and secondary consequence ("double effect") of the legitimate just war aim of repelling the unjust attack. Just war thus came to incorporate the idea that a justified use of force must satisfy the intention to use force for purposes of self-defense, resisting unjust aggression, and restoring peace.

Just war has never allowed that a use of force could directly intend the killing of an enemy, and, related to this, a criterion of proportionality developed over the centuries that insisted that a use of force must always be proportional to the end of restoring peace. Hence certain weapons and war activities that violated this sense of proportionality have always fared poorly under just war, from the medieval practice of well poisoning to the more modern condemnation of weapons like dum-dum bullets or nuclear, biological, and chemical weapons. All of these weapons of mass destruction are disallowed under just war as having an effect disproportionate to the end of restoring peace. Such weapons cannot confine the use of force to the immediate situation and circumstance nor direct them to combatants. Such weapons inflict continued destructiveness on noncombatants far beyond the conflict situation in both space and time.

After Aquinas, the Spanish Scholastics Vitoria (d. 1546) and Suárez (d. 1617) and the Protestant Dutch theologian Hugo Grotius (d. 1645) offered further developments in the idea of just war.[4] They faced a world transforming in a secular direction, not only because the Reformation had unleashed a disintegrating effect on the idea of a Christian commonwealth, but because of the emergence of the nation-state. The nation-state usurped the Church as the new center of political authority, and the secularizing influence threw into some doubt moral appeals that claimed to transcend those upheld by the state. The effect of these cultural and political shifts on just war theory was to transform just war thinking from its former emphasis on justifying war to concentrating on how to wage war in such a way as to limit its destructiveness (*jus in bello*). This shift took on urgency because of the carnage created by the religious wars of the sixteenth century. This environment of destruction prompted some thinkers to reflect on what I have in these pages called "generic holy war." That is, the question began to be asked how all parties in a bloody conflict could justify their acts of violence by appealing to God's will. It was descriptively the case that in the religious wars everyone prayed to God for victory and vindication, and eyes began to open to the irony — and the absurdity — of such a situation.

In the Reformation and beyond into the post-Reformation era, just war thinking shifted from stress on justified causes of war to the issue of means.[5] New attention was paid to the issue of proportionality, and for the first time the moral doctrine of double effect was invoked beyond killing of combatants to include now justification for the killing of noncombatants. The double-effect defense was now extended to cover noncombatants, who were deemed to be exempt as morally legitimate targets of a use of force. When noncombatants were killed, as was inevitable, double effect allowed that their deaths were, in a sense, regrettable yet allowable so long as they were not intended and every effort was made to avoid them. It is perhaps worth noting that even in the contemporary world, the development of increasingly sophisticated weaponry designed to effect destruction of military targets while seeking to avoid civilian casualties (smart-bomb technology, for example) springs directly from the just war requirement concerning noncombatant immunity. Just war theory came to have more and more of an influence in secular thinking, and in the seventeenth century, Hugo Grotius would even write that just war must be grounded in a morality that is true "even if there were no God, which God forbid."[6] Both Hobbes and Locke continued to advance the secularizing turn away from divine law and toward natural law, and the effects of this shift persist today, playing an important role even in contemporary UN deliberations and resolutions.[7]

Just war clearly has a history in Western philosophical and religious thought, and it is not a static history. Just war has evolved and modified over the centuries, and in the background is the consistent view associated with the theory that war is a terrible state of affairs, much to be avoided, and that violence must be restrained, even in justified uses of force. Accordingly, just war as a theory aimed at resisting evil also necessitates restraint of violence. As Roman Catholic theologian Richard McBrien has written, "The purpose of just war theory, therefore, was not to rationalize violence but to limit its scope and methods."[8]

The idea of just war is readily available today both in secular and religious worlds. Not only Christianity but Islam and Judaism invoke specific action guides — conditions and criteria of justice — that aim at the restraint of violence in the use of force, and in that they are consistent with the spirit of just war teaching. Just war provides a framework to guide moral reflection and articulates specific criteria of justice that can be used in deciphering the moral meaning of particular conflicts. Just war does not of itself settle any particular issue concerning the use of force in any particular conflict. As a tool for use in the moral reflections of critically minded citizens who worry about violence and its use by the state, just war provides a structure for deliberating the moral meaning of conflicts, doing so in ways that exemplify commitment to life-affirming values.

Policy makers, political leaders, and military leaders often invoke just war ideas in contemplation of a use of force. We

saw this in the Gulf War of 1991 as well as in the open-
ended war on global terrorism currently under way.[9] The
statement that "our cause is just" enunciated many times by
President George W. Bush in the wake of the September 11,
2001, terrorism attack was an appeal to just war theory —
and the president and his advisors were fully cognizant of
that. Military people in leadership positions have ordinarily
cut their teeth on just war theory and rely on it as they frame
military action.

Political and military leaders, however, can also misrep-
resent just war. They can proceed to commit to a use of
force having announced that they have applied the theory
and met the tests of justice, as if the theory can be held
in the dock and brought in to sanction a policy decision
with a final stamp of moral approval. Just war, however,
is not like a seal to be kept in a velvet bag. It is, rather, a
workhorse notion that is to be applied throughout the entire process of deliberating the meaning of a conflict and
how best to respond to it. Just war is a conversation starter.
The theory assumes that people of good will can debate and
discuss particulars and share information relevant to determining whether a proposed use of force is, or is not, morally
justified. The conversation just war begins is not value neu-
tral. As a reasonable theory, just war assumes war to be an
unwanted evil and pays respect to that assumption by insisting that any prospective use of force satisfy stringent tests
to determine whether moral permissibility can be granted
and under what conditions. Determining the moral permissibility of a prospective use of force is not equivalent to the

cynical practice of appealing to the theory or parts of it in hopes of garnering additional political support.

Although just war theory can be abused, and I say more about that momentarily, its great value lies in its ability to call rational persons together for moral conversation. In that conversation, participants engage one another using a common language and avowing common value concerns, and they can proceed to debate and even to disagreement having focused the conversation on relevant justice concerns, which the theory has set before them.

A contemporary account of the theory of just war is now in order, and in the presentation that follows, my purpose is to stress the moral presumption against using force that underwrites the theory. The secularization of just war theory has obscured this moral presumption, and failing to give it proper attention in the totality of the theory has, I believe, contributed to just war theory being abused and even demonically used. I contend that a theory of just war lacks philosophical coherence if this presumption against the use of force is not in place, and that articulating the theory must affirm this presumption as operational and functioning to guide action in the life-affirming direction of restraint and even, surprisingly, an avowed preference for nonviolence.

A Contemporary Formulation of Just War Theory

Just war theory is best known for enunciating various criteria, which, if met, establish that a use of force has met moral muster. The following lists represents a contemporary way of articulating those criteria:

- The war must be sanctioned by a legitimate and competent authority.
- The cause must be just.
- There must be a right intention and announcement of that intention.
- Combat or use of force must always be a last resort.
- One must have a reasonable hope of success in going to war.
- By going to war one must preserve values that otherwise could not be preserved.

These are a contemporary formulation of the *jus ad bellum* criteria that establish whether a war or use of force is itself morally justifiable. In addition, two other criteria, reflecting the *jus in bello* tradition, articulate constraints on the actual conduct of a war, guiding action with respect to the means of warfare:

- Noncombatants must be protected from harm (noncombatant immunity).
- A use of force cannot employ weapons or uses of force that are disproportionate to the end of restoring peace.

This list of criteria articulates the action guides that govern a prospective use of force, and they conform such prospective uses of force to the requirements of justice. These criteria require some interpretation, and I offer the following comments and qualifications as clarifications of the theory.

1. *The just war criteria guide action and direct reflection to morally relevant concerns, even principles of a sort.*[10] Taken together as a single action guide made up of many parts, the criteria act to constrain the use of force. Applying these eight criteria to any particular conflict invites moral deliberation on the possibility of a justified use of force, and the theory effects moderation by urging restraint. Just war theory is, in fact, a morally moderate ethical position because by its application, individuals can find themselves able to say that some wars or uses of force satisfy these criteria and others do not. The theory guides towards justice. It can thus be said to participate in framing action in such a way that the action will conform to a vision of goodness, wherein justice and restraint in the use of force are essential.

These guidelines, furthermore, do not function as a justification for war. Rather, they allow people to address situations that pose threats to human well-being and to the goods of life. Justice itself requires that the threat be resisted. Using force is not a first response but a last resort, and the idea of using force is itself the topic of deliberation. The theory guides deliberation and action toward the end of resisting the threat to human well-being and doing so by means that preserve the goods of life. Just war provides a way to confront conflict and then oppose violence as a preferred way of responding to the conflict. The theory seeks to preserve the goods of life and restore the condition of peace, which just war acknowledges as its default position.

Religion that incorporates this mode of moral thinking into its religiously framed ethical systems will sponsor activity designed to resist evil and injustice and respond to conflicts that pose threats to human well-being. Because the aim of the theory is to protect the goods of life, including life itself, from injustice and destructive aggression, the theory could be said to be grounded in a life-affirming vision that endorses active resistance to evil. But whereas resistance in this theory moves away from nonviolent resistance by allowing the possibility of uses of physical force, the actions of resistance must themselves be subjected to moral scrutiny. In just war theory uses of force must themselves meet the tests of justice so that they can be said to be morally justifiable actions that are restrained, proportionate, and just. The theory focuses on justice and offers no support for using force from motives of vengeance or retaliation. Such motives could be assumed to be inimical to the just war perspective because they so easily lend themselves to demonic destructiveness.

2. *The just war criteria are action guides, but they are contentless with respect to the details of any particular conflict.* The criteria, then, invite persons into a conversation about empirical particulars. In other words, these criteria require that debate and deliberation attend to the full range of empirical concerns involved in a particular conflict. Just war theory does not exist to justify war, but to frame rational debate. It points to common, universally valid concerns that would attend any conversation or debate over the issue of using force and doing so in a morally justified way. It requires that persons take on the mantle of citizenship and

acquire information about the great conflicts of their times so that they can then assess the moral meaning of all that they have learned. Just war theory assumes honesty and integrity in the flow of information. The framework of just war cannot itself be engaged if the conversation about the meaning of situations and conflicts does not take place due to information being withheld or distorted. Just war requires a full and honest accounting about particulars and in that is an ethic for engaged citizens.

Whether a war or use of force is morally justified is determined by testing the particulars of a conflict against the theory, then debating the moral meaning of those empirical matters in light of the criteria. Are the three intentions given for the American participation in the Gulf War of 1991 — to preserve the American oil supply, to provide humanitarian aid to a nation unjustly attacked by an aggressor neighbor, and to create a new world order — all morally equivalent? Can nuclear weapons serve as a proportionate means of response? Can well poisoning or arming police with hollow-pointed bullets be justified? Is retaliation a just cause for using military force in the wake of a terrorist attack?

All kinds of questions and empirical issues can be brought forward and then discussed against the criteria established in the theory, and the theory directs debate to the moral meaning of the empirical issues under discussion. So terrorist attacks, for example, however much they may be motivated by a desire to resist injustice or oppression, are disallowed under the theory because they direct violence at noncombatants, thus violating the noncombatant immunity provision. Acts deemed terrorist fail other criteria as well in particular instances, but terrorism is defined in terms of a particular feature — attacks on noncombatants — that can never pass just war muster and will always violate that criterion. Just as "murder" defines a killing that cannot be justified, "terrorism" comes to identify a use of force that cannot be justified. The term, then, is pressed into service, as "murder" is, to point to acts that are unjustifiable by definition.

Establishing that an act is justifiable — or unjustifiable — requires that the action be analyzed. As not every killing is murder, neither is every use of force, even lethal force, a terrorist act. These conclusions must be established by deliberation and analysis, and by referencing relevant facts and information to the action guides of the just war theory. Just war requires that every action undertaken in a forceful response to conflict be subject to analysis, and analysis requires information even before it begins the work of guiding moral interpretation. Just war implicitly condemns restricting information relevant to establishing moral meaning, or, worse, providing misinformation designed to garner support for a proposed use of force that those in a position to control information might distort for self-serving purposes. Just war is designed to operate in a context of good faith, with openness and an honest sharing of information.

3. *When applying the just war criteria, justification for a use of force does not rely on meeting select criteria: all of them must be met; all, not just some, must be satisfied.* Abuses of just war theory occur at precisely this point. Government officials often shorthand the theory to make it appear as if a just war requires meeting only a couple of

criteria, when in fact there are many. Or the theory is mis-represented by making it appear that in order to justify a war of indeterminate duration, the theory need only be appealed to once — at the beginning. That is to misunderstand the theory and how radically it serves justice.

Just war theory insists that its criteria be applied to any and all uses of force, and those criteria can rightly be said to attend a conflict from the moment force is first used to the moment the use of force ceases. Every action in between is subject to analysis under just war, and for this reason many uses of force that seem to be justified at the start fail to meet just war criteria soon after. Particular actions that fail to meet just war criteria, even though undertaken in a conflict where justification seemed clear, subvert the moral justification for the entire conflict. This is the reason just war theory is so often distorted, because it establishes stringent demands that are exceedingly difficult to meet, if not so much in the first moment of defensive response, then in the follow-up uses of force. The problem with just war for those who wield political and military power is that just war can establish moral warrants that justify a use of force one day, but then, depending on how the conflict proceeds, deny justification the next. The consequence of removing justification from a use of force is implicit in the theory: a use of force that cannot be justified ought not to be undertaken. Once invoked, the just war criteria are in constant play and remain so as long as force is used.

4. *The just war criteria are stringent. Just war theory does not submit to a one-time application, but applies to a use of force from inception to conclusion.* Accordingly, as wars

go on and the tendency to use more and more force affects deliberations and action dynamics, just war presses harder and harder, making moral justification for particular uses of force more, rather than less, difficult. Very few wars can meet the just war tests. They may begin with a justified response to, say, an attack, such as that experienced by the United States at the beginning of World War II. But then wars seem inevitably to push against the restraint of the theory, so that just war can easily condemn such actions as, say, the Allied bombing of a civilian city like Dresden. Such an attack not only can be described as terrorist, but that particular attack was even formulated as such by those in the Allied command who authorized it. Such actions knock the moral props out from under the edifice of a just war.

Just war theory has the logical effect of leading to a form of practical pacifism without also committing one to theoretical pacifism. The theoretical pacifism to which I refer is that of the absolutist pacifist who would deny the good of practical reasonableness and oppose all resistance to injustice and evil. Just war opposes theoretical pacifism of this sort and offers a guideline for resisting evil with the possibility of actually using force if the threat to human life and well-being is momentous and all other nonviolent uses fail or can have no further effect. Just war, like nonviolent resistance, is a theory focused on resistance to evil, but where just war differs is that it holds open the door to an actual use of force, and the theory then proceeds to establish the tests of moral justification that would, as a matter of last resort, allow a use of force in, say, acts of self-defense or in humanitarian interventions. Using force in these situations

would protect persons from unjustified killing, be it genocide or some other form of politically generated terrorism,
whereas an absolutist nonresistance perspective would not
act to oppose such violence.

I say just war theory leads to a kind of practical pacifism because the criteria are so stringent, and so hard to
meet, that in fact very few uses of force ever do meet them,
even after an initial justification has been established. Just
war theory provides the means for establishing justification for a use of force, but beyond that it also provides the
framework for critically analyzing how that use of force in
resistance to evil and injustice is being formulated and enacted. Just war theory, in other words, provides the structure
of moral analysis that allows persons to condemn acts and
projects of force devised to respond to injustice. This is not
the absolutist pacifist's objection — that nonresister's objection that all uses of force are wrong and unjustifiable, nor
even the nonviolent resister's objection that nonviolence is
a preferable means of resistance. Just war theory entertains
the possibility of resisting evil and injustice by using force,
but then requires that the act of forceful resistance to injustice must itself satisfy the requirements of justice articulated
in the theory. When those requirements are not met, the theory of just war provides the structure for morally analyzing
not only the original threat to peace and human well-being
but the response to it, either proposed or under way. Just
war theory ought not to be considered the snuggly friend
of those who wield power, for those who fail to meet the
requirements of justice in their response to injustice find just
war theory a powerful tool of moral critique, condemning

injustice however and whenever it may appear — and by whomever.

As mentioned, the consequence of failing to meet the stringent requirements of just war restraints leads to an action consequence: force ought not be used. It is beyond dispute that war is not an area of human activity where justice is ordinarily promoted, and just war theory seeks to conform action in war to a standard of justice while aiming at the end of peace. Just war, then, is a critical theory that enables persons to oppose particular wars or uses of force when they fail to satisfy the requirements of justice. Uses of force designed to resist evil are themselves likely to turn unjust because of the nature of warfare and politics, so that responses to injustice that are themselves unjust provoke a just war analysis. Thus can just war analysis wind up endorsing what looks to be a practical pacifism, though, as a nonabsolutist mode of thought and reflection, it would not support nonresistance or any other theoretical opposition to all uses of force in every conceivable circumstance.

5. *The just war criteria do not make sense unless they are positioned in relationship to some underlying action guide that commands moral assent and guides action prior to seeking a justified use of force.* The just war criteria, in other words, justify a use of force, but in that justification they also point implicitly to an underlying moral commitment that would allow the use of force to be justified as an exception to that underlying rule.

Discerning just war as a potentially life-affirming ethic depends upon grasping this often suppressed dimension of just war thinking. The just war criteria, recall, establish a moral test that can either permit a use of force if the test is passed or disallow a use of force if the test is not passed. As important as the criteria of just war are to the integrity of the theory, the philosophical issue of importance concerns the moral backdrop where action is guided prior to any effort to invoke the criteria and justify a use of force as an exception. A simple question of logic is at stake. Given that a use of force must be justified, failure to meet the tests of justice (just war criteria) require that whatever action guide is operational prior to making the exception be reinstated and reaffirmed as the normative and operational action guide. An example can make this clear. The stealing of food might be morally justified in a certain situation, and justification could be generated to support such an act. A theory of "just stealing" would generate conditions of moral justification that would establish such a test, and they would undoubtedly embrace such particulars as the imminent threat of death from starvation if food is not secured, no alternative sources of food are available, and so on. But prior to generating a theory that might justify an act of stealing food, moral persons would necessarily affirm the regulative force of an action guide that disallows stealing. Stealing neither reflects commitment to a vision of goodness nor expresses the respect for persons that such a vision requires. So if a proposed act of "justified" stealing is submitted to the test of justice and fails to meet that test, the regulative and operational rule or action guide that ordinarily prohibits stealing reasserts itself and remains in effect, continuing to guide action and governing moral meaning.

Just war theory, I claim, arises out of a general moral position comparable to that governing stealing. A justified act of stealing does not make sense except in a context where action guides disallow stealing. Just war criteria, by the same token, do not make sense except in relation to a similar moral context where the idea of using force or going to war is, as a matter of general moral affirmation, disallowed.

The governing action guide in relation to which people may seek to generate a justified exception can be referred to as a "moral presumption." A moral presumption articulates in a nonabsolutist way the action guide that holds until such time as an exception to it can be justified. A justified act of stealing is generated as an exception to a moral presumption against stealing; similarly the just war criteria guide the process of making an exception to the moral presumption at issue in just war theory. That reasonable and widely accepted moral affirmation may be expressed in these simple words: *force ought not to be used to settle conflicts.* This presumption establishes a life-affirming foundation for just war. Furthermore, by articulating the general moral affirmation that governs action until such time as the just war criteria are met and allow for a justified exception to them, this presumption renders just war theory philosophically coherent. Without this presumption being in effect, the just war criteria fail to effect their purpose, which is to restrain uses of force and reassert that even uses of force when justified must be directed toward effecting justice and restoring peace.

The moral presumption at issue in just war theory is suppressed in almost all presentations of the theory, but it is, in my view, the critical feature of the theory and the one most in need of clear articulation. This moral presumption turns the just war model of addressing response to conflict away from demonic possibilities toward life-affirming values expressive of a vision of goodness. The role of the moral presumption at issue in just war theory merits some further elaboration.

The moral presumption at issue in just war theory establishes the basic moral orientation, the moral lean or "principle" that is in place, operational, and directing action to avoid and even suppress use of force. This presumption governs action and moral meaning until such time as the various criteria are met and a justification for use of force is thereby established. I have invoked the language of "moral presumption" because it exposes by definition a nonabsolutist perspective. Yet it invokes a sense of agreement about moral meaning that reasonable persons can nigh unto unanimously avow. Just war criteria then come to serve as the means by which that moral presumption can be lifted to justify an exception in a particular circumstance or situation. Just war theory is really a "presumption/exception" ethic, and I would invoke that language were it not so aesthetically distasteful — and were "just war" not so readily available to illustrate and embody this mode of moderate moral reflection out of the well-worn traditions of Western moral thought.

The criteria of just war establish the conditions that would justify making an exception, but the moral presumption identifies the center of value that holds and will continue to hold whenever an exception to it is not forthcoming. Only in relation to a "moral presumption" opposing use of force can we devise the possibility of a use of force exempt from the control of that presumption. Then satisfying the criteria for a justified exception may, it is true, allow for a use of force, but the criteria then so constrain action that the force authorized must be limited and aimed at restoring the presumption back to its original position as a governing action guide. Reason readily assents to the idea that presumptively or ordinarily "force ought not be used to settle conflicts." By identifying this rule of action as a "presumption" I seek to call attention to the fact that the rule or principle at issue is not an absolute principle, and if not absolute but a rule for which exceptions can be made, then the criteria themselves are simply a way of articulating the requirements for making an exception.

Just war theory, then, is grounded in a moral presumption against the use of force, and that presumption is by definition life-affirming. The life-affirming character of the presumption affects the use of force itself, because the criteria necessarily constrain action and then seek to stop use of force altogether as the moral presumption is reinstated to its governing position over action. Just war, I acknowledge, bears an unfortunate linguistic designation in that the term "just war" seems to suggest that the theory is designed to justify war. But the theory is designed to confirm the compelling rational position that force ought not to be used to settle conflicts, and if an exception seems warranted, that exception must itself be argued for and morally justified.[11]

Moral presumptions must be constructed so rationally — that is, so broadly — that their appeal to moral meaning is unmistakable and nigh unto universally acceptable.[12] What rational person would disagree with the proposition that force ought not ordinarily be used to settle conflicts? My own work in ethics has used this "presumption/exception" model, which I find exemplified in the ancient tradition of just war theory, to look at other troubling issues, including medical ethics issues, including abortion, and most recently capital punishment. Let me say just a word relevant to the capital punishment issue to suggest how a moral presumption actually works and how it must be formulated.

Constructing a moral presumption to govern actions related to killing, which is what is at stake in war, abortion, nontreatment of neonates, or capital punishment, is difficult and requires nuance. But a presumption must be formulated in terms that make a broad and unmistakable appeal. The presumption must then be articulated so that its governing force over action reflects the realities of the moral life. Hence, one does not formulate a moral presumption about capital punishment by declaring, say, "Capital punishment is a justified killing" or "The execution power of the state is clearly immoral." To get at the moral presumption that governs use of the death penalty, we must seek out the undergirding presumption that connects state killing to the particular form of state killing involved in capital punishment. The presumption then is not about the death penalty per se, a restricted idea over which there is enormous disagreement and moral controversy, but over some broad, rationally compelling idea that can be formulated as follows: the state ought ordinarily not kill its citizens. The state can and does kill its citizens, but reasonable people do not want to endorse such killing as a good action that as good is to be recommended and shared and enhanced. Even those who support the death penalty seem in agreement that it is and ought to be exceedingly rare and restricted to application in certain kinds of what we might think of as emergency or extraordinary situations. Rational persons, even those who find rational justification for the death penalty, do not endorse state-sponsored execution as a good to be cherished and expanded under the general moral view that states should as a matter of ordinary practice kill their citizens. Execution killing is broadly understood as some kind of exception, and it is an exception to a presumption that states ought not ordinarily kill their citizens.

A morally moderate position on the death penalty can be constructed in relation to this presumption, because even opponents of the death penalty can think of examples where they might, as nonabsolutists, consent to a state-sponsored killing of a citizen. Certain police actions come to mind, for example, in which a killing can be determined to be morally justifiable for reasons having to do with self-defense or the defense of others who are threatened with lethal harm. On the basis of the presumption against the state ordinarily killing its citizens, one can then ask whether capital punishment constitutes a kind of killing of citizens that establishes a morally justified exception to the presumption against such state killing. The presumption against the state killing its own citizens establishes the issue of fundamental agreement, and the justice question then is whether good reasons sufficient to lift the moral presumption against capital punishment can be advanced so that an exception might be made. I have elsewhere constructed a theory of "just execution" and, having researched the execution practice, concluded that the American practice of execution fails to meet the requirements of justice.[13] Moral moderation shows with respect to the moral presumption that the state ought not ordinarily kill its citizens because in some cases such killing could be morally justified and in others not. Certain defensive police actions might satisfy the requirements of justice, but the death penalty happens to be a form of state killing that does not.

A Defense of Just War as a Model for Moral Thinking

Just war as a model of moral thinking avoids extremes and seeks out middle ground on the basis of moral presumptions, which are articulations of common ground. But just war theory can itself be employed to serve a variety of interests. Like pacifism and holy war, just war presents life-affirming and demonic possibilities. Any use of force justified by the theory must conform to a life-affirming vision of goodness. The theory engages people amid situations of conflict where moral discernment is required, and it assumes and affirms the moral context of human existence, including the reality of freedom, human finitude, and the autonomy of human persons as moral agents. Just war confronts rather boldly the imperfect and complex world, which is the context for people making moral decisions, and just war requires of those who would employ it a reaffirmation of the goods of life. This mode of moral approach, applicable to other issues, opposes absolutism while seeking to advance a vision of life-affirming goodness. When joined to religion, the morally moderate approach of just war can serve to express life-affirming values and thereby resist the temptation of the demonic turn.

On the other hand, just war can be invoked under the pressures of military or political self-interest to authorize violent action under cover of moral justification when moral justification ought not be claimed. Just war can serve political and military projects of self-deception, lending itself to demonic endorsements of destructiveness and repression. Hitler believed his incursion into Poland was not only justified but even morally just (I assume), as were his extermination policies. Some kind of invocation of "just war" can be expected whenever political or military authority exercises destructive power and appeals to some version of just war to support the effort. This represents just war in the demonic turn. But as a life-affirming ethic that presumes the use of force to be a deplorable evil, just war also provides the moral resources for critiquing, and then opposing, self-deceptive projects of violence, destruction, and oppression.

Approaching ethics via the articulation of presumptions and the morally permissible exceptions seems to me to create a mode of moral analysis that is eminently practical, reasonable, and commendable. By eschewing absolutism and endorsing an approach of moderation, this mode of ethical operation avoids extremes while taking up a position in opposition to absolutism in moral thinking. Absolutes lead to contradiction. Absolutes serve the demonic.

The model of ethics I am advocating — the model that articulates commonly held rational presumptions as well as the criteria tests that would allow for a just lifting of those presumptions in special cases and situations — is applicable to any moral issue. The approach offers an alternative to deontological, consequentialist/utilitarian, and even axiological or virtue-based ethics. It is a reason-based approach to the articulation of moral meaning and addresses moral problems in ways that avoid absolutism while embodying a vision of goodness. It accomplishes this end with attention to the luminosity of goodness.

The idea that we ordinarily ought not settle conflicts by use of force or that the state ought not ordinarily kill its citizens are propositions and affirmations that appeal to a basic moral sensibility that rational persons can be expected to share in moral community. They require no great learning but are the presumptions that are acquired as persons come to adopt a moral point of view, a view beyond ego and self-interest, and as they enter and involve themselves in the moral sphere of self-other relations. These "presumptions" appeal to goodness. The presumptions can be grounded in an epistemology of knowledge by acquaintance, but they are understandable because they are luminous rather than obscure. They are luminous with respect to goodness.

A Life-Affirming Ethic: Presumptions and Exceptions

Moral reflection that is directed and structured by the "presumption/exception" ethic of just war theory aims at preserving and promoting the goods of life. The criteria do not themselves establish that any particular use of force is justified; persons applying the criteria do that. The criteria, however, do help train moral reflection on rational discourse and empirical issues even while appealing to the common moral concerns of persons who seek to act justly and in accordance with a vision of goodness, even as they contemplate a use of force. Just war ought not to be seen as a theory to justify war but as an ethic of restraint dedicated in the first instance to the presumptive norm that force ought not to be used to settle conflicts. The theory aims to promote and protect the goods of life, including the good of life itself, through the criteria of last resort, proportional response, and noncombatant immunity; and the theory advances respect for a vision of goodness, for it is ultimately that vision that directs conversation to consideration of empirical issues, then to moral interpretation of those issues.

Just war theory as a paradigm case for structuring an ethic of justified exceptions to moral presumptions is life-affirming. By definition it is a nonabsolutist "exception" theory. When religious systems affirm this kind of nonabsolutist ethical reflection, they can attach life-affirming values to all they commend by way of religiously motivated action. That is, the ethic that seeks to express the religious vision is itself turned toward conforming action to goodness and aims at preserving the goods of life and especially the good of life itself. This mode of moderate moral reasoning, then, can express through religion a vision of goodness by requiring that injustice be resisted while also demanding that any use of force employed to oppose injustice be limited and morally justified. The end of such action is the life-affirming end of restoring peace and putting back in place the moral presumption against the use of force to settle conflicts. Religion that so conforms to a life-affirming ethic shuns the demonic and renders the expression of religious values themselves nonabsolutist.

Just war opposes injustice, and it seeks to restrain violence every step of the way, not only the violence of the aggressor who has resorted to violence, but the violence that can be unleashed in responding to the threat such an aggressor poses. This mode of moral response avoids a use of force up to the point where continued use of nonviolence actually puts the goods of life at risk of loss and destruction. Just war provides a way to oppose violence and respond to violence with restraint, with a judgment that all means short of using force must be tried prior to using force. It then requires that when force is used to combat force, it must be used in a way proportionate to the threat posed. In all these things, this mode of moral reasoning shows itself guided by life-affirming commitments. It is a theory of defense. It is nonaggressive, reason-based, and by definition opposed to absolutism. The theory would oppose any use of force that sought justification in appeal to generic holy war, and it would declare such an appeal an expression of religion having gone demonic. It would, furthermore, adjudge the absolute pacifism of nonresistance an irrational capitulation in the face of evil, discerning in the refusal to resist evil a condoning of the very violence such pacifists claim to abhor.

If nonviolent resistance represents one clear form of a life-affirming ethic, just war theory suggests another life-affirming possibility. These two approaches may in fact differ only at one significant point, which is on the issue of "last resort." Nonviolent resistance would hold to the technique of nonviolent response past the point a just war advocate would deem reasonable and acceptable. But despite that disagreement — which is not insignificant and each side would have compelling rational arguments to make in defense of its position — both of these life-affirming modes of ethical reflection have found their way into religious ethics. Both function to serve a vision of goodness while resisting the demonic turn in religion.

Conclusion

Summary of the Argument

Religion and morality both know and fear violence. Religion has always found occasion to express itself in activities of violence and destructiveness. "Religion invariably strives to subdue violence, to keep it from running wild," writes René Girard, but he no sooner offers this observation than he qualifies it by pointing out the paradox of the religion-violence connection. Girard notes that religion sponsors violence through the symbolically destructive activity of ritual, specifically, ritual sacrifice, which then protects the religious community from even greater violence. Ritual, in other words, performs violence in order to keep violence at bay.[1] Violence affects every "altar" religion where sacrifice, however sublimated and transformed, provides the conduit of communication and action in the human relationship to ultimacy, whether the objective of such ritual is sacrificial appeasement or relational restoration. Religion, then, knows violence and seeks to keep it away, yet it relies on ritualistic practices that have the

[264]

effect of putting violence at the very heart of the religious enterprise.

The moral point of view also engages the issue of violence, but it advances the view that violent acts are always suspect because they can be presumed to negate goodness. Violent acts inflict harm and injury. They violate the relational integrity of persons. Violence increases suffering, denies people respect, and not only subverts the goods of life but poses a threat to the good of life itself.

The meaning of violence in religion is somewhat ambiguous, because religion is caught in a paradoxical relationship with violence. Religion can inspire violence; by examining so mundane a religious activity as ritual we can discern how religion incorporates violence into the heart of religious life. When ultimacy is absolutized and religion turns demonic, ultimacy itself comes to serve as the sanction for a religious turn away from a life-affirming vision of goodness. An absolutized ultimacy asserts a power capable of breaking the bonds of moral restraint and drawing people into extremist attitudes and action.

Moral reflection, however, does not find itself so easily positioned in paradox. Moral reflection generated from a vision of goodness inevitably condemns violence for the wrongs it does as well as the harm it inflicts on people. The life-affirming decision to conform religion to the vision of goodness at the heart of the moral enterprise yields but one logical outcome, namely, an opposition to violence grounded in a decision to be religious in a life-affirming rather than a demonic way. Life-affirming religion always manifests a repugnance to violence, but that sense of what religion is and what it ought to be is always grounded in what is at its heart a moral, rather than a religious, understanding.

However religious people act with respect to violence, they do so based on the expectations for action they associate with ultimacy. This book has concerned itself with the relation of religion to moral understanding. The argument I have advanced is that religion is itself subject to moral interpretation and construction, which is to say that we decide in a moral sense how to do religion and how to be religious. The options are limited. Religion can serve a vision of goodness and thus support a life-affirming stance, or it can turn demonic and inspire powerful destructiveness. People choose one path or the other by translating into action their understanding of ultimacy, and by conforming action to the motives, intentions, and purposes they discern in ultimacy itself. Ultimacy, as we have seen, can endorse action projects that express a vision of goodness — or not.

We have noted that religion can serve ends that from a moral point of view are disintegrating, subversive of freedom, and destructive of the goods of life, including the good of reason and even the good of life itself. Religion that serves these purposes attacks the vision of goodness that sustains moral vision and understanding, and such religion, when it makes such a turn, can be deemed "demonic." The demonic turn occurs at the point ultimacy becomes absolutized.

"Demonic" is a term that springs from religious consciousness itself, and it points to morally defective religion that has turned away from goodness toward ends that do not participate in goodness, even if the practitioners of such religion claim otherwise. Demonic religion is, from the moral point of view, self-deceptive, and goodness itself provides the object in relation to which self-deception arises. Demonic acts, however, fail to manifest the luminosity of goodness even as practitioners of demonic religion protest and deny, rationalize and intricately explain how destructive acts are creative or murderous acts are life-affirming.

Religion that is life-affirming is not life-affirming because it is religious. Religion can claim description as "life-affirming" because religious people choose to serve a moral vision of goodness through their religion. Because ultimacy inspires human beings to act in certain ways and religious people attribute their motivation to ultimacy itself, the motives and intentions located in the heart of ultimacy fall subject to moral inquiry. Ultimacy is never simply an idea but always a motivating force for acting in certain ways. Ultimacy is not, in this sense, above moral critique; neither can ultimacy be deemed, from a moral point of view, detachable from a vision of goodness.

As religion can incite violence, so too does it offer responses to violence that can be either life-affirming or demonic. We saw in the pacifism chapter how nonviolence could serve a vision of goodness and advance a life-affirming religious vision. We contrasted nonviolent resistance, a life-affirming response to evil and injustice and violence, to the absolutized pacifism found in the thought of Leo Tolstoy, which illustrated how even pacifism can turn demonic. We then considered holy war, and concluded that despite the possibility of the rare life-affirming instance, holy war as a generic concept must be deemed demonic. We considered just war, noting how this often misunderstood perspective on the use of force is actually shaped by life-affirming values. The philosophical reconstruction of just war offered in these pages, however, fails to obscure that many invocations of just war have been employed to justify destructive means in pursuit of destructive ends, so that just war, too, is susceptible to the demonic turn.

The demonic turn is an ever-present possibility in the religious realm of meaning and relationship, and the demonic possibility is made available and rendered attractive because it is sponsored by an ultimacy that itself is turning absolutist. I conclude with a few additional remarks about the meaning of absolutism in the moral life.

Absolutism: A Final Moral Reflection

The mode of moral reasoning exemplified by just war refuses any appeal to moral absolutes. Absolutes, I have argued, express values that simply fall outside the fallible world of self-other relatedness. Absolutes are, when all is said and done, inappropriate to moral thinking, even when we consider such a hard — and fair — question as this: "Are there not some actions so heinous that we should simply say that that act is morally wrong, in every case, at every time — absolutely wrong?"

I would reject an appeal to absolutes even here. And let us take a terrible example of such a heinous act, say, the torturing of a child for purposes of sexual gratification. Is such an act not absolutely wrong?

Before answering, let me ask back, "Why do we feel such a need to invoke the idea of 'absolute' in such a situation? What does such a qualification add to the moral meaning?"

I understand that those who appeal to absolutist language to condemn such actions — and I think we all do; I do as well — ordinarily mean to intensify moral outrage by such language. The language of "absolutely" can certainly serve as a linguistic intensifier. But if what is meant by appealing to "absolutely" is some literalistic appeal to moral absolutism, then we must consider the implication that a person who commits an act that is absolutely wrong should, as a matter of logic, also be absolutely responsible.

Attributing absolute responsibility to fallible human beings, however, implies that considerations such as mental defect or an upbringing where perpetrators may have suffered such torturous abuse themselves must have "absolutely" no bearing on evaluating the moral meaning of these acts. The idea of absolute responsibility should point us to interpreting the act in question as springing from a fully responsible intention to undertake such an act. Absolute responsibility necessitates the conclusion that moral meaning can be obtained independently of any issue of mental defect or social context. The appeal to absolutism has the decided advantage of eliminating any notion of *social* responsibility and thus blunting any questions about the kind of societal context and corporate responsibility that could be assumed when such acts occur. The appeal to absolutism, if it be literal rather than literary (i.e., linguistic intensifier), atomizes the act and infuses it with absolute responsibility. To say an act is absolutely wrong logically necessitates

[269]

that the person who commits such an act be held absolutely responsible.

I have argued that absolutism leads to contradiction, necessarily and inevitably. Where is the contradiction in saying a child sex torturer has done something absolutely wrong? It is to be found in the idea that an absolutely wrong act attaches absolute responsibility to the person who commits such an act. A problem arises, however, in holding individuals absolutely responsible for a wrongful deed, for attaching absolute responsibility to an individual necessarily implies that no further attribution of responsibility can even be considered. So in the presence of an absolutely wrong or evil deed committed by an individual who is absolutely responsible, the moral community that surrounds that individual is relieved from accepting *any* responsibility for the child torturer's evil deed. That in turn implies that the moral community is helpless to affect such behaviors, and because the moral community is helpless it cannot possibly do anything preemptively to prevent such absolutely wrong acts from occurring. Not being responsible for such behaviors and not being able to do anything about them anyway — because all that affects such an act of wrongdoing is enclosed in a private and atomized intentionality apart from any relationship with the moral community — the moral community could rightly conclude that it actually ought to do nothing to address the possibilities for such behaviors preemptively. The moral community is not responsible for these behaviors and it could not do anything about them anyway. For the moral community to think that it could would be to deny that such acts are absolutely wrong. For the moral community to think that it should act preemptively would require the moral community to accept a responsibility for people and what they do at the very moment it is denying responsibility and the possibility of preventing such behaviors.

This foray into the circular logic of absolutism illustrates the kinds of problems one gets into when one takes the linguistic intensifier "absolutely" and turns it into a philosophical stance that the wrongness of such acts is and can be known to be absolutely wrong. The move into literal absolutism leads to the idea that absolutely wrong acts cannot be prevented, and furthermore, *that we should not try to prevent them,* for the simple reason that we cannot. And we should not, for we are not responsible. They are acts outside of any social context. Even trying to understand such acts is folly, for such knowledge would only be used to try to discern an etiology in a broader sphere of human relatedness, which is what the absolutism would deny.

Saying "the torture of children for purposes of sexual gratification is absolutely wrong" is, if taken literally as an absolutist statement, to say something beyond that these acts are morally wrong and reprehensible. The absolutism entails the view that such acts are not of such concern that we, collectively or corporately, should do anything to try to prevent them or see them as any kind of societal problem. Because they are actions construed in the context of absolutism, their intentionality is atomistic, and the fact that people who commit such acts of abuse have in all likelihood suffered such abuse themselves is idle information that has no prescriptive meaning. Absolutism cleans up the moral universe and removes moral problematics from any arena of responsibility except that of the individual perpetrator, who then is condemned as one who must assume absolute responsibility for an act that is absolutely wrong.[2]

The approach to ethical reasoning through moral presumptions does not accede to this point of view, and it would even object to the view that adults who torture children for purposes of sexual gratification are absolutely responsible. If moral presumptions are luminous with respect to goodness, clearly the idea of an adult person torturing a child for purposes of sexual gratification is not luminous with respect to goodness, and we can easily interpret the act itself as wrong, terribly wrong, even evil. But what is added by saying this is absolutely wrong, that it is to be examined without context or qualification? Absolutism adds certainty about moral meaning when interpreting such matters. But the approach of presumption/exception understands such a move as unwarranted and refuses to admit the infallibility of human knowing. The absolutist's lack of humility in claiming absolute knowledge and thus moral certainty is, from the moral point of view, to be feared, for it expresses overvaluation and then fanaticism. The claim to absolutism, as I have argued, leads to contradiction and inevitably so; it eventuates in self-deception and expresses a turn toward the demonic.

Persons who torture children for pleasure could be, if we consider the complexity of the situation for a moment, persons suffering severe mental and emotional affliction. That is to say that to the extent that their rationality is affected by mental and emotional disorder, they ought not to be considered fully endowed members of the moral community but sufferers, persons limited in their rational, thus their moral, capacities by reason of defect. This should not affect our judgment of their acts, for their acts stand in the glare of moral illumination as contemptible. But recognizing defect ought to affect our sense of the person's responsibility for the acts and, beyond that, affect what must be done by those of us in moral community who have to deal with such persons when they violate the relational integrity of others, as well as legal norms. I want to claim that from a moral point of view nothing is added to the moral meaning of a wrongful act by qualifying it as "absolutely" wrong. From the moral point of view, it suffices to adjudge the act wrong.

If we were to articulate some broad moral presumption to the effect that human persons are sexual beings and that sexuality, being ingredient in the goods of life, is good and ought to promote life and pleasure, then this act of child torture would violate that presumption and we could, as thoughtful people, explain why. We could talk about relational violation, lack of consent, abuse of power, and so on. I would not assume that any effort would be made to put forth criteria that might establish a test that would allow for a justified exception to the moral presumption against child torture, for so strong is the presumption against it that any test we might devise would focus more likely on criteria for assessing the extent of the perpetrator's responsibility. We could say, "What happened here is wrong," and we could reach wide consensus on that judgment and evaluation.

Adding "absolutely wrong" to that judgment adds nothing to the moral evaluation of the act except to signal that some who might say this want to connect their moral judgment with absolutism, and that ought to give us pause. The moral life does not need absolutism. The moral life stands in opposition to absolutism so people committed to the moral life can, without contradiction and without self-deception, pursue the goods of life and live out of a vision of goodness.

The moral response to that incident of sexual abuse ought to include active and compassionate concern for the victim, who needs to be surrounded with care and attention. As for the perpetrator: The perpetrator has abused the foundational condition of life in moral community, which is freedom. The perpetrator ought therefore to be removed from the free world of self-other interactions and have freedom restricted, even taken away. People living and working in moral community would have to decide how that is accomplished, whether as incarceration for a crime or as restraint for a serious mental affliction and moral disorder, for which the whole concept of moral responsibility is challenged if not actually undermined. This way of considering the moral issues does not prevent us from drawing clear moral conclusions, and it does seek to face the complexity of persons and their self-other relatedness. This way of thinking through moral issues refuses to absolutize any part of the evaluation and interpretation process. By that refusal of absolutism we thereby refuse to erode the moral sphere of self-other relatedness. We uphold the moral life as encompassing of persons in relationship; we affirm the moral context as necessitating the inclusion of both freedom and responsibility; we identify the moral life not with a judgmentalism centered on certainty but with a sensitivity to others in the context of human fallibility.

The "presumption/exception" ethic based on the just war model of moral thinking is moderate and grounded in freedom, in the fallibility of human knowing. This way of thinking subjects religion itself to evaluation in light of a vision of goodness, and it respects that the religious and moral spheres of existence are separate and involve distinct relational possibilities. The problem is not that morality demands that religion conform to a vision of goodness, but that religion sponsors actions that are subject to moral evaluation and does so by using ultimacy as an absolutist foundation for moral knowing and action. When this occurs, we get holy war and religious fanaticism in moral matters, and these fracture the integrity of the moral life with the overbearing and finally unbearable weight of absolutism. Moral understanding cannot bear the weight of absolutism.

Religion as a Moral Project

This book began by reminding readers that religion is powerful and dangerous — and never not dangerous. People choose out of their life histories and characters how they are religious, and I have attempted to articulate in these pages the moral grounding of religion in what I have called the basic religious option between life-affirming and demonic religious possibilities.

That the power of religion must never be underestimated is a lesson of September 11, 2001. Now, in the wake of September 11, 2001, Americans face an uncertain future knowing that difficult decisions lie ahead, not only on the newsworthy issues of foreign policy and military conflict, but on issues related to religion and ethics. Among the questions that continue to lie before us are these: What is the power of religion, and what are its dangers? What do individual Americans understand about Islam and about how the community of Muslims around the world views Muslim extremists? Why is it that monotheistic religions seem so enmeshed in histories of exclusionary conflict and violence, even as they continue to grow leaders who oppose violence and who seek to conform religious faith to a vision of goodness?

If the position I have been arguing for in these pages has merit, the questions that religious people must answer about their faith are not religious but moral: How do I choose to be religious? Do I use religion demonically? Can I discern the temptation of the demonic? Can I see it in the religious practices of others? What must I do to prevent my conceptions of ultimacy from being overtaken and suppressed by absolutist thought? The moral point of view offers something other than a descriptive or value-free articulation of a problematic. It commends to persons that they decide to be religious in a way that affirms life and the goods of life, while opposing all that in the name of religion leads to violence and to injury and destructive harm.

As religion contributes to the problem of violence in the world, so also can it contribute to the solution. In the end, the turn away from vindictiveness, resentment, retaliation, and vengeance ethics, and actual resorting to violence, can be effected through religion that conforms itself to a vision of goodness. Religion thus presents every person of faith with a basic moral project that must be undertaken in the context of religious faith. That project asks simply, yet reasonably, "How do you choose to be religious?"

Religion itself cannot answer this question. The choice about how to be religious is, rather, a moral question. All persons of faith must, in their traditions and interpretations of tradition, find that moral center of religious understanding that affirms a universal vision of responsibility, where all are responsible for each one, and each one for all.

Notes

Preface

1. Diana Eck, *A New Religious America: How a "Christian Country" Has Now Become the World's Most Religiously Diverse Nation* (New York: HarperSanFrancisco, 2001), 98.

2. Ibid., 97.

1. The Power and Danger of Religion

1. For a wonderful exploration of the notion of scarcity and divine stinginess, see Regina Schwartz, *The Curse of Cain* (Chicago: University of Chicago Press, 1997).

2. For such an interpretation see Cuthbert A. Simpson, "Exegesis" (for Genesis), in *The Interpreter's Bible,* ed. George Arthur Buttrick (New York: Abingdon-Cokesbury Press, 1951–57), notes on v. 5, 518.

3. T. William Hall, ed., *Introduction to the Study of Religion* (New York: Harper & Row, 1978), 4.

4. I would suggest that the "peaceful" impulse is revealed only in the wake of the Abel murder, when Yahweh banishes Cain but preserves his life, thus refusing to exact blood for blood already shed. There is, thus, a restraint on blood-shedding violence in the penalty phase of the Cain conviction before Yahweh. Yahweh's action constitutes a qualified movement away from violence and an appearance of religion's attachment to nonviolence. This act is then reinforced

by Yahweh's protection of Cain, which is accompanied by a curse on any who would harm him. Yahweh's peculiar but still essentially nonviolent response to the murder of Abel may reflect some consciousness on the part of Yahweh that he bears considerable responsibility for what happened, though the lack of detail in the story must relegate such a thought to wild speculation.

5. These statistics have been taken from George Gallup Jr. and D. Michael Lindsay, *Surveying the Religious Landscape: Trends in U.S. Belief* (Harrisburg, Pa.: Morehouse Publishing, 1999): 11, 9, 25, respectively, to cited statistics.

6. The definition of religion given previously from Hall, *Introduction to the Study of Religion,* invokes a "that which" of ultimacy put in terms of unrestricted or ultimate value, which then becomes the core value of the religious sphere of meaning, just as goodness is the core value of the moral sphere. See n. 3. Religious thought that is respectful of the object of ultimacy often relies on such language — i.e., "that which" — in order to avoid hardening a metaphor into something graspable and manageable when ultimacy ought not be thought of in such terms. Even popular music demonstrates this basic insight: See the 1981 George Harrison song, "Life Itself," which includes a lyric descriptive of ultimacy, "You are the essence of that which / We taste, touch and feel."

7. This assumes, of course, that life itself is not identified as the ultimate value, which theists would not do.

8. Abraham, going to the mountain to sacrifice his son as directed by God, may not have been happy about the prospect, for he did love dearly his son. But constituted as a religious person motivated to act by a divine command, Abraham proceeds to the place of sacrifice on the understanding that as much as what he does will offend morality, the meaning of what he will do is not ultimately moral, but religious. He can interpret religiously the act of killing his son, which is apparently what Yahweh wanted him to do, which is what the "test of faith" is about. He really does deserve the biblical characterization "father of faith." But it should be remembered that by subordinating the moral to the religious understanding, Abraham is

willing in the name of religion to defy morality. I would assume that the terrorists who acted out of religious motivations in the September 11 attacks were essentially in the same psychic/spiritual place: willing to defy the lower-order good of morality for the "higher," transcendent good of religion. In other words, they operated out of a vision of goodness that was defined as good, not morally but religiously.

9. See Hall, *Introduction to the Study of Religion*, 16. This is still the best definition of religion available.

10. See Germain Grisez, *Beyond the New Morality* (Notre Dame, Ind.: University of Notre Dame Press, 1974), for an analysis of religion as a basic good.

11. I'm not thinking so much of the book of Jude in the New Testament as I am the story of David's conquest where "the Lord gave victory to David wherever he went" (2 Sam. 8:6, 14). David made "servants" of those he defeated: some he killed and others he made pay tribute; and Solomon who "conscripted forced labor out of all of Israel" (1 Kings 5:13).

12. A few fanatical and religiously inspired opponents of abortion hold that abortion service clinics are legitimate targets for religious violence. The amazing contradiction is that by so doing they put at risk of harm, even death, the mothers, hence the fetuses, whom they are committed to saving absolutely and at all costs. Absolutism works like this in real life. As the contradictions of absolutism express themselves, the adherent of absolutist thought justifies contradictory notions, arguing, for instance, that killing is a way to preserve or promote life. Such claims are dangerous. They make sense to the fanatic who suspends reason, so fanaticism is dangerous. Fundamentalism is dangerous. These expressions of absolutist thought are put into action when the action itself contradicts the meaning imputed to it. It becomes dangerous when the motive for action — pursuit of some good — is turned inside out and an evil is accomplished under cover of a justification grounded in goodness.

13. See Regina Schwartz, *The Curse of Cain*, for a thought-provoking, full defense of such a perspective.

2. Being Religious: The Life-Affirming Option

1. Gabriel Marcel, *Mystery of Being,* vol. 1, *Reflection and Mystery* (Chicago: Henry Regnery, 1950), 260.

2. William C. Chittick, " 'Your Sight Today Is Piercing': The Muslim Understanding of Death and the Afterlife," in *Death and the Afterlife: Perspectives of World Religions,* ed. Hiroshi Obayashi (New York: Praeger, 1992), 136.

3. Thus is the finger dipped in seder wine in regret that freedom came at the price of loss of life.

4. A. M. Hocart, *Social Origins* (London: Watts, 1954), 87; quoted in Ernest Becker, *Escape from Evil* (New York: Free Press, 1975), 6.

5. Ibid.

6. René Girard, *Violence and the Sacred* (Baltimore: Johns Hopkins University Press, 1979), 92.

7. The Roman Catholic Church's sacramentalizing of the fetus presents a perspective on abortion as a religious (e)valuation drawn out of the particularities of the Christian symbol system we know as the Roman Catholic Church, rather than as a moral view that could command universal assent.

8. Karen Armstrong, *Muhammad: Biography of the Prophet* (New York: Harper & Row, 1992), 259.

9. Reasonable people universally concluded that the terrorist acts of September 11, 2001, failed to enact any vision of goodness, so that any claim that these were religiously inspired acts led many to conclude that these acts were perversions of religion or even expressions of false religion. But to the extent they were grounded in an understanding of ultimacy, however confused or untrue to Islamic teaching those particular acts were, they were religious. That an evil act is untrue to religion is a hard case to make if ultimacy is present in the meaning of the action. The evaluation of those acts as horrendous and deplorable did not emerge from a religious point of view, but from a moral point of view. Their failure to embody goodness was an evaluation undertaken not against the standard of ultimacy but against the standard of goodness.

10. A certain critique of moral meaning can be invoked at this point, namely, the viewpoint that if we try to establish a universal moral meaning we simply impose our relative idea of a universal moral meaning. Such a perspective holds that no universal moral meaning exists, but only the ambiguity and relativity of cultural and thus moral difference. After all, we live in a world where we have come to appreciate the relativity of moral practices and are conscious of the dangers we pose to the well-being of others if we try to impose on others our ethnocentric values and particularized moral views. Some assent to the reality of moral or ethical relativism seems almost a necessary prelude to any discussion about moral meaning, for "moral" seems to imply that moral assessment and evaluation are relative, imprecise, and so fluid as to make what is right, good, and fitting nothing more than equivalent to "you have your opinion and I have mine." That is as far as we can go. Sensitivity to differences between people and cultures is itself an expression of moral concern for the well-being of others. But such sensitivity ought not to be confused with a relativism that denies any normative concept of goodness at the heart of the moral enterprise, one that says moral meaning is localized and has no relevance beyond one's own group or community. Moral relativism is an incoherent perspective that reduces moral meaning to an assertion of power, and, incidentally, denies any notion of moral progress. The curious thing about moral relativism is that very few people, even very few of the people who advocate or espouse a relativistic moral world, actually live in such a world. I would say much in defense of relativism as a sociological fact of culture. Accordingly, I affirm, as many rational persons would, *cultural* relativism: the idea that practices and values differ from one culture to another, with a value foregrounded in one culture being perhaps backgrounded in another. I can affirm the need for sensitivity towards those who background cultural and even moral concerns that in another society may be foregrounded. And I note that even before postmodernist thought elevated to an ideological premise that difference and relativity are all we can really say about morality, the view has been widespread that no commonly accessible and reason-

related moral vision holds beyond the relativities and contingencies of a group.

11. See Aristotle, *Nichomachean Ethics,* Book I, section vii for a discussion of this.

12. I draw this list from a general framework of goods of life from Germain Grisez and Russell Shaw, *Beyond the New Morality: The Responsibilities of Freedom,* 2d ed. (Notre Dame, Ind.: University of Notre Dame Press, 1980), 61–62.

13. For a provocative essay on goodness and its visibility see Philip Hallie, "From Cruelty to Goodness," reprinted in *Vice and Virtue in Everyday Life: Introductory Readings in Ethics,* 3d ed., ed. Christina Hoff Sommers and Fred Sommers (Fort Worth, Tex.: Harcourt Brace, 1993), 9–14.

14. For a brutally frank discussion of this question, see Gore Vidal, *Perpetual War for Perpetual Peace: How We Got to Be So Hated* (New York: Thunder's Mouth Press/Nation Books, 2002).

3. Being Religious: The Demonic Option

1. "When psychiatry and psychotherapy speak of 'overvalued' ideas and images, they basically mean by this simply that in the individual case in view of the concrete totality of the psychic household too much psychic energy and energetic intensity is given to a particular idea." Josef Rudin, *Fanaticism: A Psychological Analysis* (Notre Dame, Ind.: University of Notre Dame Press, 1969), 71.

2. Ibid., 73.

3. Ibid., 94–95.

4. R. M. Hare, *Freedom and Reason* (London: Oxford University Press, 1963), 153.

5. Paul Tillich, *What Is Religion?* trans. and ed. James Luther Adams (New York: Harper Torchbook, 1963), 85.

6. Paul Tillich, *Systematic Theology,* vol. 3, *Life and the Spirit: History and the Kingdom of God* (Chicago: University of Chicago Press, 1963), 105.

7. I would point the interested reader to the pages in *Systematic Theology* where Tillich deals with the demonic, most notably

3:102–6, and then throughout the volume. See Vernon R. Malow, *The Demonic: A Selected Theological Study: An Examination of the Theology of Edwin Lewis, Karl Barth, and Paul Tillich* (Lanham, Md.: University Press of America, 1983), for more detail on the role of the demonic in twentieth-century Christian thought.

8. Tillich, *Systematic Theology*, 3:102–3.

9. I mention this well-known example of Hebrew-Jewish resistance to Roman authority, which took form as murder-suicide. Despite the role that Masada continues to play even in contemporary Israel, given that Israeli soldiers take their oaths of allegiance at Masada, I count the murder-suicide under the category of demonic because that is where it belongs in the account I am offering. A scholarly debate rages over the accuracy and historicity of Josephus's account, and I offer my skepticism of that account and do not think that Masada ended as Josephus claims.

10. I am not intending here to be appealing to a strictly Kantian notion of practical reason as distinguished from theoretical reason. The Kantian distinction holds that warrants of reason are defensible although not theoretically demonstrable. All I mean by "practical reason" is the kind of logic that holds in the moral realm of human action and behavior directed to and guided by the central concern of goodness. Practical reason is directed to a discernment of the logic of action in relation to goodness; it invokes will and emotion as essential to the process of discerning and accessing the meaning of action and the beliefs that would attend the interpretation of action.

11. Cited in Lloyd Steffen, *Executing Justice: The Moral Meaning of the Death Penalty* (Cleveland: Pilgrim Press, 1998), 103.

12. See "Text of Anonymous Letter Claiming Responsibility for Pensacola Clinic Bombings," in *Abortion: A Reader*, ed. Lloyd Steffen (Cleveland: Pilgrim Press, 1998), 447–48. The writer advocates violence and even "deadly force" against those working at the Pensacola clinic, because this is the way "to stop the slaughter of innocents. We WILL put an end to the murder of babies."

13. The Pensacola bomber writes at the conclusion of her letter, "So, I do not feel that I have done anything wrong." See *Abortion: A Reader,* ed. Steffen, 448.

14. Because of some public mention concerning activities I was engaged in opposing the Westboro Baptist Church of Topeka, Kansas — an anti-gay Christian Church — I was sent anonymously a pamphlet entitled "Intolerance of, Discrimination Against and the Death Penalty for Homosexuals Is Prescribed in the Bible," by Pastor Peter J. Peters. This publication was produced by Scriptures for America in LaPorte, Colorado, fourth printing in November 1993. The publication wonderfully illustrates demonic absolutism in its advocacy of death for homosexuals. The author reminds readers that this is the punishment prescribed by the Hebrew Bible for homosexual activity. Demonic religion often appeals to absolutist solutions, and execution is nothing if not absolutist.

15. See Gore Vidal, *Perpetual War for Perpetual Peace: How We Got to Be So Hated* (New York: Thunder's Mouth Press/Nation Books, 2002).

16. Ernest Becker, *Angel in Armor: A Post-Freudian Perspective on the Nature of Man* (New York: George Braziller, 1969), 111.

17. See Søren Kierkegaard, *The Concept of Anxiety* (Princeton, N.J.: Princeton University Press, 1980) for explication of this notion.

18. See Robert Solomon's analysis of "dread" and "anxiety" in *The Passions: The Myth and Nature of Human Emotions* (Garden City, N.Y.: Doubleday Anchor Books, 1977), 300–301, 287–89, respectively.

19. I have done this elsewhere: Lloyd Steffen, *Self-Deception and the Common Life* (New York: Peter Lang, 1986).

20. Tillich, *Systematic Theology,* 3:103.

21. See Edgar Allan Poe's short story "The Black Cat" for a dramatization of such clearheaded perversity.

22. Paul Tillich, *The Protestant Era,* abridged ed., ed. James Luther Adams (Chicago: University of Chicago Press, 1957), 174.

23. D. Mackenzie Brown, *Ultimate Dialogue: Tillich in Dialogue* (New York: Harper, 1965), 59.

24. Ibid., 30.

25. Tillich, *Systematic Theology,* 3:381.

26. Gay religious leader Mel White once told in my hearing of an incident where a caller on a radio show he was doing held that his homosexuality was such an abomination in his religious view that the caller went on, in White's presence, to support the scriptural warrant that homosexual people should be killed.

4. The Pacifist Option

1. Another form of utilitarianism, act utilitarianism, evaluates every act in accordance with a principle of maximizing utility (happiness or benefit or pleasure) to the greatest number. Rather than abiding by a principle or rule like "force should not be used to settle conflicts," this form of consequentialist thought would evaluate anticipated outcomes and then decide if utility is enhanced by using force, or not using force, and then recommending action on the basis of that evaluation.

2. J. C. C. Smart, "Utilitarianism," in *Vices and Virtues in Everyday Life,* 5th ed., ed. Christina Sommers and Fred Sommers (Fort Worth, Tex.: Harcourt College Publishers, 2001), 99–101.

3. George Rapall Noyes, *Tolstoy* (New York: Dover, 1968), 3.

4. Leo Tolstoy, "What Is Religion and of What Does Its Essence Consist?" in *A Confession and Other Religious Writings,* trans. Jane Kentish (Harmondsworth, U.K.: Penguin Books, 1987), 113–14.

5. Aylmer Maude, *The Life of Tolstoy: Later Years* (London: Constable and Co., 1910), 353.

6. Leo Tolstoy, "The Law of Love and the Law of Violence," in *A Confession and Other Religious Writings,* trans. Jane Kentish (Harmondsworth, U.K.: Penguin Books, 1987), 176.

7. Ibid., 174.

8. Ibid., 174–75.

9. Quoted in Noyes, *Tolstoy,* 239.

10. Maude, *The Life of Tolstoy,* 366.

11. Noyes, *Tolstoy,* 246. Noyes provides the contrast with Rousseau.

12. Leo Tolstoy, *The Law of Love and the Law of Violence,* trans. Mary Koutouzow Tolstoy (New York: Rudolph Field, 1948), 126–27; Penguin edition, see p. 228.

13. Noyes, *Tolstoy,* 282–83.

14. Ibid., 284.

15. Ibid., 249.

16. Ibid., 311.

17. Daniel Rancour-Laferriere, *Tolstoy on the Couch: Misogyny, Masochism, and the Absent Mother* (New York: New York University Press, 1998), 87.

18. E. B. Greenwood, "Tolstoy and Religion," in *New Essays on Tolstoy,* ed. Malcolm Greenwood (Cambridge: Cambridge University Press, 1978), 170.

19. M. K. Gandhi, *Non-Violent Resistance (Satyagraha)* (New York: Schocken Books, 1951), 3.

20. Ibid., 17.

21. Ibid., 10.

22. Ibid., 381.

23. Ibid., 363.

24. Ibid., 281.

25. Ibid., 376.

26. Ibid., 294.

27. Ibid., 294.

28. Ibid., 60.

5. The Case of Holy War

1. For more on the idea of *hērem,* see Bruce M. Metzger and Michael D. Googan, "Ban," in the *Oxford Companion to the Bible* (New York: Oxford University Press, 1993), 73.

2. For pointing out this passage and discussing the significance of it with me, I wish to thank my colleague, Benjamin G. Wright, who also directed me to the best book on *hērem,* Susan Niditch, *War in the Hebrew Bible: A Study in the Ethics of Violence* (New York: Oxford University Press, 1993).

3. Gerhard von Rad, *Holy War in Ancient Israel,* trans. Marva J. Dawn, introduction by Ben C. Ollenburger (Grand Rapids: William B. Eerdmans, 1991).

4. Ben C. Ollenburger, "Introduction," in von Rad, *Holy War in Ancient Israel,* 8–9.

5. Ibid., 16.

6. For more discussion of the scholarly controversy see ibid., 29–30.

7. Ibid., 31.

8. Ibid., 39.

9. Having made this comment, I now need to qualify it to say that this is more of a theory issue than practice issue in many Muslim countries. The constitution of Egypt, for instance, states that law will be founded on the *shari'ah,* or Islamic code, but outside family law, this is not how law is applied. Saudi Arabia may be the only Muslim country where the influence of European law is negligible.

10. Even in America, this separation is not so widely respected as many believe, as is evidenced by all the First Amendment litigation that winds up in the courts for constitutional review. Prayer in school, display of the Ten Commandments in public settings, crèches on courthouse lawns, and even a religiously avowed idea of "person from the moment of conception" position in the abortion debate: all of these issues provide evidence that many Americans want to push religion across the constitutional divide and let religion explicitly direct politics and the scope of governmental action in the society.

11. So distinctive is that movement that a respectful encounter with Islam at some point forces a recognition that Islam — an Abrahamic form of monotheism committed to a theology, and even to values of social justice, more akin to Christianity and Judaism than to, say, Buddhism — is not itself a religion that easily elides into the American myth of a Judeo-Christian tradition. Sufism is somewhat of an exception, but even though Rumi is today the biggest-selling poet in the United States, his sales numbers would not compare to the writings of the Dali Lama or Thich Nhat Hanh. The irony, of course, is that many Americans have embraced Buddhism as a

digestible complement in their search for spirituality, though Buddhism is much more dissimilar to Christianity and Judaism than is Islam, which understands itself to be the final evolution of Western monotheistic thought and religious practice.

12. The Qur'anic prohibition on suicide, unqualified, is to be found in the Qur'an at 2:195; 4:29. As I remark later on, Islamic rules of warfare constrain the use of violence and correspond strikingly to features of what developed in the Western just war tradition.

13. Seyyed Hossein Nasr, *Muhammad: Man of God* (Chicago: KAZI Publications, 1995), 45.

14. The Battle of Badr was a raiding party in which the Muslim force was seriously outnumbered yet won the day. I am not establishing how I think this particular battle might or might not fit the criteria of a morally justified use of force, except to say that in the moral arena, everything is up for interpretation even if, in the end, clear moral determinations can be made. I have opted here to accept Professor Nasr's interpretation of Badr as morally justified for the sake of argument. I also acknowledge that survival of the *umma* or community was at stake, so that any conflict with the Meccans could be deemed defensive.

15. The only unforgivable sin in Islam is polytheism (idolatry), and the Muslim understanding is that God wills that as a general principle Muslims are to fight against it. Muhammad's polytheist combatants at Badr were bent on the very destruction of Islam.

16. See n. 13 for bibliographic reference.

17. W. Montgomery Watt, *Muhammad: Prophet and Statesman* (London: Oxford University Press, 1961), 171–72.

18. Karen Armstrong, *Muhammad: A Biography of the Prophet* (New York: HarperSanFrancisco, 1992), 207.

19. Ibid., 207–8.

20. Watt, *Muhammad*, 173.

21. Armstrong, *Muhammad*, 208.

22. I do not mean to suggest that reason-based, as opposed to revelation-based, arguments are foreign to Islam, for surely they are

not. But clearly the religion-culture relationship has evolved differently in Islam than it has in Judaism and Christianity, and that is the result of such matters as the Qur'an, which holds a status quite distinct from that of the Bible in Judaism and Christianity.

23. Although scholars of Islam emphasize things differently, Simon Wood, to whom I am indebted for his guidance in these matters, has ordered the authority for law as Qur'an, *hadith, qiyas,* and *ijma'*, with *ijma'* being infallible as a process but not in terms of content. So, for example, a scholars' consensus may be infallible in the moment for a given situation, but may be overturned by subsequent *ijma'*.

24. This discussion is based on "How the Door of Ijtihad Was Closed" at *http://www.islamicvoice.com/june98/islamic.htm.*

25. By suggesting a broad cultural contour, I run the risk of portraying this movement against interpretive flexibility in monolithic terms, which I certainly do not want to do. I do not mean to suggest that there was — or is — no resistance to those opposed to innovation in Islam. Islamic modernism, in fact, developed in response to the resistance to innovation, symbolized by the closing of the gate. In addition, it is argued in Shi'ism that the gate of *Ijtihad* was never closed, so that Shi' has two source authorities: the Qur'an and *Ijtihad.*

26. Fazlur Rahman, *Islam* (Garden City, N.Y.: Anchor Books, 1966), 95.

27. Rudolf Peters, "Jihad," *The Encyclopedia of Religion,* ed. Mircea Eliade (New York: Macmillan, 1987), 8:89.

28. As I did not report on all that scholars are able to tell us about holy war in ancient Israel, neither do I intend to provide a thorough or exhaustive treatment of jihad as a holy war–related notion in Islam. Holy war in Israel and jihad in Islam are actually topics of serious and important scholarly investigation, and readers who seek more complete scholarly investigation of these ideas may consult appropriate resources. I have found particularly helpful James Turner Johnson, *The Holy War Idea in Western and Islamic Traditions* (University Park: Pennsylvania State University Press, 2001); Majd Khadduri, *War and Peace in the Law of Islam* (Baltimore: Johns

Hopkins University Press, 1955); and Rudolph Peters, *Jihad in Classical and Modern Islam* (Princeton, N.J.: Marcus Wiener Publishers, 1996).

29. I am indebted to Islamic scholar Simon Wood of Temple University, who discussed these various issues with me.

30. Peters, *Jihad in Classical and Modern Islam*, 1.

31. Ibid., 116.

32. Peters, "Jihad," 8:89.

33. Peters, *Jihad in Classical and Modern Islam*, 116.

34. Ibid.

35. Seyyed Hossein Nasr, *Islamic Spirituality: Foundations,* World Spirituality 19 (New York: Crossroad, 1987), 167.

36. Peters, *Jihad in Classical and Modern Islam*, 120.

37. Ibid., 121.

38. Ibid., 89.

6. Case of Just War

1. Marcus Tullius Cicero, *De Officiis/On Duties,* trans. Harry G. Edinger (New York: Bobbs-Merrill, 1974), I, (34), 19.

2. Ibid., 217.

3. Bernard T. Adeney, *Just War, Political Realism, and Faith* (Metuchen, N.J.: Scarecrow Press, 1988), 24.

4. For an excellent discussion of the history of just war in the medieval period, see James Turner Johnson, *Just War Tradition and the Restraint of War: A Moral and Historical Inquiry* (Princeton, N.J.: Princeton University Press, 1981).

5. Richard P. McBrien, *Catholicism: Study Edition* (Minneapolis: Winston Press, 1981), 1036.

6. Adeney, *Just War, Political Realism, and Faith*, 43.

7. See the outstanding "Secular Just War Theory" chapter in Kenneth L. Vaux, *Ethics and the Gulf War: Religion, Rhetoric, and Righteousness* (Boulder, Colo.: Westview Press, 1992), 120–45.

8. McBrien, *Catholicism: Study Edition*, 1036.

9. I was critical of the way policy makers twisted and molded just war thinking immediately prior to the 1991 Gulf War, and my

comments on this can be found in Lloyd Steffen, *Life/Choice: The Theory of Just Abortion* (Eugene, Ore.: Wipf and Stock Publishers, 1999), 8–10.

10. I say "of a sort" because the "principles" or propositions at issue here are not absolute, and some ethical perspectives, particularly some versions of deontological or Kantian ethics, would consider a principle by definition to be an exceptionless rule.

11. For a more in-depth discussion of what constitutes a moral presumption and how it embodies a vision of goodness, see my *Life/Choice*, 30–34.

12. Scholars and critics have pointed out to me that the language of "moral presumptions" was central to Philip Wogaman's ethics project in his book *A Christian Method of Moral Judgment* (Philadelphia: Westminster, 1976). In that book, Wogaman both discusses moral presumptions and articulates specific Christian moral presumptions. I can acknowledge that my own invocation of the term has come about not from Wogaman, whose work I did not know, but from wanting to devise a shorthand for signifying how a moral rule could be universal without also being absolute, and that is what I think a presumption by definition accomplishes. (Wogaman does not attend to absolutism or the philosophical problems I attach to it.) I do avow connection to those who have advanced prima facie ethics in the Western tradition of ethical discourse, and invoke "moral presumption" as a way that accepts that perspective but then attaches to it a reason-based, natural law ethical thinking that presumptions, I think, also endorse. Wogaman's own philosophical critique of presumptions defines a presumption more as a prejudice or bias, and his clear intent was to inquire into the meaning of Christian moral presumptions and ask how they might be rendered identifiably Christian. Wogaman's valuable and insightful project I would interpret as distinct from my own. My own project with respect to "presumptions" has been to assert them as universal but nonabsolutist moral agreements that bind together moral communities, which I worked out in *Life/Choice: The Theory of Just Abortion*. As universal but nonabsolutist, they authorize exceptions, and the just war model

[293]

seemed to me to demonstrate how an exception could be generated in accord with principles of justice. Presumptions then explain how practical reason functions, and are so broad, when correctly articulated, that reasonable people of any time or cultural setting can accept them as regulative action guides that it would be irrational to reject. Wogaman, I was pleased to discover, did discuss just war and the whole idea of exceptions in his 1976 book, calling just war a "useful model" (51) for moral inquiry. Independently of Wogaman, I have attempted to expose the extent of that usefulness, using this model as a practical alternative to Kantian and utilitarian and communitarian approaches on specific issues. Readers seeking a more exhaustive examination of presumptions in ways directed that elucidate especially Christian ethics should consult Wogaman's important book.

13. See my *Executing Justice: The Moral Meaning of the Death Penalty* (Cleveland: Pilgrim Press, 1998).

Conclusion

1. René Girard, *Violence and the Sacred* (Baltimore: Johns Hopkins University Press, 1977), 20.

2. The death penalty symbolizes, as well as enacts, an absolutist action in that it imposes a punishment beyond reach of correction or qualification. It is imposed on the assumption that the person subject to execution is absolutely responsible for some absolutely wrong offense, and this attribution of absolute responsibility necessitates the absolute and unqualifiable final solution of death. For more discussion of this logic on this issue see my *Life/Choice: The Theory of Just Abortion* (Eugene, Ore.: Wipf and Stock Publishers, 1999), 129–33.

Index

Index